The Economics of Tax Policy

THE ECONOMICS
OF TAX POLICY

edited by

MICHAEL P. DEVEREUX

Oxford University Press
1996

Oxford University Press, Walton Street, Oxford OX2 6DP

Oxford New York
Athens Auckland Bangkok Bogota Bombay
Buenos Aires Calcutta Cape Town Dar es Salaam
Delhi Florence Hong Kong Istanbul Karachi
Kuala Lumpur Madras Madrid Melbourne
Mexico City Nairobi Paris Singapore
Taipei Tokyo Toronto
and associated companies in
Berlin Ibadan

Oxford is a trade mark of Oxford University Press

Published in the United States
by Oxford University Press Inc., New York

British Library Cataloguing in Publication Data
Data available

Library of Congress Cataloging in Publication Data
The economics of tax policy / edited by Michael P. Devereux.
Includes bibliographical references.
1. Taxation. 2. Fiscal policy. I. Devereux, M. P.
HJ2305.E26 1996 336.2—dc20 96–10754
ISBN 0–19–877429–X
ISBN 0–19–877430–3 pbk

1 3 5 7 9 10 8 6 4 2

Typeset by Hope Services (Abingdon) Ltd.
Printed in Great Britain
on acid-free paper by
Bookcraft (Bath) Ltd
Midsomer Norton, Somerset

PREFACE

This book contains six surveys of different aspects of tax policy. Each survey was first published in the journal *Fiscal Studies*. In addition, there is an Introduction to general economic issues in tax policy. Each chapter aims to present the current state of thinking on particular tax policy issues. As with all papers appearing in *Fiscal Studies*, they are written in non-technical language in the hope that they will be accessible to readers from a wide variety of different backgrounds—in fact, anyone with an interest in tax policy.

The idea of a series of surveys in *Fiscal Studies* arose when I took over as Managing Editor of the journal, with Mark Pearson, in 1991. At around the same time, the Institute for Fiscal Studies was granted Research Centre status by the Economic and Social Research Council (ESRC). The new status enabled the Institute to move into a period of a greater financial stability.

The Institute was founded in 1969 and the highlight of its first decade was setting up the committee chaired by Professor James Meade which produced the pathbreaking report *The Structure and Reform of Direct Taxation* (Allen & Unwin, 1978). This report is a prime example of the kind of research which the Institute has aimed to produce ever since. It brims full with excellent and original economic analysis (the economists on the committee were well chosen: apart from James Meade, they were Tony Atkinson, John Flemming, John Kay, Mervyn King, and Cedric Sandford). But what sets the report apart is its attention to detail: the analysis of the existing tax system and the routes by which sensible reform could be achieved are painstakingly addressed.

The Institute changed shape at the end of the 1970s, with the appointment of John Kay, first as Research Director and then as Director. John set up an in-house research team for the first time and launched (among other things) the journal *Fiscal Studies*. By the time John moved on in 1986, the research of the Institute was well established, and since then it has continued to grow and to make an ever-increasing impact on tax policy through a number of channels from research papers published in academic journals to its own reports to media appearances and advice to political parties.

Throughout its life, the Institute has been fiercely independent in the political environment. Has it been influential in affecting tax policy in the UK, Europe, and elsewhere? Certainly it is possible to point to specific tax reforms which have been directly or indirectly influenced by the Institute's research. But the greater need is to improve the general level of understanding of tax policy; in the words of the founders of the Institute: 'to alter the climate of opinion within which changes to the British tax system were considered' (*Fiscal Studies*, (1990), p. 3). In John Kay's words: 'It is often tempting for scholars to believe that the best route to policy influence is to whisper in the Minister's ear but, in reality, that whisper will be lost in the clamour of vested interests and day-to-day political pressures. It is in the broader climate of opinion that good ideas will tend, over time, to outlive the bad, and rational argument to defeat the protestations of the self-interested' (*Economic Journal*, vol. 100 (1990), p. 21).

The survey articles collected in this book are intended to contribute to developing the climate of opinion which will result in good tax policy. In particular, they are intended to celebrate the new status of the Institute, to summarise what we know about the economics of tax policy at the beginning of the life of the Research Centre, and also to point to where future research—at the Institute and elsewhere—should take us.

Many people, at the Institute and elsewhere, have played direct and indirect roles in shaping this book. It is impossible to name them all, and the following list is inevitably far too selective. In particular, my co-Managing Editors (at various times) of *Fiscal Studies*—Mark Pearson, Michael Ridge, Paul Johnson, and currently Rachel Griffith and Ian Preston—have played important roles. Richard Blundell, Andrew Dilnot, Malcolm Gammie, and Stephen Smith, as the current leaders in various capacities of the Institute, have created a stimulating research environment and have given specific help to this project (two of them, of course, as authors).

Special mention, however, should be made of John Kay. Apart from being a member of the Meade Committee, John effectively set up the Institute as an independent economic research centre in 1979. It was his intellectual clarity and drive which were primarily responsible for the Institute becoming an important voice in tax policy in the UK and Europe. John has written widely on tax policy issues and, as the quotation above indicates, he has been typically lucid on the ways in which good ideas are transformed into policy. As a former student of his (one of several involved in the work of the IFS), I cannot resist the temptation to quote the remainder of his thoughts on the subject from the *Economic Journal*: 'Amid the demands for "relevant" research, it is easy to forget that the principal route by which scholars exert influence is—as it always has been—through their students' (ibid.).

M.P.D.
November 1995

CONTENTS

LIST OF FIGURES

LIST OF TABLES

NOTES ON CONTRIBUTORS

MICHAEL P. DEVEREUX is Professor of Economics and Finance at Keele University, UK, and Research Fellow of the Institute for Fiscal Studies. He has been a Managing Editor of *Fiscal Studies* since 1991.

RICHARD BLUNDELL is Professor of Economics at University College London, Research Director of the Institute for Fiscal Studies, and Director of the ESRC Centre for the Microeconomic Analysis of Fiscal Policy based at the Institute for Fiscal Studies.

ROBIN BOADWAY is Professor of Economics at Queen's University, Canada.

CHRISTOPHER HEADY is Professor of Economics at Bath University, UK, and Research Associate of the Institute for Fiscal Studies.

MICHAEL KEEN is Professor of Economics at Essex University, UK, and Research Fellow of the Institute for Fiscal Studies.

JACK MINTZ is Arthur Andersen Professor of Taxation at Toronto University, Canada.

STEPHEN SMITH is Reader in Economics at University College London and Deputy Director of the Institute for Fiscal Studies.

DAVID WILDASIN is Professor of Economics at Vanderbilt University, USA.

INTRODUCTION

Devereux,
Michael P.

Tax policy wins and loses elections. Governments are commonly expected to engineer a tax-cutting budget just before an election. President Bush was elected on the strength of his famous slogan 'read my lips—no new taxes' and he subsequently lost the presidency after he failed to keep his promise. Margaret Thatcher was deposed as Prime Minister at least partly because of her insistence on the poll tax. Yet the level of political debate on tax issues is usually pitifully low. The basic rate of income tax is frequently called on to represent the entire system. One party would cut it, while another would raise it to pay for education. But what of social security contributions, VAT, excise taxes, inheritance tax, capital gains tax, corporation tax, and countless tax breaks of various kinds? On average there were over 200 pages of new tax legislation per year in the UK in the 1980s. Anyone who thinks that the level of taxation in the UK has fallen since 1979 because the basic rate of income tax has fallen from 33 per cent to 24 per cent should think again.

This book analyses tax policy in the context of rigorous economic analysis. It consists of six independent surveys, by different authors, on central issues in the economics of tax policy. An overriding—but not the only—concern is about how taxes affect economic behaviour. Consider some examples.

How does the level and form of saving depend on tax? For example, can taxes help to explain the phenomenal growth of saving through pension funds and owner-occupied housing in the UK? The answer is yes: savings in both of these forms are tax advantaged relative to other forms of savings. If you put your money in a bank, you will pay tax on the nominal interest you receive. Given that nominal interest rates usually rise with inflation, this can mean that your tax liability may exceed the real return. By contrast, if you put your income in a pension fund, you get a tax rebate for the amount you have contributed. Although your eventual pension will be taxed, you will also receive a lump sum tax free. The tax treatment of housing is equally advantageous, although more complicated. We return to it below as an example of what can go wrong in designing tax policy.

What of the supply of labour? At first sight it may appear that tax is unlikely to affect the supply of labour, since most workers either work a fixed number of hours per week, or have an income which is independent of hours worked or effort put in. While this may still be true of a large number of workers, however, labour markets are becoming increasingly dominated by the prevalence of part-time work with variable hours. And there are many other margins on which tax may be important. An important one is the participation decision. In the 1970s and early 1980s in the UK, many unemployed workers would have been worse off in work than out of work—the so-called unemployment trap. Even those in work were not immune. Many low-paid workers would have seen their net income fall if they earned a higher gross income; in effect they faced effective marginal tax rates of over 100 per cent—the so-called poverty trap. These traps were not due simply to the formal tax system, but to the combination of income tax, social security contributions, and the withdrawal of benefits paid during spells of unemployment or low earnings.

Investment is a vital component of a healthy economy, and a popular view is that the government should design the tax system to encourage more investment. Business groups continually lobby for higher allowances for capital expenditure or cuts in the corporation tax rate. But, while they would undoubtedly gain from a cut in the tax rate, for example, this would do little to stimulate investment—indeed it might even deter investment. The reason is that the value of tax allowances falls with the tax rate, so that, even though the return to the investment pays lower tax, the net effect on investment incentives is likely to be small.

Governments also frequently aim to divert investment from one region to another. At the same time they compete with governments of other countries for inward international investment. But competition between governments is likely to drive down the tax rate on investment in all countries—several theoretical studies predict that the only stable outcome would be when all taxes on investment have been abolished. One possible way of avoiding this is for governments to agree to harmonise their taxes. Countries within the European Union have agreed to restrictions on VAT rates within their borders,[1] but we are still a long way from any such agreement on taxes on investment.

Another area in which governments aim to promote good behaviour—with more justification—is the environment. The 'Toronto target' is to reduce carbon dioxide emissions back to their 1990 levels in order to combat global warming. How might governments achieve the major changes in energy use that would be required to stabilise CO_2 emissions permanently? One way would be to impose limits or quotas on activity which results in such emissions. Probably a better way would be to use the tax system to encourage producers and consumers to switch to less polluting types of activity. There is plenty of evidence that such taxes can work. Successive rises in the tax on leaded but not unleaded petrol in the UK have had dramatic effects on the behaviour of motorists.

Of course, tax policy is not just about encouraging good things and discouraging bad things. Nor is it just about raising the required revenue with the minimum amount of distortion to economic activity, and with the minimum cost of collection. It is also about fairness. A poll tax is a classic example of a tax which does not distort choices of economic activity: you have to pay the tax whatever you do. What caused rioting in British streets when Mrs Thatcher's government introduced the Community Charge was the fact that everyone, rich and poor, had to pay the same amount.[2] So the tax was regressive in the sense that the poor paid a higher proportion of their income than the rich.

But designing a tax system which is fair requires looking at all taxes, not just one. Some taxes are more progressive, some more regressive. We cannot say that the British tax system was regressive because of the Community Charge any more than we can say that it was progressive because of a large number of bands for income tax, with rates at their peak rising to 98 per cent. (The existence of a 98 per cent tax rate is in any case not a sign of real progressivity, since those who were wealthy enough to face such a tax rate could also generally afford to pay for legal advice on how to avoid it.)

Moreover, fairness also requires us to look at what governments do with tax revenue. A large part of government expenditure throughout the developed world takes the form either of direct transfers to, or of subsidies to the activities of, selected groups. Transfers include state

---

[1] The original EC Treaty provides for a common system of VAT within the Community.

[2] The Community Charge was, in almost all respects, a poll tax. Strictly, however, since its level varied between localities, there was in principle an incentive to move to a lower-taxed area.

pensions, unemployment benefit, and income supplements paid to the less well off. Subsidies include the provision of free education and health—these are essentially transfers from those who do not consume these goods (the healthy and childless) to those who do (sick parents with large families).

Many of these issues are discussed in detail in this book, although no claim can be made that it is comprehensive in its coverage. Below is a brief introduction to some of the central policy issues discussed in the surveys. Before that, however, it is worth considering some of the reasons why tax policy is not as straightforward as it might at first seem (and is often assumed to be). Two examples illustrate many of the issues: the taxation of housing and the taxation of labour income. The details concern the UK tax system.[3]

1. Fundamental Concepts in Tax Policy

1.1. Effective incidence and tax capitalisation—a case study of mortgage interest tax relief

The appropriate tax treatment of owner-occupied housing depends on the conceptual base of the tax—as discussed below, the two main options are the comprehensive income tax and the expenditure tax. Here we consider just one aspect—relief against income tax for payments of interest on borrowing to purchase a house. In principle, both the comprehensive income tax and the expenditure tax would give such relief for such interest payments. However, in the UK at least, tax relief for interest payments is rare and for most individuals is confined only to this one case.

Tax relief for interest payments on owner-occupied housing represents the last vestiges of the 1803 tax system which gave relief for all interest payments. Over the intervening two centuries, interest relief has been cut back, but governments have always refrained from removing it from owner-occupied housing (so far at least). One important reason for not removing the relief is the problem of tax capitalisation discussed below. Another appears to be that successive governments have favoured a 'property-owning democracy' and have been willing to maintain the tax

---

[3] An excellent survey of the British tax system, containing an eloquent summary of the issues is Kay and King (1990). A shorter, but also excellent, account of British tax reform and the issues concerned is Keen (1991).

relief apparently to persuade individuals to purchase their own houses rather than rent.[4]

The issue for our purposes is the probable effects of such interest tax relief: will it encourage individuals to purchase their own houses rather than to rent a property? Two problems arise in attempting to answer this question. The first is one of *effective tax incidence*: who benefits from the tax relief?[5] To begin with, it is important to note that the effective tax incidence is completely independent of the *formal tax incidence*. The latter simply describes who receives the tax rebate from (or who sends the cheque to) the Inland Revenue. Under the present system in the UK, the borrower pays interest net of tax and the lender receives a tax rebate. But this has no implications at all for who actually benefits from the rebate.

It is not necessarily the case that the borrower will benefit from the full amount of the tax relief. If there were a perfectly competitive market in the provision of mortgages, with a perfectly elastic supply of funds at the ruling interest rate, this is exactly what we would observe. Lenders would compete to offer the cheapest possible mortgage; any tax relief would be used further to reduce the cost to borrowers. But take an opposite extreme, a single monopoly lender. In the absence of tax relief, the profit-maximising approach of such a lender would be to charge a higher interest rate, with consequently a lower amount of lending in total. Introducing tax relief is likely to encourage the monopolist to raise the gross interest rate still further. If, as is likely, the net of tax rate fell, then the tax benefit would be shared between lower costs for lenders and higher profits for the monopolist. The demand for mortgages would increase, but not by as much as in the perfectly competitive case: the impact of the tax relief would be blunted.

There is evidence that in the UK at least part of the benefit is captured by the lender. In the UK there are two standard types of mortgage. A repayment mortgage has a fixed monthly repayment. The proportion of that fixed amount which constitutes interest falls over time as more principal is repaid. But there is a more tax-efficient form of mortgage: an endowment mortgage is one in which no principal is repaid during the life of the mortgage. This means that more interest is paid and hence more tax relief claimed. In order to be able to pay off the mortgage at the end of its life, the borrower must also save an amount which, when accumulated over the life of the mortgage, is enough to repay the principal.

---

[4] Quite why it is necessary to reduce taxes in order to persuade individuals to buy a house when in the absence of such a reduction they would prefer to rent is unclear.

[5] In discussing tax payments, this is normally asked the other way round: who bears the tax burden?

This saving generally takes the form of a life assurance fund, operated by an insurance company. If the benefits of more favourable tax treatment were being claimed by borrowers, endowment mortgages should be cheaper than repayment mortgages. In fact, the costs are very similar. This suggests that much of the tax benefits of endowment mortgages are being captured by the lenders and insurance companies.

So the first problem with attempting to encourage home ownership in this way is that the tax revenue foregone may actually be lining the pockets of lenders more than reducing the costs of borrowing. That is the problem of effective incidence. A second problem is *tax capitalisation*. It is likely that, in introducing the tax relief, at least some of the tax benefit is captured by borrowers in a lower net cost. A lower cost is likely to increase demand, which, in turn, is likely to push up the price of housing as well as expand the supply of owner-occupied housing. In an extreme case, if the supply of owner-occupied housing is fixed, the rise in house prices will be the *only* effect of a lower cost of borrowing. If the supply increases to meet the extra demand, then introducing the tax relief will have had at least some effect on the numbers owning their own house. But almost certainly this will be offset by a price rise. Who benefits from this price rise? Existing owners, who see a one-off increase in their wealth. Since the tax relief was actually introduced in 1803, then, other things being equal, we can safely assume that the main beneficiaries are no longer with us.

But tax capitalisation is a trap for the unwary policy-maker. One of the reasons the tax relief has never been abolished is the issue of who would lose if the relief were to be abolished. As house prices fall, the answer is again existing owners—but this time the owners at the time the tax relief is abolished; in fact, those who bought their houses at the higher prices induced by the relief may find themselves in the position that the value of their house would be lower than their outstanding mortgage—the 'negative-equity' problem. So the government cannot easily abolish the relief. What it has recently done, however, is to limit the relief to loans up to £30,000—a figure which has not changed for more than ten years and which has consequently become much smaller relative to the average house price. More recently still it has also reduced the rate at which the tax relief can be claimed. With these reforms in progress, however, we would expect and we continue to observe a slump in house prices. With these reforms, we would also expect endowment mortgages to become less popular—and there are signs that this too is happening.

1.2. Tax incentives and the excess burden— a case study of labour supply incentives

The issue of tax incentives is clearly important in understanding the impact of tax on the demand for housing. But to study the nature of incentives more closely we turn to another example: labour supply. It has frequently been argued that reducing income tax rates would encourage people to work longer and harder. This argument has been used to reduce higher rates of income tax in many countries. At first sight, one may wonder whether this would be good thing—after all, people generally tend to prefer leisure to work. But the issue is really the extent to which the tax system discourages work. More precisely, the welfare costs of taxation in this instance depend on the extent to which individuals' marginal decisions are influenced by tax, giving rise to an 'excess burden'.

To bring out these issues, consider the very simple case of a worker paid by the hour who can choose how many hours she would like to work. The tax system allows her to earn a fixed amount—the tax allowance—tax free but charges a fixed rate on all income above this amount. Much of Chapter 3 is concerned with extending this example to more complex cases, but for the time being we leave those to one side.

It is useful to consider the effect on her work of two tax reforms. The first is to reduce the tax allowance. This makes our worker unambiguously worse off. If she works the same number of hours she will pay more tax and have a lower income. Consequently she is likely to work more hours, trading less leisure time against a smaller reduction in post-tax income. This effect is known as the *income effect*. The impact on incentives is purely through a change in total income—which could be measured by the average tax rate. Her post-tax wage rate for any additional hour worked—affected by the *marginal* tax rate—is unchanged.

The other tax reform is an increase in the tax rate. Here again there is an income effect, since again her total post-tax earnings will be lower for the same number of hours worked. Again, the income effect will tend to result in more hours worked. In this case, however, the post-tax wage rate per hour is now changed: the return to working one additional hour is now lower. Choosing between one extra hour of leisure and the smaller additional income derived from one extra hour of work, our worker will be pushed towards more leisure by the increase in the tax rate. This is the *substitution effect*. Since the income effect and the substitution effect push (in this case) in opposite directions, we cannot be sure whether our worker will choose to work more or less following a change in the tax rate.

So much for incentives. What are the welfare implications of increasing tax? It is useful again to answer this question by considering income and substitution effects. Consider first the income effect. This exists because of a transfer from our worker to the government (and hence to society at large). Clearly our worker is worse off because of the transfer. But there is an offsetting gain in permitting higher public expenditure. Any tax levied must have an income effect and hence this kind of welfare loss.

The welfare loss due to the substitution effect is more subtle, however. To understand this, compare the tax system just described with a lump-sum tax (or poll tax), where our worker makes a single tax payment irrespective of how much she works. Then the *marginal* tax rate she faces is zero. For any additional hour she chooses to work she will earn the gross wage rate. Given this higher wage she is likely to decide to work longer hours—the trade-off between additional leisure and additional income is shifted back in favour of income. Society as a whole would be better off in this case. Not only does she gain—engaging in work which she would like to do but would be deterred from by a positive marginal tax rate— but her employers gain additional work, which they are willing to pay for.

There is therefore a corresponding welfare loss when the marginal tax rate is not zero. This is additional to the welfare loss due to the income effect, and it differs from it in one important respect: there is no offsetting gain to anyone in society. If we think of the welfare loss due to the income effect as the 'normal' burden of taxation, which everyone would immediately acknowledge, then the welfare loss due to the substitution effect can be thought of (and is generally referred to) as the *excess burden*. Since the 'normal burden' is unavoidable and is in any case offset by the use of the income, it is size of the excess burden which is generally used to measure how efficient the tax system is.

A tax system based exclusively on a poll tax would be completely efficient—there would be no substitution effect and no excess burden. But this example only illustrates the fact that the efficiency of the tax system—while very important—is not the only criteria by which to judge its performance. With these fundamental concepts in mind, we turn now to consider some of the most central issues in tax policy.

2. Central Issues in Tax Policy

Tax liabilities are determined by two factors: the tax base and the tax rate (or rates). The rules of the tax base define the way in which different forms of income, expenditure, wealth, or any other factor determine what is to be taxed. The tax rate determines the proportion which is taken in tax. Not surprisingly, then, the two central policy issues in taxation are how the tax base is defined and what rates are charged. The remainder of this chapter introduces a selection of four of the policy issues discussed in this book, beginning with the tax base and tax rates. Of the four, the definition of the tax base is probably the most important and more space is therefore devoted to it.

Many of the issues are discussed in several places in this book. For example whether the tax base should be income or expenditure is addressed in Chapter 2 in the context of personal saving. But it is also of crucial importance for the taxation of companies, discussed in Chapter 4. The importance of the tax rate is discussed in the context of optimal taxation in Chapter 1 and the impact of taxation on labour supply in Chapter 3. The remaining two issues introduced here are the taxation of international flows (Chapter 5) and environmental taxation (Chapter 6).

2.1. What should the tax base be: Income, expenditure, or a hybrid?

There are two main contenders for the optimal tax base (although all real-world tax systems have so far been a mixture of the two): comprehensive income or expenditure. A comprehensive income tax aims to tax all income, including any change in wealth as it accrues; this is equivalent to taxing current expenditure (or consumption) plus the net change in wealth. By contrast an expenditure tax would not seek to tax the change in wealth; equivalently it would not seek to tax the return to saving. The debate over which of these is more appropriate has continued since Kaldor first proposed an expenditure tax in 1955 (Kaldor, 1955), but was given greater impetus by two reports proposing an expenditure tax published in the 1970s: the Meade Committee report in the UK (Meade, 1978) and a US Treasury report in 1977 (US Treasury, 1977). The debate continues, however: two more recent reports also favouring various

10   *Michael P. Devereux*

forms of an expenditure tax are the Economic Council of Canada (1987) and the IFS Capital Taxes Committee (1994).

There are three important issues in the choice of a tax system: economic efficiency, equity, and administration. We examine the choice between these two tax bases on each of these grounds. In places we also consider the merits of real tax systems which tend to incorporate elements of both ideal forms of tax (as well as rather less ideal features). Before doing so, however, it is useful to distinguish between three different forms of an expenditure tax.

The most straightforward way of taxing only expenditure is through an indirect tax, such as VAT. If we were serious about introducing an expenditure tax, we could abolish all income taxes, corporation tax, and capital gains taxes, and simply increase the rate of VAT and extend its coverage to all goods and services to recover the lost tax revenue. The main drawback from such a tax would be its lack of progressivity—under a single rate of VAT on all goods, the rich would pay the same proportion of their expenditure in tax as the poor (and a lower proportion of their income). However, there are ways in which this lack of progressivity could be avoided.[6]

A second—and rather obvious—way of not taxing the return to saving is simply not to tax the return to saving. Thus, interest and dividends received, and capital gains and imputed rents on assets owned would all be tax exempt. Such a tax is—perhaps confusingly—commonly labelled a pre-paid expenditure tax (PET).[7] The third main candidate is what is commonly referred to as a registered-asset expenditure tax (RET). The RET is a more subtle way of not taxing the return to saving. It works by permitting saving in the form of special registered assets to be undertaken from gross income—that is, before tax is paid. The return to saving is, however, taxed when the money is withdrawn from the registered asset and spent on consumption goods. Registered assets would include a wide range of savings instruments—bank accounts, company shares, pension funds, and so on. The net effect of giving tax relief when the sav-

---

[6] One way would be for wages and salaries paid to the labour force to be deductible from VAT, and taxable instead as earned income. Individuals would receive a tax allowance which would generate progressivity in the system as a whole. This is the core of the 'flat tax' proposal of Hall and Rabushka (1983), which has received considerable attention in the USA.

[7] Despite arguing against an expenditure tax, Nigel Lawson, then Chancellor of the Exchequer, introduced elements of a PET—the Personal Equity Plan (PEP)—into the UK tax system in 1986. This has been extended in various forms since, including the Tax Exempt Special Savings Account (TESSA). However, both have restrictions on the form of the saving.

ing is made, but taxing the return to saving, is that the rate of return earned on the saving is not reduced by tax (if the tax rate does not change over time); it is in this sense that the return to saving is not taxed. In effect, the government becomes a partner in the saving. It contributes a proportion of all saving (through the initial tax relief) but keeps the same share of all returns.

There are several differences in the effects of the PET and RET. Here we consider two. The first concerns the taxation of returns over and above a 'normal rate'—the *economic rent*. Under a PET the economic rent is not taxed, since it is treated in the same way as all other returns to saving. Under a RET, however, since the government shares in all the returns to saving, it also claims a share of the economic rent. In present value terms, then, the RET is likely to generate a higher tax revenue than a PET charged at the same rate. This distinction has important consequences for the existence of a separate tax on companies (discussed more fully in Chapter 4). With a PET in operation in the personal sector, a corporation tax based on economic rent may be justified in the corporate sector (this is essentially what the IFS Capital Taxes Committee (1994) proposes). However, with a RET in operation in the personal sector, this economic rent is already taxed; this makes the case for a separate corporation tax much weaker.[8]

A second difference is one of timing. Under a RET, the government in effect must contribute to the saving up front, receiving its reward at some later date. Under a PET, the government avoids the up-front contribution. If the government's discount rate is the same as the rate of return on the saving, however, the present value of these two streams of tax revenues is the same. Whether this is an important argument in favour of the PET therefore depends on the government's discount rate and whether it faces any financial constraint.

Given these different structures, we can now return to examining the choice between a comprehensive income tax and an expenditure tax.

---

[8] The argument for a separate corporation tax is perhaps strongest if the aim is a comprehensive income tax. This is because it is in principle necessary to tax shareholders on the increase in their wealth due to profits made by companies which they own. However, this raises the issue of the relationship between the corporation tax and the personal income tax; if shareholders also pay tax on the dividends they receive, they will have paid a double layer of tax. To avoid this, many tax systems at least partially integrate the two taxes, although in a variety of different ways—see Chapter 4.

2.1.1. *Economic efficiency*

At first sight it may appear obvious that the expenditure tax must be more efficient. Any tax on the return to saving may generate a substitution effect, in which individuals save less than they otherwise would. If so, lifetime consumption patterns are distorted by tax and there is an excess burden. However, things are not that simple, since both forms of tax also distort labour supply decisions. A tax system which did not distort any economic activities would be optimal. But if some economic activities (e.g. the supply of labour) are already affected by tax, then it is not necessarily the case that the tax system should aim to avoid other distortions (e.g. in saving behaviour). We must consider the second best case where some tax-induced distortions already exist.

The circumstances under which it may be optimal to tax the return to saving are discussed in Chapter 2 and will not be repeated here. Two general points can be made, however. First, it has been shown that there exist circumstances—albeit rather special—under which it would be optimal not to tax the return to saving, whatever the tax rate on labour income. Second, even if it turns out to be optimal to tax the return to saving, it is unlikely that it should be taxed at the same rate as labour income, as the comprehensive income tax would do. On balance, though, it is unlikely that the superiority of one of these tax bases over the other can be demonstrated by recourse to arguments about economic efficiency.

However, an important question is 'do existing "hybrid" systems create any special economic inefficiencies?'. Either 'ideal' base on its own would generate a 'level playing field', in the sense that saving in the form of different assets would be taxed in the same way. However, under existing systems this is not the case: as noted at the beginning of this chapter, some assets are more favourably treated than others. As a result, savings tend to flow into the tax-favoured assets.

One of the central results in economic theory which helps to answer this question is that, under certain conditions, the tax system should not prevent *production efficiency*. Production efficiency holds if all activities generate the same rate of return at the margin.[9] If it did not hold, total wealth could be increased by transferring resources to activities which generate a higher marginal return and away from activities which generate a lower marginal rate of return. If savers invest in alternative assets or activities up to the point at which their post-tax marginal rate of return on each asset is the same, then production efficiency requires marginal

---

[9] Diamond and Mirrlees (1971).

effective tax rates on all assets or activities also to be the same. If some assets are taxed under a comprehensive income tax base, others under an expenditure tax base, and still others under some other arbitrary tax base (as if often the case), this will clearly not be true. There is therefore a case for believing that a 'hybrid' system tends to depress economic welfare.

The conditions for production efficiency to be optimal are fairly stringent, however. They are that economic rents are taxed at 100 per cent and that the government is unconstrained in the tax instruments which it might employ. In the absence of these conditions other taxes are likely to distort economic behaviour, and we are back to the position in which, if behaviour is already distorted, then an absence of distortions in the form of saving may no longer be optimal. However, it is unlikely that the arbitrary marginal effective tax rates which have been observed in practice are likely to be optimal either. In the end, the issue must come down to empirical estimates of the likely size of the welfare loss created by non-uniform marginal effective tax rates; evidence is sparse, but at least one recent paper suggests that the welfare loss is small.[10]

2.1.2. Equity

As noted in Chapter 2, Kaldor originally proposed the expenditure tax largely on equity grounds—that expenditure is a better measure by which to compare the well-being of individuals than is income. It is easy to think of examples of and counter-examples to this proposition. One of Kaldor's examples (Kaldor, 1980) compared an Indian prince using up his stock of gold with the beggar outside the palace gates. Neither has any income, yet clearly the prince is better off and the difference in welfare is closely connected to the size of expenditure. As Kay (1990) points out, however, if the prince's wealth had been derived from a lifetime's earnings from hard work, on which tax had been paid, there may be grounds for believing such an income tax to be fair, even if he pays no additional tax when he spends his accumulated wealth. Of course, it is more likely that his gold was inherited—but then the issue of equity also depends on the tax treatment of inheritance and gifts.

A more convincing argument begins with the observation that, over a lifetime, income must equal expenditure, since 'we bring nothing into the world and we take nothing out'.[11] On these grounds, then, income and expenditure over one's whole life are equally valid ways of making comparisons of fairness. But an expenditure tax would have no impact

[10] Auerbach (1989)

[11] 1 Tim. 6: 7. Inheritances are a form of income and bequests are the last big spend.

on the timing of expenditure over a lifetime: the present value of tax is unaffected by when the spending takes place. This is not true of a comprehensive income tax. Since returns to saving are taxed, someone who consumes early in life will pay lower tax in present value terms than someone who consumes late in life. There is no obvious reason why this should be the case, and so this argument favours the expenditure tax.

2.1.3. Administration

It is on administrative grounds that the proponents of expenditure taxation have probably the strongest case. And this case is largely to do with the problems of implementing a true comprehensive income tax. Such a tax must, in principle, measure and tax all changes in an individual's net wealth. There are two quite separate problems with this.

The first is that such changes are not easily measured. It may be possible to revalue my house each year, but what about my yacht, my Rembrandt, my pension fund, and—most difficult of all—my human capital?[12] The tax base must also be based on real increases in wealth, after allowing for inflation. Clearly it is not feasible to measure each individual's wealth at any moment in time, let alone once a year. The second problem is that, even if everyone's wealth were measured each year and tax were assessed, it is unlikely that everybody would be able to pay that tax. If my house rises in value by £20,000 in one year and my marginal tax rate is 40 per cent, the Inland Revenue will demand £8,000. Yet, if I have no source of income, I will be unable to pay without selling my house.

By contrast, both forms of the expenditure tax avoid these problems. The PET needs only to determine whether income received constitutes a return to saving as opposed to labour income. Since they are not taxed, accretions to wealth can be ignored. The RET essentially taxes only withdrawals from registered assets. Both are based on identifiable cash flows, not on changes in asset values. Of course, there are many administrative issues involved in either form of tax. However, none is as difficult to deal with as those of the comprehensive income tax.[13]

[12] Graduating with a degree in economics should increase one's human capital and there are estimates of how much higher one's earnings will be relative to not having a degree. However, there is a large variance of earnings in practice. The graduate who has committed himself to a life as a monk would have a case for arguing that he ought not to be taxed upon graduating. On giving up holy orders a year later, however, he should expect to be taxed.

[13] The Meade Committee (Meade, 1978) and the IFS Capital Taxes Committee (1994) examine in detail how a RET and PET, respectively, could be administered.

2.2. What should the tax rate schedule be?

In popular debate the primary role of the tax rate schedule is often thought to be in determining the fairness of the tax system. And it is further thought that the income tax schedule must consist of a number of increasing rates in order to make the system progressive. Neither of these propositions is correct.

We have used the term progressive already in this Introduction: it is now time to define it more precisely. An income tax is 'progressive' if the proportion of income taken in tax rises as income rises. This is a statement about average tax rates: the *average* tax rate increases as income increases. However, a typical tax schedule allows a certain amount of income to be tax free. Income above this level but below the next threshold is taxed at a relatively low rate. Beyond that threshold, additional income is taxed at a higher rate, and so on for the total number of bands of income. So the rate schedule determines *marginal* rates—that is, how much tax I will pay on an additional pound of income. It is not necessary to have a large number of bands for the tax system to be progressive. A linear income tax with just one rate and a tax-free allowance is also progressive. Indeed, over large ranges of income it may even be more progressive than a system with a large number of bands with increasing rates.

Of course, the degree of progressivity desired in the tax system is a matter of political or ethical judgement. Adam Smith stipulated that the tax system should demonstrate 'equality'. This turns out to mean proportionality—that all taxpayers pay the same proportion of their income in tax. Most would now argue in favour of some degree of progressivity (measured over the whole of the tax system). More generally, as discussed above, it is not clear that income is the best measure of ability to pay.

But in any case, the structure of tax rates is also important in determining the economic efficiency of the tax system, as measured by the excess burden. As discussed above, in considering efficiency we are primarily concerned with *marginal* rather than *average* tax rates, since the excess burden depends on the size of the substitution effect, which in turn depends on the marginal tax rate. We have already considered the unemployment and poverty traps, which are caused by excessively high marginal rates, largely as a result of withdrawal of benefits as a person finds work or receives an increase in his or her gross wage. A practical proposal to eliminate such problems is a 'negative income tax', proposed by many commentators, of whom Tobin et al. (1967) were one of the first. The idea here is that below some threshold, low-income households would receive a payment rather than pay tax. The rate of credit could be integrated into the tax schedule itself, with the result that marginal tax rates could be considerably lower and the unemployment and poverty traps eliminated.

One extreme version of the importance of marginal tax rates is the 'Laffer curve'. This is based on the initial observation that no tax revenues would be raised either at a rate of zero or at a rate of 100 per cent (there would be no point in earning any income if you did not keep at least some of it—at least unless you were particularly public-spirited). This implies that there must exist a revenue-maximising tax rate which is less than 100 per cent. This is not a particularly earth-shattering claim. But what lies behind the claim is the belief that the disincentive effects of high tax rates are large; as tax rates are reduced, so more income is generated (and so the tax base is increased) and tax revenues can actually rise. No one would deny that tax rates at 99 per cent would have considerable disincentive effects. However, the proponents of the Laffer curve claimed that even at much lower tax rates a reduction in rates may increase revenue. Certainly this view was influential with the Reagan administration in the early 1980s in the USA. However, the Reagan response—cutting tax rates—appears to have done more to increase rather than decrease the US budget deficit.

More serious analysis of the impact of tax rates on economic behaviour is widely available in the economics literature. Chapter 3 contains a description of empirical work in measuring the impact of tax on labour supply. The thrust of the argument is that there is no single answer to this question. Rather, to understand the macroeconomic impact of tax reform, it is necessary to identify a range of responses across a number of different groups of individuals with different characteristics: men and women, couples and single people, with and without children, old and young, rich and poor, and so on. There is no reason to expect the same response to a change in the tax rate from all of these people; but only a detailed microeconometric analysis can shed light on these differences. In identifying such responses, it is also necessary to model the structure of the tax system carefully; for example, we expect—and we observe— groups of taxpayers at kinks in the tax schedule.

Chapter 1 contains a survey of some of the theoretical work on designing an 'optimal' tax schedule. Without surveying the survey here, some points are nevertheless noteworthy. First, there is an inescapable trade-off between economic efficiency and equity. As we have already noted, a classic example of an efficient but inequitable tax is the poll tax. Basing the tax system on income (or expenditure), however, induces behavioural responses which create a higher welfare loss the higher the marginal tax rate. Because of this, it is often thought that a more redistributive government should have a steeply rising schedule of tax rates.

However, an important lesson from optimal tax policy analysis is that this is not so: as Chapter 1 notes, it is not the case that 'a redistributive government must use an income tax schedule with increasing marginal rates', at least over all ranges of income. A famous result of the optimal tax literature (due to Mirrlees, 1971) is that the marginal tax rate of the person with the highest income should be zero. The practical implications of this are small. But what has much more practical significance—with considerable administrative convenience—is that Mirrlees also showed (and others have confirmed) that that the optimal income tax schedule can be well approximated by a linear income tax (i.e. a single marginal rate). As noted above, progressivity can be achieved through substantial tax allowances.

2.3. How should international income flows be taxed?

Economic activities in one country affect the welfare of residents in other countries. An obvious example concerns the environment: acid rain in Norway may originate in British power stations. But there are many others. The day trippers on the ferry from Dover to Calais are not just enjoying a day out; they are taking advantage of the lower taxes on alcohol and tobacco in France. The tax breaks on inward investment into one European country may persuade Nissan to build its European factories there rather than another country.

These 'fiscal externalities' have important implications for the design of tax policy. But exactly how they impact depends on the degree of international agreement between countries. At one extreme, governments could act purely in the interests of their own citizens, maximising domestic welfare, possibly at the expense of welfare abroad. At the other extreme, governments might maximise joint welfare between countries.[14] The real world has elements of both. For example, there exists a web of double tax treaties between pairs of countries which define how certain international flows between the two are to be taxed—in effect, each government makes a deal with the other, presumably in the best

---

[14] Of course, arguably we would be lucky to have a government which consistently followed either course.

interests of both. Aside from such treaties and occasional discussions about harmonisation or approximation within the European Union, however, governments generally set their tax systems independently.

The international dimension is, in fact, simply one element in what has been called 'fiscal federalism'—the design of tax systems across many jurisdictions, whether local authorities in the UK, states in the USA, or countries in the European Union. In designing taxes in a multijurisdictional world, the notion of production efficiency again comes to the fore.

Consider setting VAT rates in the European Union, given that all governments agree to cooperate with each other. Suppose an Italian clothes designer sells her products in London, and suppose the VAT rates in Italy and the UK are different. Should the clothes be subject to the British rate since they are purchased in London (the destination principle), or should they be subject to the Italian rate since they were produced in Milan (the origin principle)? Under the destination principle, all producers selling clothes in London face a common tax rate. If equivalent goods are sold for the same price, producers then receive the same price net of tax. Under perfect competition, this implies that marginal costs are equal across producers: the same output could not be produced more cheaply by reallocating it among producers. This implies that production efficiency holds which, as we have seen, is optimal under the conditions discussed above. As discussed more fully in Chapter 5, this 'creates a presumption for a destination-based system', although there are a number of caveats which are discussed there.

The notion of production efficiency is also important in setting taxes on capital income. The Italian clothes designer need not make the clothes in Milan: she could do so in London. Assuming that she continues to live in Milan, however, her earnings must eventually be repatriated to Italy. This raises a similar issue: should she be taxed on those earnings at the Italian tax rate (a residence-based tax) or at the British tax rate (a source-based tax). If the member states of the European Union cooperate with each other, joint welfare is again maximised by achieving production efficiency (subject to the same conditions). It turns out that this requires a residence-based tax. The intuition is that the location in which production takes place should not be distorted by tax considerations. If it is cheaper to produce in Milan in the absence of tax, the tax system should not mean that production instead takes place in London. A source-based tax which was lower in London than in Milan may induce production to take place in London; that would imply higher costs and lower joint welfare than if production took place in Milan. However, a residence-based tax would not affect the location of production—as long as our Italian designer continues to live in Italy. Production efficiency is still relevant even if countries do not cooperate. However, in this case, governments should not aim to equalise net of tax production costs and hence marginal rates of return across the world. Rather, each government should aim to equalise the marginal social return *to that country* of its worldwide investment activity. Suppose, for example, that our designer earns a pre-tax rate of return of 15 per cent on her British activities, which is reduced to 10 per cent by British tax. Achieving production efficiency in Italy requires that this net marginal return of 10 per cent be taxed at the same rate as activities taking place in Italy. The Italians should not be interested in the pre-tax rates of return and the proportion captured by the British Inland Revenue: they should be concerned only with the return net of British tax. The Italian designer then faces a higher combined tax rate when operating in the UK rather than in Italy. However, what matters is the social rate of return, rather than the (pre-tax) private rate of return. Italian tax revenue is presumably spent in ways which are beneficial to Italians. But British tax revenue generally does not benefit Italians—unlike Italian taxes, British taxes are simply a cost to be deducted from the Italian tax base.

So there is no simple answer to the question 'how should international income flows be taxed'. As Chapter 5 concludes: 'Some surveys answer questions, other pose them. This one has been largely of the latter type.' Part of the problem lies in identifying the aims of individual countries. Beyond that, however, the economic models which have so far been developed tend to be relatively simple. It is likely that this will continue to be a growth area, both for research and—as the world becomes more integrated—for tax policy-makers.

2.4. How should environmental taxes be designed?

The environment is another area in which there exist externalities to economic activity. These may be positive—I may enjoy looking at my neighbour's garden—or negative—my enjoyment of my own garden may be reduced by the smoke from the nearby power station. Environmental taxes are one way of attempting to deal with negative externalities. Taxing the power station in proportion to its polluting emissions is likely to encourage it to reduce such emissions. Yet environmental taxes must be subject to all the questions which arise with other taxes. What is the effect on incentives? What is the effective incidence? What is the excess burden? What are the capitalisation effects?

Taxes on emissions themselves are known as Pigouvian taxes (after Pigou, 1920). More common, probably because of the difficulties of measuring emissions, are approximate Pigouvian taxes, based on an indirect alternative. The distinction between leaded and unleaded petrol is one example. Clearly, there may often be substantial savings in administrative cost in using such approximate taxes, since the tax base is chosen to be relatively easily observed. Approximations usually cause problems in tax policy, however: the 'windows tax' was introduced because it was easier to count the number of windows than to measure directly a household's income or wealth; it was supposed that the two were highly correlated. Not surprisingly, however, after its introduction, windows were boarded up and the correlation between the number of windows and income fell sharply. This is a problem of incentives: successful approximations in environmental taxation are likely to be cases where it is easier for the polluter to reduce emissions than to avoid the tax by some other means—that is, where there is a high degree of 'linkage' between the tax and the emissions.

With Pigouvian and approximate Pigouvian taxes there are also questions regarding incidence and tax capitalisation. Suppose that a polluting (privately owned) power station was subject to a tax on emissions. Depending on the market structure of the provision of power, the owners of the power station may be able to pass on most of the cost of the tax to consumers. The degree to which emissions are reduced would then depend on the degree to which consumers are prepared to reduce their consumption of power in response to higher prices. If the net profits of the owners are reduced, then the market value of the power station would fall. A new owner would not bear any part of the tax burden—it would be borne by the owner at the time the tax is introduced. These issues relate both to efficiency and to equity: on the one hand, we are interested in how successful the tax will be in reducing emissions; on the other, we may also be interested in who bears the cost of the tax.

An alternative market-based approach might be Pigouvian subsidies rather than taxes: in this case, polluters would be paid per unit for reducing their emissions. With perfect information, this may in principle be just as economically efficient as a Pigouvian tax; only the distribution of post-tax income would be different. However, there would be a number of problems, even aside from the distributional issues. Most importantly, it would be necessary to determine the baseline from which abatement is measured. For example, we might expect emissions to rise rapidly while the government was debating the bill to introduce subsidies, so that the baseline and hence abatements may also be higher. In addition, the higher profits derived by subsidised polluters may affect the industry structure and afford polluters protection in the changing economic environment.

More fundamental, however, is the question of whether even precise Pigouvian taxes are an appropriate means of reducing environmental pollution. The main alternative to taxes is direct regulation, such as a quota on emissions. A number of issues arise in choosing the most effective form of emissions control. However, taxes—or other market-based approaches—are more likely to achieve an economically efficient outcome. A tax on emissions will favour those with low emissions or those who can relatively easily reduce their emissions. By contrast, a quota will give no incentive to reduce emissions below the level of the quota. Further, its treats all polluters in the same way—for some it would be very costly to reduce their emissions, for others rather cheap, but this makes it difficult to design quotas which equate the marginal social costs and marginal social benefits of polluting emissions.

An additional benefit from environmental taxation is to raise revenue: there may be a so-called 'double dividend'. It is, however, important to be precise about what this double dividend is. First, there can be a double dividend only if the required amount of total tax revenue can otherwise be achieved only through taxes which distort economic behaviour. But this depends on the size of the excess burden imposed by the existing tax system. If a 'first-best' system of taxation already exists, there is little gain in raising even more revenue. However, if the existing tax system does distort behaviour, we are in a 'second-best' world; here the gains from distorting some polluting activities are difficult to determine and will depend, among other things, on the effects on labour supply and other factor markets.

References

Auerbach, A. J. (1989), 'The deadweight loss from "non-neutral" capital income taxation', *Journal of Public Economics*, 40, pp. 1–36.
Diamond, P. A., and Mirrlees, J. A. (1971), 'Optimal taxation and public production I; Production efficiency and II: Tax rules', *American Economic Review*, 61, pp. 8–27, 261–78.
Economic Council of Canada (1987), *Road Map for Tax Reform*, Ottawa: Minister of Supply and Services Canada.

Hall, R. E., and Rabushka, A. (1983), *Low Tax, Simple Tax, Flat Tax*, New York: McGraw-Hill.

IFS Capital Taxes Committee (1994), *Setting Savings Free: Proposals for the Taxation of Savings and Profits*, report of a committee chaired by Malcolm Gammie, London: Institute for Fiscal Studies.

Kaldor, N. (1955), *An Expenditure Tax*, London: Allen & Unwin.

—— (1980), 'Indian tax reform', in *Reports on Taxation*, London: Duckworth.

Kay, J. A. (1990), 'Tax policy: a survey', *Economic Journal*, vol. 100, pp. 18–75.

—— and King, M.A. (1990), *The British Tax System*, 5th edn., Oxford: Oxford University Press.

Keen, M. J. (1991), 'Tax reform', *Oxford Review of Economic Policy*, vol. 7, no. 3, pp. 50–67.

Meade, J. E. (1978), *The Structure and Reform of Direct Taxation*, report of a committee chaired by J. E. Meade, London: Allen & Unwin.

Mirrlees, J. A. (1971), 'An exploration in the theory of optimum income taxation', *Review of Economic Studies*, vol. 38, pp. 175–208.

Pigon, A. C. (1920), *The Economics of Welfare*, London: Macmillan.

Tobin, J., Pechman, J. A., and Mieskowski, P. M. (1967), *Is a Negative Income Tax Practicable?* Washington DC: Brookings Institution.

United States Treasury (1977), *Blueprints for Basic Tax Reform*, Washington DC: Government Printing Office.

OPTIMAL TAXATION
AS A GUIDE TO TAX POLICY

CHRISTOPHER HEADY

1. Introduction

The purpose of this chapter is to survey the field of optimal taxation. In order to provide a focus, it will concentrate on attempting to answer the question of whether, and to what extent, the literature on optimal taxation can provide guidance in the practical determination of tax policy. This focus means that the survey will be selective, and will neglect many intellectually interesting results that have not yet been developed to provide clear policy conclusions.

It is an interest in tax policy that has led a number of economists to undertake research on optimal taxation, and so one might expect the link between the research and the policy-making to be clear. However, the level of abstraction of much of the research, together with the extensive use of (sometimes difficult) mathematics, has caused many policy-orientated people to discount its practical value. It is dismissed as being 'academic', with little or no practical value. For some, the mere title of the field is off-putting: how can any aspect of public policy, with all its political constraints and administrative problems, ever hope to be optimal? Particularly, how can anything as unpopular as taxation be described in such terms?

As somebody who has contributed to the literature on optimal taxation, I would like to think that it can be helpful to practical policy-making. It has certainly been used by some economists (including

The author would like to thank Michael Devereux and Michael Keen for their helpful comments on an earlier draft of this chapter. Any remaining errors are the author's responsibility.

First published in *Fiscal Studies* (1993), vol. 14, no. 1, pp. 15–41.

myself[1]) who have been asked to advise governments on tax policy. However, like any theory, it has practical limitations and it must therefore be applied with great care. This survey is intended to indicate both the strengths and weaknesses of optimal taxation as a guide to policy-making.

The survey starts in Section 2 by looking at the basic ideas of optimal taxation, answering such questions as what is the point of optimisation, what is it that is being optimised, and what constraints are considered? The chapter then proceeds to look at the optimisation of particular aspects of the tax system: Section 3 deals with income taxation and Section 4 with commodity taxes. Finally, Section 5 concludes by summarising the main lessons of optimal taxation and commenting on their practical applicability.

2. The Basic Framework

This section presents the basic ideas that lie behind all analysis of optimal taxation. It deals with (1) the criteria for optimality, (2) the specification of social welfare, (3) the modelling of disincentives, and (4) problems of application.

2.1. The criteria for optimality

Since the time of Adam Smith, and even earlier, economists have thought and written about the effects of taxation. In doing so, they have frequently tried to describe what they regarded as desirable characteristics of tax systems. Smith (1977: bk. 5, ch. 2) listed 'four maxims with regard to taxes in general':

 (i) equality: that people's tax payments should be in proportion to their income;
 (ii) certainty: that tax liabilities should be clear and certain, rather than arbitrary;
 (iii) convenience of payment: that taxes should be collected at a time and in a manner that is convenient for the taxpayer; and
 (iv) economy in collection: that taxes should not be expensive to collect, and should not discourage business.

---

[1] For example, Heady and Mitra (1992) and Heady et al. (1992).

The second and third maxims have not been widely discussed in the economics literature, perhaps because they are self-evidently desirable. However, the ideas contained in them are frequently incorporated in statements of taxpayers' rights.

It is the first and the last maxims that have absorbed the main interest of economists. The idea of equality has been widely discussed, and is still a major part of the evaluation of any tax policy proposal. However, Smith's idea of equality (tax payments in proportion to income) is not the only one that has received support. Musgrave (1959: chs 4 and 5) provides a history of differing views on what constitutes a fair distribution of the tax burden. The administrative costs and the effects on incentives (the discouragement of business) have also been widely discussed. Taxation proposals have therefore frequently been analysed in terms of three criteria:

(1) the need for taxes to be fair (although fairness means different things to different people);
(2) the need to minimise administrative costs; and
(3) the need to minimise disincentive effects.

The difficulty with having three separate criteria is that a particular policy proposal will typically satisfy one criterion but not another. For example, in choosing between the poll tax (Community Charge) and a local income tax to finance local government expenditure, most people would regard the local income tax as fairer but it would have a greater disincentive effect on labour supply than the poll tax. In order to come to a decision, it is necessary to weigh the fairness advantage of the local income tax against its disadvantage of discouraging work (not to mention taking account of the different administrative costs).

The approach of the optimal taxation literature is to use economic analysis to combine these criteria into one, implicitly deriving the relative weights that should be applied to each criterion. This is done by using the concepts of individual (or household) utility and social welfare.

Social welfare is seen as an indicator of the well-being of society and is taken to depend on the utilities of individuals. However, social welfare is not necessarily seen as simply the sum of individual utilities; it can also depend on how equally these utilities are distributed. It is typically assumed that social welfare decreases as inequality of utility increases. In this way, the concept of social welfare reflects one idea of fairness in the tax system: that taxes are fair if they reduce the degree of inequality. Thus an attempt to maximise social welfare will involve an attempt to achieve one interpretation of criterion (1).

Criterion (2) will be reflected in social welfare because higher administrative costs will require a greater amount of gross tax revenue to be collected to finance government services, thus reducing individual utilities. Criterion (3) is incorporated because the discouragement of work will distort the economy and lower people's utility and hence social welfare. In this way, all three criteria are converted to aspects of social welfare and become commensurable, and so the policy that should be chosen is the one that gives the highest level of social welfare.

This is one of the main ideas behind optimal taxation, but it is typically not carried through completely. Economists have found it very difficult to model the relationship between tax rates and administrative costs. They have, therefore, usually ignored administrative costs in their analysis and have concentrated on criteria (1) and (3). Effectively, they have been trying to determine the tax systems that will provide the best compromise between equality (or fairness) and efficiency (or incentives). This neglect of administrative costs is a major shortcoming of much of the literature on optimal taxation, and is a topic to which we shall return later in this paper.

These same basic ideas have also been applied to the study of tax reform, where the aim is to identify whether specific (and typically small) tax changes will raise social welfare. There is clearly a close connection between the analysis of optimal taxation and tax reform: an optimal tax system is one in which there are no possible reforms that will increase welfare. Indeed, most of the models used in tax reform analysis reflect the approach described in this chapter. The only difference is that the aim is not to find the best tax system, but to find a better one. A useful exposition to tax reform analysis is given in Ahmad and Stern (1991).

The more modest aims of tax reform analysis lead to smaller informational requirements: it is necessary to know only how economic agents will respond to fairly small changes in taxes, rather than the large changes that might be involved in a move to the optimal tax structure. This is clearly an advantage, and it is worth noting that a country that follows a sequence of tax reforms that improve social welfare will eventually approach optimality. However, it is often not a good idea for a country to change taxes repeatedly and, as will be shown in this chapter, there are a number of optimal tax results that are not very sensitive to the precise specification of individual economic behaviour. These results give a clear idea of some major characteristics of the desired final tax structure, whether it is approached in a series of small steps or in one large change.

None the less, it would be foolish to suppose that any country could redesign a tax system and get everything first time. A practical approach to tax policy should combine the insights of both optimal tax theory and tax reform analysis.

2.2. The specification of social welfare

In many areas of economics, it is common to measure the well-being of people by their real after-tax incomes. However, as mentioned above, the literature on optimal taxation is based on the concept of utility. It is, therefore, worth considering why income is not suitable for this analysis. There are three reasons.

First, people often respond to increased taxation by working harder, to reduce the fall in their after-tax incomes. Their increased work effort clearly represents a cost to these people,[2] and this cost should be added to the observed reduction in real after-tax income to arrive at the total cost of the tax increase. This total cost would be reflected in a utility measure that took account of the disutility of work.

Second, in considering the extent of inequality, real after-tax income can be misleading. If everybody received the same hourly wage, but some worked more hours than others, there would be inequality in terms of income but the equity argument for taxing high earners more than lower earners would be weak. After all, anybody could choose to work the longer hours.[3] However, if the same degree of earning inequality was due to differences in wage rates, the equity argument for redistributive taxation would be considerably stronger. If utility was used instead of income as a basis for inequality measurement, the differences in work effort would be taken into account; the case of equal wage rates would show a smaller degree of utility inequality than the case with differing wage rates.

Third, when taxes are applied to consumption goods, relative prices will change and consumers will respond by changing their consumption patterns. This should result in a change in the weights used in the price index that converts nominal to real income. It is not possible to ensure that the weights change properly without knowledge of consumer preferences as represented by a utility function. It is then more convenient to use the utility function directly.

---

[2] If it were not a cost, they would have chosen the higher level of work effort before the tax increase.

[3] We are assuming here that there are no differences in family circumstances that affect the hours people can work.

These three arguments justify the use of looking at utility functions of the form:

$$\text{Utility} = u(x_1, \ldots, x_n, L) \tag{1}$$

where x_i is the consumption of good i and L is the quantity of labour supplied.[4]

When interest is concentrated on income taxation alone, the consumption levels of individual goods are not significant. It is only the total command over consumption goods, represented by income, that is important. The utility function can then be written as:

$$\text{Utility} = u(Y, L) \tag{2}$$

where Y is real after-tax income.

As we shall see in Sections 3 and 4, there are general theoretical results that are independent of the form of these utility functions. However, for quantitative applications, estimates of these functions are essential.[5] In the case of the simplified form (2), estimates can be obtained from studies of labour supply such as those reviewed by Bundell (1992). For the general form (1), a complete demand system must be estimated.[6]

Although statistical methods can supply the form of the utility function, they cannot determine its scale: any increasing transformation of an estimated utility function would be consistent with the same observations. The scale must be fixed by the user in a way that yields the most insight into the problem being studied. In some cases, the utility function can be scaled so that utility is proportional to income, or, at least, so that changes in utility are proportionate to changes in income.[7] Then the scale can be chosen so that a one-unit increase in income (at the current prices) produces a one-unit increase in utility. This makes interpretation of results straightforward, as utility is clearly seen as real income with an adjustment for labour supplied. However, this is not always possible, with the consequence that results are more difficult to interpret.

When the individual utility functions have been determined, they must be aggregated to form social welfare. Once again, there are general

---

[4] Although savings are not explicitly included in this utility function, they can be represented as consumption of future goods. The implications of this are discussed in Section 4.3.

[5] In practice, the use of statistical methods to identify the correct functional form can be very difficult. Many studies concentrate on estimating the parameters corresponding to a pre-specified functional form.

[6] For example, Ebrahimi and Heady (1988) use estimates from Blundell and Walker (1983).

[7] The two cases are those of homothetic and quasi-homothetic preferences, respectively.

theoretical results that do not depend on the method of aggregation, but quantitative results require a specific method. The simplest method, often referred to as 'utilitarianism', is to add the utilities:

$$\text{Social welfare} = \sum_h u^h \tag{3}$$

where u^h is the utility of individual (or household) h.

If the utility functions have been scaled to represent income (adjusted for labour supply), the measure of social welfare is simply a labour supply adjusted measure of national income.

The problem with the social welfare function (3) is that, just like national income, it takes no account of income distribution. If our idea of a fair tax system is one that reduces inequality of utility, our social welfare function must place more weight on utility gains of poor people than those of rich people. This is achieved in most studies by using the following formulation, which transforms utility:

$$\text{Social welfare} = \frac{1}{1-\epsilon} \sum_h (u^h)^{1-\epsilon} \qquad \text{for } \epsilon \neq 1 \tag{4}$$

$$\text{Social welfare} = \sum_h \log(u^h) \qquad \text{for } \epsilon = 1. \tag{5}$$

Concentrating first on expression (4), note that for $\epsilon = 0$ it is the same as expression (3). So when $\epsilon = 0$, there is no concern for inequality. However, when ϵ is positive, increases in u^h are transformed into less than proportional increases of

$$\frac{1}{1-\epsilon} (u^h)^{1-\epsilon}.$$

This implies that less weight is attached to a given absolute increase of utility for somebody with high utility than for somebody with lower utility. The social welfare function therefore embodies a preference for equalising utility. The strength of this preference increases with the value chosen for ϵ. As ϵ approaches infinity, the extent of the preference for equality becomes so strong that only the utility level of the worst-off person has any weight in the social welfare function, representing the view proposed by Rawls (1971). Expression (4) is indeterminate for $\epsilon = 1$ and must be replaced by (5) in that case.

The value chosen for ϵ has a particularly straightforward interpretation if the utility function is proportional to adjusted income. Consider two people, one with twice the adjusted income of the other. The weight placed on additional income going to the poorer person relative to that for the richer person is give by 2^ϵ. Thus, if $\epsilon = 1$ the relative weight is 2, and if $\epsilon = 2$ the relative weight is 4. Thought experiments of this sort allow one to think what a reasonable value of ϵ might be.

Before moving on to discuss disincentives, the consequences of this social welfare formulation can be illustrated by considering a case in which there are no disincentive effects: labour supply is fixed. In this case, it is straightforward to show that the optimal tax policy under social welfare function (3) would involve levying taxes so that the marginal utilities of income were equalised. In the case of social welfare function (4), it would be the marginal transformed utilities that would be equalised. If, in addition, we assumed that all utility functions were identical and everybody worked the same number of hours, both (3) and (4) imply that optimal taxation would produce a perfectly equal distribution of after-tax income.

This result demonstrates that we have departed from Adam Smith's idea of fair taxation: that taxes should be proportional to income. Instead, the objective is to minimise inequality, and in the absence of disincentive effects the inequality can be reduced to zero without any efficiency loss.

There are at least two good reasons for abandoning Adam Smith's principle of fairness: (1) keeping taxes proportional to income at all levels will cause great hardship for people at or below the poverty line, and (2), as argued above, it should be utility rather than income that represents ability to pay. None the less, the idea that the aim of tax policy is to eliminate all inequality has been used in attempts to discredit optimal tax theory and requires some comments.

First, the equality result obtained above depends crucially on the assumptions of identical utility functions and equal labour supply. If people have different needs (perhaps because of illness or numbers of children) or differ in their labour supply, equality of after-tax income is no longer desirable. Thus hard work would still be rewarded.

Second, in practice, disincentive effects prevent the equality result from being implemented. The goal of equality must be qualified by the need for incentives: this is the trade-off between efficiency and equity. The question of what would be desirable without disincentive effects therefore becomes rather irrelevant. All that is important is the wish to reduce inequality below its current level, and even that wish will be offset to some extent by a wish to maintain the efficiency that is also required to maximise social welfare.

2.3. The modelling of disincentives

All taxes affect behaviour to some extent: it is simply impossible for an individual to pay a higher tax bill without reducing consumption, increasing income, reducing savings, or increasing borrowing. The approach of the optimal tax literature is to model this response to taxation in a manner that is consistent with the specification of utilities discussed in the previous section and to trace through the consequences of such behaviour.

This approach can be illustrated with the example of optimal income taxation in a model where labour supply response is the only disincentive problem. In this case, the utility function (2) for each individual is used both to predict how that person will alter his or her labour supply when taxes are changed and to evaluate the resulting level of individual utility. The changes in labour supply will then be used to calculate the change in tax revenue, while the changes in utilities will be used to calculate the change in social welfare. The optimal tax system will be the one where it is impossible to increase social welfare without reducing overall tax revenue.

The requirement to raise a specific amount of tax revenue[8] is obviously fundamental, for otherwise taxes could just be reduced to zero. It has two important implications. First, it means that the solution to the optimal tax problem will depend on the size of the revenue requirement. Second, it means that the tax changes that are considered should be revenue-neutral. For example, an increase in the standard rate of income tax would allow an increase in the personal allowance so that the 'average taxpayer' will continue to pay the same amount of tax.

The importance of this last point becomes clear if we divide the effect of a tax change into an 'income effect' and a 'substitution effect', just as in the standard economic analysis of price changes. The income effect of a tax increase is that it reduces after-tax income and so increases the individual's labour supply, in an effort to ameliorate the reduction in consumption. The substitution effect is that the marginal return to work is reduced, thus leading to a reduction in labour supply. The fact that these two effects go in opposite directions means that the effect of an income tax increase on labour supply could be in either direction, depending on which effect is stronger. However, in revenue-neutral tax changes the average taxpayer does not have an income effect, so the substitution

---

[8] Most of the optimal tax literature takes the revenue requirement as given by a pre-specified level of government spending. The reasons for this level of government spending, and its possible optimisation, are not considered.

effect operates only for that person. Other taxpayers will experience increases or reductions in taxes, but the resulting income effects will probably approximately balance out. Thus, overall the substitution effect will prevail: an increase in the standard rate of income tax that is used to finance an increase in the personal allowance will generally reduce total labour supply.

This dominance of the substitution effect that results from revenue neutrality applies to all optimal tax problems, and leads to an emphasis on the compensated elasticities of supply and demand in the evaluation of the distortionary effects of taxation.[9]

Returning to the example of income taxation, why does it matter that a higher tax rate with higher personal allowances will reduce labour supply? After all, the objective is to maximise social welfare, not the size of the national income. The answer is that, by choosing to work less on average, workers will have lower incomes and thus will pay less taxes. Thus a change that would have been revenue-neutral for a fixed level of labour supply will, as a result of the reduction in work, produce a revenue loss. It is this revenue loss that represents the 'excess burden' of taxation. It requires an increase in tax rates to offset it—an increase that will reduce social welfare and counteract, at least in part, the gain in social welfare from the reduction in inequality that is produced by the increase in tax progressivity. The factors that determine whether the overall effect on social welfare is positive or negative will be discussed in Section 3.

The approach in other areas of optimal taxation is basically similar to that described above for income taxation and labour supply. There is, therefore, no need to discuss them separately. However, it is worth pointing out that any modelling of disincentive effects is likely to be selective. For example, income taxation can affect other decisions apart from labour supply, such as educational choice, savings decisions, and even the decision to evade taxes. Models have been constructed to look at these different disincentive effects separately or in conjunction with labour supply, but there is no model that combines them all. This is probably because the complexity of such an omnibus would be too great to yield any useful insights.

---

[9] A compensated elasticity measures the strength of the substitution effect alone, indicating the response to a price change under the assumption that the individual is compensated (positively or negatively) to maintain his or her real income. This is appropriate because of the revenue neutrality of the tax changes being considered.

2.4. Problems of application

Before proceeding, it is important to note the aim of optimal tax analysis. It is to describe the taxes that governments should set, not to explain the taxes that governments do set. One might like to think that governments do what they should, but there are a number of reasons for believing that they do not. A close relationship between the prescriptions of optimal tax analysis and the tax systems that are actually implemented should not necessarily be expected.

The idea of what should be done must, of course, be based on ethical views. In the case of taxation, the role of ethics is confined to the view that is taken about the importance of reducing inequality. In the theory, this is represented by the parameter ϵ in the social welfare function (4). Clearly, people can differ in their views about a reasonable value for ϵ, and so it is standard practice to calculate optimal taxes for several different values.

It might be thought that appropriate choice of ϵ could rationalise almost any tax system, but that is not correct. The studies discussed below show that variations of ϵ often have fairly modest effects on optimal tax rates, and typically have a very small effect on the relative size of different taxes. The range of optimal taxes that are calculated for different values of ϵ is both inevitable and desirable: one cannot believe that people with different views on inequality would choose the same rate of income tax.

The usefulness of the optimal tax results will depend in part on the realism of the economic models that are used in their derivation. This is not to say that the presence of any unrealistic assumption invalidates the results. Rather, any practical application of theoretical analysis requires an evaluation of whether any violation of the assumptions can be expected to alter the results significantly.

One way in which many models are unrealistic has already been mentioned: their neglect of administrative costs of tax collection. To this can be added neglect of the costs to taxpayers of compliance. These costs have usually been omitted because they do not vary continuously with the tax rates. Instead, they tend to vary with such things as the number of different rates of tax or the number of tax allowances. This makes them difficult to include in the mathematical analysis.

This does not mean that administrative and compliance costs have been completely neglected. A number of studies have used administrative costs as a reason for restricting the number of tax rates or for ruling out some taxes altogether. If numerical calculations are used, it is possible to compare optimal policies that correspond to different restrictions on the number of tax rates. The difference in the optimal values of social welfare can be converted into money terms by calculating the change in total income that would produce a similar welfare change. This sum of money then represents the gain of allowing a more complex tax system, and this could be compared with the likely additional administrative and compliance costs.

Another doubtful assumption in some, but not all, models is that the economy is otherwise undistorted. Perfect competition is usually assumed, as is the absence of environmental effects and other externalities. The dropping of these assumptions would alter the optimal pattern of taxes[10] but would greatly increase both the complexity of these models and their data requirements. The application of optimal tax results in situations where imperfect competition or externality problems are significant therefore requires considerable care.

Models also differ in the extent to which they recognise the diversity of households in terms of their composition and preferences. Until now, this chapter has focused on individuals, but their position within households can affect their labour supply, their demand patterns, and their level of utility. This fact has been recognised in some of the literature, but it has been ignored in many papers in order to clarify the main point of the discussion. Obviously, practical policy must at least take account of the different needs of different demographic groups.

Finally, it should be noted that optimal tax analysis has concentrated on personal income taxes and commodity taxes, including taxes on international trade. It has not dealt with company taxation, capital gains tax, or inheritance taxes.[11] The reason for this is probably that the effects of these taxes on behaviour and utility are less well understood than the effects of personal income tax and commodity taxes. Also, issues of administrative costs and enforcement are considered as more important for these taxes. This presents an extra difficulty in devising a suitable mathematical formulation of the tax design problem.

---

[10] Some of the effects of introducing imperfect competition are discussed in Myles (1989a).

[11] To the extent that these taxes are simply seen as taxes on savings, they are covered by the analysis discussed in Section 4.3. However, these taxes also have an effect on the choice between different financial assets, and the full consequences of that have not been modelled.

3. Optimal Income Taxation

The first analysis of income taxation using the methodology described in Section 2 was by Mirrlees (1971). This paper stimulated a number of further studies, each analysing the same basic model of the economy, often referred to as the 'Mirrlees model'.

The two fundamental assumptions of the Mirrlees model are: (1) the only disincentive effect of taxation is on the number of hours supplied by each worker and (2) differences between the wages of different workers are produced by differences in their fixed productivities. The fixed productivities of assumption (2) imply that relative pre-tax wages are fixed.

The Mirrlees paper considered the problem of designing an optimal non-linear income tax in which the marginal tax can vary as income rises. However, it is also interesting to consider the design of simpler tax systems with a constant marginal rate: an optimal linear income tax. It is also important to consider the implications of changing the two key assumptions. These three topics are now discussed in turn.

3.1. Non-linear income taxation

Much of the discussion in Mirrlees (1971) is technically difficult, but the main ideas can be understood without going into the technicalities.

The fundamental policy issue is whether it would be a good idea to increase the rate of income tax and use the proceeds to fund an increase in tax allowances, thus reducing after-tax income inequality.

Because we are dealing with non-linear taxation, it is possible to consider the effect of changing the marginal tax rate over a short range without changing the marginal tax rate at any other incomes. The people with incomes below the range of tax increase will be unaffected by this change. People with income below the range of tax increase will be unaffected by this change. People with income within the range will experience an income effect from the higher taxes which would tend to increase their labour supply. However, they will also experience a substitution effect tending to reduce their labour supply because of the reduced reward for additional work. Because the increased tax rate applies only to a small proportion of their income, the size of the reduction in after-tax income will be small and so the income effect will generally be less than the substitution effect. Therefore, the labour supply of this group will be reduced and they will therefore probably pay less tax.

People with incomes above the range will not experience a substitution effect, because their marginal tax rate has not changed. However, they will pay more tax, because of the higher rate applied to some of their income. This will have an income effect, causing them to work more and so pay yet more tax.

Overall, there are three effects of the tax increase on tax revenue and welfare: (i) the tax payments of people with the increased marginal rate will probably fall, (ii) the tax payments of people with income above the range of increase will rise, and (iii) the utility levels of both groups affected by the tax increase will fall.

If the net effect of (i) and (ii) is negative, there is no extra revenue available to fund an increase in tax allowances and so the increase in the marginal tax rate is clearly not desirable. This is most likely to occur either if effect (i) is large, because of a high compensated elasticity of labour supply, or if effect (ii) is small, because the number of people above the range of increase is small.

If the net effect of (i) and (ii) is positive, the revenue gain from the tax increase must be weighed against the utility loss of effect (iii). This can be done by calculating the welfare gain that would be produced by using the additional revenue to increase tax allowances. It is then a matter of weighing the utility loss to higher-income people against the utility gain to lower-income people.

Overall, therefore, the net effect on social welfare will depend on four factors:

(1) the compensated elasticity of labour supply: a high elasticity will mean that the net revenue gain is either small or negative, so the tax increase is less likely to increase social welfare;

(2) the degree of concern for inequality, as represented by ϵ in equation (4): the higher is ϵ, the smaller is the relative weight placed on the utility losses of the losers from the tax increase, and so the tax increase is more likely to increase social welfare;

(3) the degree of income inequality: a high level of inequality implies a greater income difference between the (relatively poor) gainers and the (relatively rich) losers from the tax change, implying that a greater relative weight should be attached to the gains, and that the tax increase is more likely to increase social welfare;

(4) the proportion of the population above the range of the tax increase: the higher is this proportion, the greater is the amount of gain to the poorest, and so the tax increase is more likely to increase social welfare.

One implication of factor (4) that has attracted considerable attention in the theoretical literature is that the marginal income tax rate for the person with the highest income should be zero. This is because there is no extra revenue to be obtained by raising it above zero, and so no reason to distort that person's labour supply decision.

The argument really needs to be more complicated, because the government cannot know in advance the precise level of the highest income. A full analysis involves consideration of the probability distribution of incomes, and the result becomes less sharp: the marginal tax rate should approach zero as incomes become very high, provided that the probability density declines at a sufficiently fast rate.

However, from a practical policy point of view, the importance of this result does not lie in its precise form: tailoring the very top of the income tax schedule to minimise the disincentive effects for a very small number of people can hardly be seen as a major policy issue.[12] Rather, its importance lies in it being a counter-example to the widespread belief that a redistributive government must use an income tax schedule with increasing marginal rates. Here is a case where, however strong is the wish to increase the utility of the poor, the marginal tax rate declines at the top of the income distribution.

This theoretical result can be derived only for the top of the income distribution. However, Mirrlees (1971) also calculated complete optimal income tax schedules for some specific numerical examples. These show a very gentle decline in the marginal tax rate over most of the income distribution. The decline is so slight that the optimal income tax schedule can be approximated fairly well by a tax system with a constant marginal rate: a linear income tax.[13]

This finding has considerable practical significance because it suggests that there is no conflict between theoretical optimality and administrative convenience. All the advantages of a single marginal rate, most notably the ability accurately to withhold taxes from multiple sources, can be achieved with no worsening of the inescapable trade-off between equity and efficiency.

It is important to realise that a linear income tax can achieve significant redistribution. Personal tax allowances that are a substantial

[12] This point is reinforced by calculations of optimal income tax schedules reported in Tuomala (1990), which show substantial positive marginal rates even for people in the top 1 per cent of the income distribution.

[13] Tuomala (1990) shows that more rapidly declining marginal rates can be desirable when different parameter values are assumed. However, none of the numerical examples supports the widespread use of increasing marginal tax rates.

fraction of average income can produce considerable progressivity in the average tax rate over most of the income distribution. The constant marginal rate implies that the degree of progressivity declines (but is still positive) at high income levels. But there are so few people at those incomes that additional progressivity will yield little or no extra revenue.

3.2. Linear income taxation

The conclusion that optimal income tax schedules are approximately linear has allowed investigators to concentrate on analysing optimal linear taxation. This has the important practical advantage of greatly simplifying the calculations needed for numerical examples.

The most important study is that of Stern (1976), who took considerable care in selecting realistic functional forms and parameter values. The study uses the same basic structure as the Mirrlees model and reports the optimal tax rates that correspond to a range of values for the compensated elasticity of labour supply, the degree of concern for inequality, and the size of the government's revenue requirement.

TABLE 1.1. *Optimal tax rates for varying parameters (%)*

	$\epsilon=2$	$\epsilon=3$	$\epsilon=\infty$
Case 1	54	59	87
Case 2	68	72	94
Case 3	45	50	80
Case 4	48	53	84
Case 5	61	65	90

Note: See text for description of cases.

Table 1.1 presents a small part of Stern's results. It shows the optimal tax rates corresponding to three different values of ϵ, for each set of assumptions about the compensated elasticity of labour supply and the size of the government's revenue requirement. Case 1 corresponds to Stern's best estimate of labour supply elasticity and a reasonable value for the government's revenue requirement. The remaining cases alter one parameter at a time, keeping the other constant. Thus Case 2 reduces the value of the labour supply elasticity and Case 3 raises it, while the revenue requirement is kept constant at the value for Case 1. Similarly, Case

4 reduces the revenue requirement and Case 5 raises it, keeping the labour supply elasticity at the value for Case 1.

The results confirm the effect of the first two factors considered in the discussion of non-linear income taxation and Stern states that unreported calculations also confirm the third effect. The original fourth effect no longer applies, as the marginal tax rate is constant, but can be replaced by the effect of the government's revenue requirement. Thus the optimal marginal rate of income tax is higher for:

- lower values of the compensated elasticity of labour supply;
- higher values of ϵ, the degree of concern for inequality;
- greater inequality in pre-tax wages;
- higher government revenue requirement.

The results also confirm another important aspect of the analysis of optimal non-linear income taxation: for some parameter values, the revenue effect of raising the tax rate is negative. This implies that there is a limit to how high the tax rate should be raised, however strong is the concern for inequality. This limit depends crucially on the value of the compensated elasticity of labour supply. This shows that observable market behaviour can limit the role of the ethical views in determining tax policy: we can all agree that some tax rates would be too high.

None the less, differences in concern for inequality can generate a substantial range of optimal marginal tax rates, especially when one notes that smaller values of ϵ would produce lower optimal tax rates. For reasonable parameter values, this range includes the tax rates currently used in most OECD countries.[14] One cannot say that one of these rates is better than another without taking a firm view on how much concern should be shown for inequality.

One important feature of linear income taxation is that people with income below the tax exemption level will receive a transfer payment from the government.[15] In other words, the linear income tax

---

[14] As the Mirrlees model does not explicitly include any other taxes, any comparison between model results and actual rates should take account of all taxes that vary with income, not just the formal 'income tax'. In the UK, this would include VAT and other sales taxes, so that the model-equivalent marginal income tax for the typical taxpayer would include both the standard rate of income tax and the percentage of additional income that would go in sales taxes. The question of whether National Insurance contributions should be included turns on whether they are viewed as a tax or as savings. In the UK, the connection between marginal contributions and level of benefit is so weak that they should probably be regarded as a tax.

[15] This characteristic of optimal income tax schemes is not confined to the linear case: the non-linear calculations in Mirrlees (1971) also included transfer payments to low-income individuals.

incorporates a negative income tax system of social security. This is a feature that differs quite markedly from the practice of most OECD countries, in which social security benefit entitlement is much more complex and the implicit marginal tax rate on benefit recipients is frequently very much higher than the rate applied to non-recipients.

3.3. Changing the assumptions

Although the Mirrlees model has held centre stage in the study of optimal income taxation, there have been attempts to analyse the consequences of altering the basic model. Tuomala (1990) provides a thorough discussion of many of these alterations. Two interesting examples are the work of Allen (1982) and Atkinson (1973).

Allen (1982) considers the effects of dropping the assumption of fixed relative wages, but otherwise maintains the Mirrlees assumptions. Two types of worker are considered and their relative wages are assumed to depend on the relative supply of the two types of labour, the wage of one type declining as its supply increases. If, in the absence of taxation, one type of worker is paid less than the other, the optimal non-linear income tax will be quite different from the Mirrlees case. The poorer group will face a positive marginal tax rate, while the richer group will face a negative marginal tax rate. The reason for this is that it will reduce the supply of low-paid workers and increase the supply of high-paid workers, thus reducing the extent of pre-tax inequality. The size of this effect will clearly depend on how difficult it is to substitute one type of worker for another.[16]

This result is certainly provocative, although some of its features depend on there being just two distinct groups with an income gap between them.[17] None the less, Carruth, Heady, and Ulph (1983) show that the result can be extended to a model with a large number of different types of worker. In that case the marginal tax rate at the top of the income distribution is negative, rather than the zero of the Mirrlees model. However, it is difficult to establish the form of the complete tax schedule in a model as complicated as this. Moreover, there is little evidence on the crucial question of how difficult it is to substitute between different types of worker. This means that further work is needed before

[16] In more technical terms, it will depend on the inverse of the elasticity of substitution between different types of labour.

[17] The income gap allows the tax schedule to be manipulated to make the higher-paid group pay more tax despite their negative marginal rate.

an assessment can be made as to whether relative wage effects significantly affect the practical policy implications of the Mirrlees model.

Atkinson (1973) looks at a different type of disincentive. In his model, hours of work are fixed but the efficiency of labour depends on the educational level of the worker. Receiving education is costly and so an income tax can have a disincentive effect on educational choice. Atkinson restricts his attention to the optimal linear income tax. Although the model is concerned with a different dimension of labour supply choice—quality rather than quantity—the mathematical structure is similar to that of Stern's analysis of linear income taxation in the Mirrlees model. It is therefore not surprising that the range of optimal tax rates obtained for reasonable parameter values is similar to that obtained by Stern.

Neither of these two variations on the basic optimal income tax model provides us with much practical guidance. The most important practical result from the Mirrlees model is that the optimal income tax schedule is approximately linear. Atkinson's model does not address this issue, as it imposes linearity from the start. Allen's model casts some doubt on the desirability of linear income taxation, but there is insufficient evidence of the degree of tax non-linearity that it would imply in practice. Clearly there is room for more work here.

Finally, it is worth noting that most of the optimal income tax literature does not deal with one important practical policy issue: the extent to which demographic characteristics of households should be reflected in the tax system. For example, how should the presence of children affect a household's tax liability? This sort of question has, however, been addressed in the literature on optimal commodity taxation, and it is to this topic that we now turn.

4. Optimal Commodity Taxation

The literature on optimal commodity taxation is mainly concerned with the design of final sales taxes, such as value added tax and the excise duties on alcohol, tobacco, and petrol. However, it has also dealt with the taxation of intermediate goods and international trade, and can be used to analyse the taxation of savings.

4.1. Final sales taxes

The first analysis of optimal sales taxes was undertaken by Ramsey (1927) and considerably predates the literature on optimal income taxation. It focused on a rather different question. Instead of looking at the trade-off between equity and efficiency, it analysed the problem of designing sales taxes to raise a given amount of revenue at the least possible distortionary cost in a single-person economy (or, equivalently, an economy with many identical people).

To a certain extent, this is not a serious problem. If there is no inequality, there is no reason to avoid the use of a poll tax, which would have no distortionary cost. It is only a concern for the regression impact of a poll tax that leads to the desirability of using distortionary taxation. None the less, the results of Ramsey (1927) and of Corlett and Hague (1953) in the single-person context provided useful insights for the subsequent analysis of optimal sales taxes in an economy with inequality.

Ramsey showed that, when only a very small amount of revenue had to be raised, the taxes should produce equal proportional reductions in the consumption of each good. He then showed that this result continued to hold, even for substantial revenue requirements, if there were no income effects and if the demand curves for the goods were linear. These conditions are most unlikely to hold in practice but, as is shown in Atkinson and Stiglitz (1980: p. 372), this 'equal proportional reductions' rule can be expressed as a generally applicable mathematical condition that optimal taxes should satisfy.

Unfortunately, this condition does not provide a direct indication of which goods should be most heavily taxed. Greater intuition can be obtained by making an additional assumption: that the demand for each good is independent of the prices of other goods. Using this assumption, Ramsey derived the 'inverse elasticity rule', that goods with more price-inelastic demands should be taxed more heavily. This rule only strictly applies under the assumption of independent demands and needs considerable revision when income inequality is taken into account. However, the rule has wide influence and its basic rationale—that the taxation of inelastic goods yields more revenue because demand falls only a little—is probably partly responsible for the high taxation of alcohol, tobacco, and petrol all over the world.

Corlett and Hague (1953) approached the issue of tax design from a different perspective. Instead of asking which pattern of taxes would be optimal, they looked at a situation where there are two consumption goods taxed at the same rate and asked whether efficiency could be improved by introducing some non-uniformity (raising the tax on one good and lowering the tax on the other). They showed that, if the goods differed in their degree of complementarity or substitutability with leisure, efficiency could be improved by increasing the tax rate on the good that was most complementary (or least substitutable) with leisure and reducing the tax rate on the other good.

The intuition behind this result is as follows. A uniform tax on the two consumption goods is effectively the same as an income tax (ignoring savings). The distortionary effect is therefore one of discouraging labour supply or encouraging leisure. An increase in tax on a good that is complementary with leisure will discourage the consumption of leisure, increase labour supply, and so partially offset the original distortion.

Clearly, if uniform taxation were optimal, the introduction of non-uniformity would not improve efficiency. The Corlett and Hague result therefore tells us that uniform taxes are optimal if all goods have the same degree of complementarity or substitutability with leisure. It also suggests a result which was later demonstrated by Diamond and Mirrlees (1971): that, in this two-good case, optimal taxation involves placing a heavier tax on the good that is most complementary to leisure.

The Corlett and Hague result was obtained in a model that is basically the same as that used by Ramsey and so one should expect the two results to be consistent, as indeed they are. The relationship between the two results is explored in Heady (1987), using a diagrammatic analysis. All that need be noted here is that, in the 'inverse elasticity' case (with independent demands), it can be shown that the good which is most complementary to leisure will also be the good with the most inelastic demand curve. Thus the two results pick the same good to be most heavily taxed.

The next major step in the development of the theory of optimal commodity taxation came with the analysis of an economy with inequality by Diamond and Mirrlees (1971). They showed that the introduction of distributional considerations alters the equal proportional reductions rule substantially. The most significant alteration was that goods which are consumed particularly heavily by the poor should experience a lower-than-average proportional reduction. The extent of the differentiation in proportional reductions would depend on the degree of concern for the poor, as represented by our parameter ϵ, and the extent of differences in consumption patterns between the rich and the poor.

In the case of independent demands, the Diamond and Mirrlees result shows that the optimal tax rate on a good should depend not only on the inverse of its price elasticity of demand but also on its income elasticity, which indicates how the budget share of a good changes as income rises. The significance of this modification can be appreciated when one notes that many goods with low price elasticities: the demand for goods that are regarded as necessities will not be very responsive to changes in either price or income. For these goods, the efficiency argument for high taxation must be balanced against the distributional argument for low taxation. The question arises of whether differential taxation really is a good idea, and this has been the focus of much recent research on optimal sales taxes.

The analysis of whether differential sales taxation is desirable was encouraged by two further considerations. First, the costs of administration and compliance are much lower if sales taxes are uniform. Second, if we ignore the issue of savings (which will be taken up later), a uniform sales tax accompanied by a uniform payment to all households is equivalent to a linear income tax with a suitably chosen exemption level and marginal tax rate.[18] Therefore, if uniform sales taxes are optimal, the choice of the relative proportions of revenue to be raised by income tax and sales tax need take account only of the effect on savings and of administrative considerations, such as collection costs and the need to minimise tax evasion.

The major results on whether differential sales taxes are desirable in an economy where households differ only in their incomes and not in their underlying preferences are shown in Atkinson and Stiglitz (1980: ch. 14). An important aspect of their analysis is the role of the uniform payment to all households (or the income tax exemption level). If all goods are normal, in the sense of being consumed in larger quantities by people with higher incomes, the poor will always benefit more by an increase in the uniform payment than by the same amount of money being used to reduce the sales tax on a particular good: the reduction in sales taxes will benefit the rich more because they buy more of the good.

As empirical studies in the UK have failed to find any categories of goods that are not normal, this argument implies that the government's redistributive goals are best achieved by an appropriate choice of the uniform payment. Therefore, the issue of whether to have differential sales taxes is really one of efficiency, provided that the uniform payment is set optimally, and we are back with the Corlett and Hague question of

---

[18] The exemption level would have to be chosen so that people with no income would receive the same real payment from the government under the two schemes. The equivalent marginal income tax rate would be lower than the uniform sales tax rate. For example, a 100% sales tax halves a person's real disposable income and so is equivalent to a 50% income tax rate.

whether differential sales taxes will reduce the disincentive effect on labour supply of an income tax. As explained above, the answer depends on differences in the degree of complementarity between individual goods and leisure, and Atkinson and Stiglitz show that the condition for uniform taxation to be optimal is that the uniform payment is set optimally and that there is weak separability between goods and leisure.[19] This condition means that households with different hours of work but the same income (because of different wage rates) will choose the same quantities of consumer goods.

The intuition here is essentially the same as for the Corlett and Hague result. Consider a good that is more heavily consumed by households that take more leisure—golf clubs, for example. Additional taxation of such a good is essentially a tax on leisure and will ameliorate the effect of the tax on work. On the other hand, if one could identify goods consumed by those who work more (convenience foods, perhaps), a lower rate of tax on them would encourage work effort.

An obvious difficulty that arises in attempting to apply the Atkinson and Stiglitz result to a country like the UK is that their model ignores differences in preferences between households that might arise from differences in demographic characteristics. This is particularly significant because the arguments in favour of VAT zero-rating for some goods is that they form a large part of the budget of particular demographic groups. Thus the zero-rating of food and children's clothing is justified by the observation that families with large numbers of children are particularly prone to poverty and spend a high proportion of their budgets on these items.

Deaton and Stern (1986) extend the Atkinson and Stiglitz result to an economy with different demographic groups and show that uniform taxation is still desirable if preferences are weakly separable, provided that households in each demographic group receive an optimally chosen payment which is uniform within each group but differs between groups. The idea here is that the redistribution between groups is accomplished most efficiently by the use of direct payments to households, leaving the sales tax rates to deal with problems of efficiency.

Ebrahimi and Heady (1988) develop the Deaton and Stern analysis and apply numerical analysis to look at the question of whether it would

---

[19] This condition is slightly different from the Corlett and Hague result, because of the presence of the uniform payment. It should also be noted that the Atkinson and Stiglitz result requires that the Engel curves (the relationship between a household's demand for a good and its income) be linear, but this is not required if there is an optimal non-linear income tax.

be better to abolish the zero-rating of food and use the additional funds to finance an increase in child benefit. The numerical results confirm the Deaton and Stern theoretical result under their assumptions, but the effect of relaxing these assumptions is also investigated. Some of the results are shown in Table 1.2.

TABLE 1.2. *Optimal sales taxes with child benefit* (ϵ=1)

	(1)	(2)	(3)	(4)
Tax on energy	30%	41%	28%	35%
Tax on food	34%	40%	32%	37%
Tax on clothing	52%	41%	55%	42%
Tax on other goods	44%	40%	49%	46%
Lump sum (per week)	£28	£28	£57	£56
Child benefit (per week)	£22	£22	–	–

Note: Column (1) is based on the estimates from Blundell and Walker (1983);
column (2) is the same as column (1) but separability has been imposed;
column (3) is the same as column (1) but there is no child benefit;
column (4) is the same as column (2) but there is no child benefit.

All of the results in Table 1.2 correspond to a zero government revenue requirement (above that needed to pay for the child benefit and personal tax allowances). The personal tax allowances have been converted into equivalent lump-sum payments, and so we have the equivalent of a negative income tax. However, there is no explicit income tax in the model: all the revenue is raised by the sales taxes, which accounts for their high rates, but could equivalently be raised by an income tax and a lower level of sales taxes. That would have no effect on the degree of non-uniformity of the sales taxes, which is what concerns us here.

Column (1) represents the optimal sales tax pattern combined with optimally set lump-sum payments and child benefit. It is based on demand system estimates that allow for non-separability, and so the existence of some non-uniformity is not surprising. It shows that available empirical estimates of the degree of non-separability do justify a small amount of differential taxation, even if child benefit is set optimally. However, the welfare loss of imposing uniformity is equivalent to only 0.4 per cent of GNP and could well be outweighed by the administrative problems of non-uniformity.

Column (2) shows the effects of altering the demand system estimates to impose separability. The resulting optimal taxes are almost uniform, but not quite, because there are two of Deaton and Stern's requirements that have not been met. First, there is a condition that the Engel curves should have the same slope for all households. Second, we have imposed a uniform child benefit for each child, while Deaton and Stern allow child benefits to be set separately for families with different numbers of children. However, the non uniformity is so small as to suggest that these two theoretical conditions are of little practical importance.

Columns (3) and (4) show the optimal taxes when there is no child benefit. These results show that the desirability of uniform taxation depends crucially on the optimal setting of child benefit. If it is not set optimally, substantial non-uniformity can be justified even if the weak separability condition is satisfied.

Table 1.2 also provides an illustration of how optimal tax theory can be used to calculate the special tax treatment given to different demographic groups, a point that was found to be missing in the review of optimal income tax in Section 3. Child benefit is obviously not a tax provision, but its effects are identical to a child tax allowance under a linear negative income tax system.[20]

The optimal child benefit reported in Table 1.2 is substantially higher than the current value in the UK. However, this result should be treated with some care. As explained in Ebrahimi and Heady, this result is based on the assumption that, while children are costly to raise, they provide no benefits to the household. This is obviously untrue, for otherwise no household would choose to have children. The proper setting of child benefit must involve more complex issues than the simple economic cost of child-raising. These would include issues of parental responsibility, and the extent to which children should be allowed to suffer from the fertility decisions of their parents.

This suggests that optimal tax analysis cannot settle all issues related to the treatment of different demographic groups. However, it does not compromise the importance of the tax uniformity result: direct payments are more effective than non-uniform sales taxes in achieving distributional goals. It is only when direct payments are impracticable that non-uniform taxes should be employed.

Although the optimal tax literature has addressed the issue of differential sales taxes that might be sought on distributional grounds, it has not really confronted the issue of whether the high rates of taxation on alcohol, tobacco, and petrol are optimal. In terms of the analysis in this section, these high rates of tax can be justified only if it could be shown

---

[20] The equivalent child tax allowance is one which has the same budgetary cost as the child benefit. The linearity of the tax system and its extension to households below the tax threshold (the 'negative income tax') is necessary to ensure that, like the child benefit, the net benefit of the tax allowance is the same for all households.

that these goods are very strongly complementary to leisure. In fact, the estimation of consumer demand functions for these goods involves particular statistical problems and they are often excluded from the complete demand system estimates that are used to inform calculations of optimal tax rates. There is, therefore, no definitive answer as to whether the high rates of tax can be justified in terms of complementarity to leisure.

In fact, my guess is that such high rates of tax could not be justified in these terms alone. The calculated optimal taxes on goods that have been estimated to be particularly complementary to leisure have not been anything like as high. The justification, if there is one, for these high rates of tax must be found elsewhere: either in terms of the externalities that the consumption of these goods impose on other people (including possible costs to the National Health Service) or on the basis of a paternalistic concern for the consumer's health. As observed in Section 2.4, these concerns have not yet been integrated into the literature on optimal taxation.

4.2. The taxation of intermediate goods and international trade

In addition to introducing distributional considerations into the theory of optimal commodity taxation, Diamond and Mirrlees (1971) demonstrated an important result about the desirability of production efficiency. They showed that, even though considerations of income distribution might justify the use of distortionary taxes on the supply of factors of production or the consumption of final goods, they did not justify any distortion to the way in which production is organised.

The basic idea behind this result is that each household's level of welfare depends on the prices it receives for the labour and other factors of production that it sells and on the prices it pays for the goods it consumes. It is these prices, therefore, that determine the distribution of utility. If the government is setting all taxes optimally, it is able to control all of these prices independently of the prices that firms face in trades between themselves. For example, if the producer price of cars was to rise, the government could prevent the consumer price from rising by reducing the sales tax on cars. Thus there is no improvement in social welfare that would result from a manipulation of producer prices; all that is required of the production sector of the economy is that it should be as efficient as possible, and it is a standard result in economics that this efficiency is maximised if there is no taxation on trade between firms.

This production efficiency result has wide implications. It is straight-forward to see that it implies that turnover taxes are inefficient and should be replaced by VAT or final sales taxes. It also implies that public sector enterprises should attempt to maximise profits at market prices, in just the same way as private companies. Finally, and most controver-sially, it implies that a country that has no monopoly or monopsony power in world trade (a 'small country') should not tax either imports or exports.[21] The idea here is that international trade can be seen as just another production activity, converting exports into imports, and so should not be distorted. If substantial revenues are raised from import duties, they should be replaced by domestic sales taxes on the same goods at the same rates. These will yield at least as much revenue and will not distort production. If the resulting imports result in the reduction in the wage of people with particular skills, then it is more efficient to make transfer payments to those workers than to distort production.

A result as powerful as this must clearly rely on quite far-reaching assumptions. It certainly assumes that all markets are functioning effi-ciently and that unemployment would not result from the removal of trade barriers. Obviously, in practice, the removal of trade barriers or the exposure of nationalised industries to full market pressures might well cause problems of adjustment. The result is telling us that, once these short-term problems are out of the way, the final level of social welfare will be higher. However, it cannot tell us whether the short-term loss is outweighed by the long-term gain. This would depend on the precise nature of the adjustment process and the rate at which future benefits were discounted in comparison to current costs.

Another assumption that is required to produce this result is that pri-vate sector firms do not earn pure after-tax profits, something that would be guaranteed if there was perfect competition and constant returns to scale. That is not to say that they do not earn any accounting profits. Rather, the requirement is that they do not earn any more profit than is required to attract the equity capital in the firm. This assumption is needed because otherwise changes in producer prices will affect pure profits, and hence household utility. The assumption is almost certainly violated in the real world, but it is hard to know how important this is because of the difficulty of measuring pure profits.[22]

The final assumption is much more significant: the assumption that

---

[21] This does not, of course, alter the 'optimal tariff' argument for countries to restrict trade to exploit monopoly or monopsony power.

[22] Imperfect competition is one way in which profits can arise, and the implications of this for the taxation of intermediate goods are discussed in Myles (1989b).

the government is able to alter taxes on individual goods to manipulate their prices precisely. This is very difficult for the government to do, and the example above of compensating workers who lose out from trade liberalisation illustrates this. It would be very difficult to identify exactly which workers have suffered and calculate the precise amount of compensation needed.

The violation of this assumption opens the possibility of justifying import tariffs in terms of the need to protect particular vulnerable groups of workers. Heady and Mitra (1987) use numerical analysis to investigate the size of the tariffs that could be justified. The optimal tariffs they find are low (usually less than 20 per cent) but could be significant in their impact. However, these arguments could not justify many of the tariffs that are actually observed. They are frequently unjustifiably high and/or provide benefit to the rich rather than the poor.

The difficulties of setting optimal taxes, or any taxes at all, are greatest in underdeveloped countries. It is often nearly impossible to collect taxes directly from subsistence agriculture or the informal urban sector. In such cases, trade taxes may be the only way of collecting sufficient revenue, and, indeed, underdeveloped countries are usually much more reliant on the revenue from trade taxes than are the OECD countries. Tax issues for underdeveloped countries are discussed in Newbery and Stern (1987).

Despite the practical objections raised here to the blanket application of the production efficiency result, its practical importance must not be overlooked. It is often easy to provide some example of an assumption that is not quite satisfied, but, at least for countries like the UK, it provides a very useful benchmark that is widely applicable. It is best to presume the desirability of production efficiency, and place the burden of proof on the people who are arguing for an exception.

4.3. The taxation of savings

So far in this chapter, the issue of savings has been ignored, except to say that its existence produces the only difference in effect between a linear income tax and a uniform sales tax. However, the effect of taxation on savings is a major policy issue and there have been a number of tax changes in recent years that have been designed to encourage savings.

The issue is whether people should be taxed on their full income, including income from capital, or on their expenditure on goods and services. A tax on expenditures could be implemented either as a uniform sales tax, such as VAT, or by extending the current sheltering of certain types of savings under the income tax. There have been moves of both types in the UK since 1979: the progressive reduction in income tax-sheltered forms of savings.

Income taxation taxes both the income that is saved and the subsequent return on that saving, something that is often referred to as the 'double taxation of savings'. Expenditure taxation either allows the interest to be tax-exempt or postpones the taxation on the amount saved until it is spent, at which point both the savings and the return are taxed. Under income taxation, the saver's return on the savings is less than the rate paid by the borrower. Under expenditure taxation, the saver's return is equal to the rate paid by the borrower. Thus the income tax can be seen as discouraging saving, while the expenditure tax does not discourage it.

This makes the expenditure tax seem better. However, because it exempts savings, an expenditure tax does not raise as much revenue as an income tax with the same nominal rate. To be revenue-neutral, the expenditure tax must be levied at a higher rate. The question is whether the disadvantages of the higher rate outweigh the advantages of not discouraging savings.

The analysis of this question can become extremely difficult, as it involves people making savings decisions that will have effects for a long time into the future. However, Atkinson and Stiglitz (1980: ch. 14) show how the theory of optimal commodity taxation can shed some light on the question. They divide a person's life into two periods: work and retirement. The person earns wage income in the first period and divides the proceeds between consumption in the two periods. The total consumption in each period can be viewed as one composite good. Viewed in this way, expenditure taxation is equivalent to an equal tax rate on the two goods, while income taxation is equivalent to a higher tax rate on retirement consumption. The analysis in Section 4.1 suggests that which is better depends on whether consumption in retirement is more complementary with leisure in the work period than is consumption in the work period. If it is, income tax is better. If the two types of consumption are equally complementary with leisure (if there is weak separability), the expenditure tax is better.

This analysis has not settled the issue, partly because it is clearly a gross simplification of reality and partly because there is no conclusive evidence about the structure of people's intertemporal preferences. However, this analysis does show that the theory of optimal commodity taxation can provide some insight into the issues involved.

Unfortunately, it has not progressed far enough to yield practical policy conclusions.

Even if we cannot determine the rate at which savings should be taxed, can we presume that all forms of savings should be taxed at the same rate? This is an important practical issue because we observe a wide range of tax treatments for different forms of savings: bank and building society deposits, equities, pension funds.

This is not an issue that the optimal tax literature has addressed directly, but it could be argued that such variations in tax treatment result in different firms facing different costs of capital. If that is the case, the differential tax treatment violates the production efficiency result discussed above, which requires all firms to face the same prices for all inputs and outputs.

This argument has a strong appeal, and it is hard to see any justification for the wide range of tax treatments for different types of savings. However, the financial markets are so complex that it is often difficult to trace through the effects of all these different tax treatments and demonstrate the way in which resources are being misallocated. This is clearly an area that deserves attention in future research.

5. Conclusions

The organising theme of this survey has been the assessment of the contribution that the literature on optimal taxation can make to the formulation of practical tax policy. It is therefore appropriate to conclude by summarising that contribution.

The most important, and perhaps surprising, conclusion from the literature on optimal income taxation is that the optimal schedule can often be approximated by a linear income tax. There is certainly no reason to expect the optimal marginal rate to increase at higher income levels: any wish to increase tax progression is balanced by the fact that there are few people to pay those higher taxes. This conflicts with the practice of most countries, but perhaps the conflict arises from a lack of general awareness about how strongly redistributive linear taxation can be.

The other important conclusion about income taxation is that, although a fairly wide range of optimal marginal tax rates correspond to a reasonable range of key parameter values, these optimal rates are influenced just as strongly by estimates of (objective) labour supply behaviour as by the (subjective) degree of aversion to inequality.

Turning to indirect taxes, the most significant conclusion is that there is little or no reason to have differential sales tax rates on distributional grounds, and little reason to have them on efficiency grounds either. However, these results leave out the considerations required to provide a proper analysis of the excise duties on alcohol, tobacco, and petrol. The setting of these rates depends on matters outside the standard optimal taxation literature, such as externalities and paternalism.

The other major result on commodity taxation is the desirability of production efficiency, implying the superiority of VAT over turnover taxes, the need to run nationalised industries on market principles, and the desirability of free international trade. This result depends on some fairly strong assumptions, but forms a useful benchmark for policy decisions.

Finally, the literature on optimal tax has also been unable to resolve the important policy issue of whether we should have an income tax or an expenditure tax (whether savings should be tax-sheltered), although it has illuminated the issues involved.

The overall message that comes through from this is that optimal taxation can help in some, but not all, areas of tax policy. What is perhaps surprising is that, despite its general disregard for administrative and compliance considerations. Also, although value judgements necessarily come into decisions about rates of tax, there are a number of important tax design matters (for example, linearity of the income tax or uniformity of the sales tax) that are quite independent of such judgements.

References

Ahmad, E., and Stern, N. (1991), *The Theory and Practice of Tax Reform in Developing Countries*, Cambridge: Cambridge University Press.

Allen, F. (1982), 'Optimal linear income taxation with general equilibrium effects on wages', *Journal of Public Economics*, vol. 17, pp. 135–44.

Atkinson, A. B. (1973), 'How progressive should income tax be?', in M. Parkin and A. R. Nobay (eds.), *Essays in Modern Economics*, London: Longman.

—— and Stiglitz, J. E. 91980), *Lectures on Public Economics*, London: McGraw-Hill.

Blundell, R. W. (1992), 'Labour supply and taxation: a survey', *Fiscal Studies*, vol. 13, no. 3, pp. 15–40; repr. as Chapter 3 of this volume.

—— and Walker, I. (1983), 'Limited dependent variables in demand analysis: an application to modelling family labour supply and commodity demand

54   *Christopher Heady*

behaviour', University of Manchester, Discussion Paper in Econometrics no. 126.

Carruth, A., Heady, C. J., and Ulph, D. (1983), 'Optimal income taxation and comparative advantage', mimeo.

Corlett, W. J., and Hague, D. C. (1953), 'Complementarity and the excess burden of taxation', *Review of Economic Studies*, vol. 21, pp. 21–30.

Deaton, A., and Stern, N. (1986), 'Optimally uniform commodity taxes, taste differences and lump-sum grants', *Economics Letters*, vol. 20, pp. 263–6.

Diamond, P. A., and Mirrlees, J. A. (1971), 'Optimal taxation and public production: I and II', *American Economic Review*, vol. 61, pp. 8–27, 261–78.

Ebrahimi, A., and Heady, C. J. (1988), 'Tax design and household composition', *Economic Journal*, Conference Papers, vol. 98, no. 390, pp. 83–96.

Heady, C. J. (1987), 'A diagrammatic approach to optimal commodity taxation', *Public Finance*, vol. 42, pp. 250–63.

—— and Mitra, P. K. (1987), 'Distributional and revenue raising arguments for tariffs', *Journal of Development Economics*, vol. 26, pp. 77–101.

—— (1992), 'Taxation in decentralizing socialist economies: the case of China', World Bank, Policy Research Working Paper no. WPS820.

—— Pearson, M., Rajah, N., and Smith, S. (1992), *Report on the Czechoslovak Government's Tax Proposals*, London: Institute for Fiscal Studies.

Mirrlees, J. A. (1971), 'An exploration in the theory of optimum income taxation', *Review of Economic Studies*, vol. 38, pp. 175–208.

Musgrave, R. A. (1959), *The Theory of Public Finance*, New York: McGraw-Hill.

Myles, G. D. (1989a), 'Ramsey tax rules for economies with imperfect competition', *Journal of Public Economics*, vol. 38, pp. 95–115.

—— (1989b), 'Imperfect competition and the taxation of intermediate goods', *Public Finance*, vol. 44, pp. 62–74.

Newbery, D., and Stern, N. (1987), *The Theory of Taxation for Developing Countries*, Oxford: Oxford University Press.

Ramsey, F. P. (1927), 'A contribution to the theory of taxation', *Economic Journal*, vol. 37, pp. 47–61.

Rawls, J. (1971), *A Theory of Justice*, Cambridge, Mass.: Harvard University Press.

Smith, A. (1776), *An Enquiry into the Nature and Causes of the Wealth of Nations*, Cannan edition, London: Methuen, 1904.

Stern, N. H. (1976), 'On the specification of models of optimum income taxation', *Journal of Public Economics*, vol. 6, pp. 123–62.

Tuomala, M. (1990), *Optimal Income Tax and Redistribution*, Oxford: Clarendon Press.

TAXATION AND SAVINGS

ROBIN BOADWAY AND DAVID WILDASIN

1. Introduction

The choice of how much of society's income to consume today and how much to save for future consumption is among the most important economic decisions. It can have implications not only for the well-being of the households taking the decisions, but also for the rate at which the economy invests and grows, and therefore the well-being of future generations. The way in which savings decisions are taken is a matter of ongoing research in the literature, involving such important and unresolved issues as the degree of foresight and rationality of households, the extent to which capital markets are complete and well-functioning, the importance of life-cycle versus bequest versus precautionary motives for saving, and, more generally, the weight, if any, that current savers put on the welfare of future generations.

Taxation is one of many policies that affect the level of savings. Other significant ones include the system of social insurance, especially pensions, but also health and disability insurance, welfare services and education; transfers of various sorts; and debt policy. None the less, the principles by which saving behaviour responds to these various policies are very similar. We begin our survey with a discussion of these principles, first at the household level and then in the aggregate. Then, the effects of taxation are addressed. This is done first from a theoretical perspective, followed by a discussion of some of the main currents in the empirical literature on taxation and savings. Finally, we address some important normative or policy issues that have arisen in the literature,

The authors are grateful for the assistance provided by Travis Armour in the preparation of this chapter and to Michael Devereux and Michael Keen for detailed comments.

First published in *Fiscal Studies* (1994), vol. 15, no. 3, pp. 19–63.

focusing mainly on two issues. One is the optimal tax treatment of savings—should capital income be taxed? If so, how? The second is the more general issue of what the optimal rate of saving in the economy is.

2. The Determinants of Saving

There are several aspects of saving that differentiate it from other consumer optimisation decisions and that turn out to be important for tax analysis. For one thing, the ultimate object of choice is future consumption, of which savings is the *value* rather than the *quantity*. The price of future consumption in terms of current consumption is the after-tax discount factor. Thus, saving is the discounted present value of future consumption. Even though a fall in the price of future consumption, it may involve a fall in the level of savings, since a given amount of future consumption can be obtained at a lower cost in terms of forgone current consumption.

A second distinguishing feature of saving concerns the nature of the budget constraint. An individual's income may take the form of a stream of earnings (or other forms of non-capital income) in both present and future periods, so that the budget constraint involves a present value of earnings, referred to as *lifetime wealth*. This has two implications. First, a given stream of consumption over time will involve different levels of savings depending upon the time profile of the earnings stream. The later that earnings occur, the less savings (or more dissavings) will be required to finance a given amount of consumption. Second, a change in the price of future consumption (the after-tax discount rate) will cause a change in the present value of earnings or lifetime wealth. This change will be larger the more the earnings stream is skewed towards the future because the discount factor will be higher for earnings further in the future. This induced change in lifetime wealth caused by a change in the price of future consumption will give rise to an indirect effect on household saving behaviour, referred to as the *human wealth effect*, that is not present in standard consumer choice models (Summers, 1981).

The intertemporal nature of the saving decision gives rise to various other unique issues. For one thing, there will be *uncertainty* about the future, and varying amounts of it may be borne by the individual saver. For another, to the extent that the individual is a dissaver in certain periods, there may be *liquidity constraints* which will restrict the individual's choice. Also, there will be a variety of instruments for converting present into future consumption, including financial assets (debt, shares in firms, annuities, pension funds, mutual funds, insurance policies), real property, unincorporated business assets, consumer durables (including housing), and even investment in human capital formation. These distinctions are relevant because different savings instruments are typically treated differently for tax purposes.

Finally, saving is often seen as a vehicle for achieving altruistic objectives, particularly altruism within the family. The existence of altruism turns out to have a profound effect on the way in which taxation affects savings, as well as on the way in which we conduct our economic analysis of saving. Saving to account for altruistic motives gives rise to bequests and gifts to younger cohorts.

2.1. Individual savings

The simplest case to consider is that of a selfish individual whose economic life can be divided into two periods, who receives earnings Y in the first period only, faces perfect capital markets with full certainty, and whose only decision is how to divide the earnings into first-period consumption, C_1, and second-period consumption, C_2, so as to maximise a lifetime utility function in C_1 and C_2. The budget constraint facing the household states that the present value of consumption, discounted at the after-tax interest rate, equals earnings. The combination of present and future consumption chosen will be such that the marginal rate of substitution between the two is just the relative price of future consumption, $p = 1/(1 + r(1-t))$, where r is the interest rate and t is the tax on interest income.

The amount of saving, S (i.e. $Y-C_1$), will depend upon the earnings of the household and the relative price, p. An increase in Y will typically increase S, since the household will want to increase both present and future consumption (assuming them both to be normal goods). However, an increase in p (reduction in $r(1-t)$) will have offsetting effects on savings. The higher price will tend to make the consumer substitute present consumption for the more expensive future consumption (the *substitution effect*), thus reducing savings. At the same time, the higher price of future consumption makes the consumer worse off, since less of both goods can be bought with a given amount of income. This reduction in real income tends to cause the household to reduce both present and future consumption and so to save less (the *income effect*). Although future consumption will definitely fall, whether saving rises or falls with a fall in the interest rate depends upon the relative strengths of the income and substitution effects. Broadly speaking, the more the consumer is willing to substitute present for future consumption (the less the curvature in the household's indifference curves between C_1 and C_2), the greater will be the substitution effect relative to the income effect, and the larger positive (smaller negative) will be the responsiveness of saving to increases in the after-tax interest rate. The issue becomes an empirical one.

The above discussion assumes that all earnings are in the first period. If there are second-period earnings, there will be additional effects. The household problem now involves maximising lifetime utility subject to a budget constraint which says that the present value of consumption must equal the present value of earnings, or lifetime wealth. An increase in earnings in either period will increase lifetime wealth, and thus will increase both present and future consumption if both are normal goods. However, the effect on savings will depend upon the period in which the earnings increase. Increases in first-period earnings will increase savings as above. However, increases in second-period earnings will reduce savings, since the individual will need to borrow against the future earnings increase in order to increase first-period consumption. This *life cycle timing effect* is of crucial importance to the analysis of the effect of taxation on savings.

An increase in p (reduction in $r(1-t)$) will have the usual income and substitution effects as above, but there will now be an additional effect, the human wealth effect. The increase in p will increase the present value of future earnings, thereby causing lifetime wealth to rise. This will increase the demand for C_1, thus reducing S unambiguously. In other words, the human wealth effect will unambiguously increase the interest elasticity of saving. For a given initial value of lifetime wealth, the interest elasticity of saving will be higher, the higher is the proportion of earnings accruing in the second period.

2.1.1. Human capital investment

There are various extensions that could be added to this two-period model of savings. The first involves human capital investment, which effectively makes the earnings stream endogenous.[1] Suppose individuals can convert forgone present earnings into increased future earnings by

---

[1] Of course, earnings could also be made endogenous by allowing the labour supply to vary. Since we are concentrating on savings decisions, we ignore this possibility for simplicity.

devoting some of their time to education or training rather than working. The stream of earnings will then be chosen as that at which the marginal rate of return to human capital formation (the increment in future earnings from a marginal reduction in current earnings) just equals the after-tax discount factor defined as above. A reduction in $r(1-t)$ *increases* investment in human capital, causing current income to fall and future income to rise. This causes saving to fall, thereby reinforcing the human wealth effect in increasing the interest elasticity of saving. In effect, the individual has substituted human wealth for asset wealth (Davies and St-Hilaire, 1987).

2.1.2. Bequests

Another important extension to the two-period model is to allow for bequests. There are three main reasons for bequests: uncertain lifetimes, altruism, and strategic behaviour with respect to children.

Uncertain lifetimes. Uncertain lifetimes will result in involuntary bequests if the individual has to self-insure against the possibility of living a long life. In the two-period model, individuals may or may not live to the second period, but precautionary wealth must be held to finance consumption in case they do. If they die early, the wealth is passed on to the next generation. This motive for saving would disappear if there were well-functioning annuity markets in which the individuals could insure themselves; individuals would behave as if their lifetimes we known with certainty and the above analysis of the effects of earnings and after-tax interest rate changes would apply. An additional possibility might now be forms of income received in the second period which are contingent on being alive, such as public pensions. Since these are like annuities, they reduce the need for precautionary saving (Abel, 1985).

Altruism. Altruism towards one's heirs implies that households take decisions not only with their own lifetime utility in mind, but also with the well-being of their heirs. They will allocate their lifetime earnings between their own consumption and that of their heirs such that at the margin they are indifferent between the last pounds of their own and their heirs' consumption. An increase in income will partly go to consumption for one's heirs as well as one's own consumption. Thus, there will be an additional factor tending towards an increase in saving out of income increases. An interesting case is that in which all households care for the level of utility attained by their immediate heirs. In this case, indirectly they care for their heirs' heirs (since this affects the utility of their heirs), and for their heirs' heirs' heirs, and so on into the indefinite future. In taking decisions about how much to leave to their immediate heirs, they behave as if their own utility function included the consumption of all future heirs. This is referred to as a *dynastic utility function,* or a utility function with an infinite time horizon. The intertemporal allocation of consumption across various members of the dynasty can be determined by maximising the dynastic utility function subject to the present value of wealth available to the entire dynasty into the infinite future. To the extent that this is the case, it has an important policy implication. Consider an increase in an individual's income which is offset by a reduction in the income of their heir (or their heir's heir, and so on) such that dynastic wealth is unchanged. In this case, the pattern of consumption across members of the dynasty will remain unchanged. The income transfer will be exactly offset by changes in bequests in the opposite direction. This idea that intergenerational transfers imposed on households by, say, the government will be completely undone by changes in bequests is known in the literature as the *Ricardian equivalence theorem* (Barro, 1974).[2]

Strategic bequests. Finally, bequests may be 'strategic' in nature, given by selfish parents conditional on their children performing certain duties or services, such as staying in the family business, caring for parents in old age, and so on (Bernheim, Shleifer, and Summers, 1985). The greater the promised bequest, the more services might the children be expected to perform. Strategic bequest models focus attention on the effect of tax and other policies on the bargaining strength of parents and children within the family; whereas altruistic parents would simply pass incremental social security benefits on to their children as bequests, strategically motivated parents would use the prospect of higher benefits to elicit additional assistance or other transfers from their children. The strategic-bequest model may also have important implications for the effect of estate taxation on savings. Estate taxes effectively increase the price of child services relative to current consumption, reducing the demand for these services and hence the level of parental saving.

---

[2] There is an enormous literature on the issue of Ricardian equivalence and the circumstances under which it applies. A summary of opposing positions can be found in Boadway and Wildasin (1993).

2.1.3. The multi-period case

The results of the two-period model apply in the multi-period case, along with some additional results. Consider the selfish consumer who obtains an exogenous stream of earnings over a given (working) portion of the life cycle and converts it to a stream of consumption. The basic results can be illustrated supposing that lifetime utility is just the sum of utilities of consumption achieved in each period, discounted at the rate δ. In this case, the marginal utility of consumption falls from one period to the next at the proportional rate $r(1-t)-\delta$, which is generally taken to be positive. If the elasticity of the marginal utility of consumption is constant and denoted η, consumption rises at the proportional rate $(r(1-t)-\delta)/\eta$. All saving is for life-cycle smoothing purposes. The savings profile is hump-shaped, rising in the early part of the life cycle, then falling, and eventually becoming negative as wealth is run down in retirement. Saving may also be negative at the beginning of the life cycle. Define *lifetime wealth* in any period as the sum of asset wealth and human wealth (the present value of future earnings). Consumption in each period can be shown to be proportionate to lifetime wealth in that period, where the propensity to consume rises with age, but can rise or fall with the after-tax interest rate (Beach, Boadway, and Bruce, 1988). Since the present value of future earnings falls with a rise in the interest rate, the human wealth effect from a rise in the interest rate causes a decrease in current consumption.

Suppose income increases unexpectedly in some period. Lifetime wealth then rises, as does the lifetime consumption profile. Saving will increase in the short run as well as in some following periods, and the asset accumulation profile will shift upwards.[3] If income rises in one period and falls in another, there will be a change in saving, even if the lifetime consumption profile is unchanged. For example, an increase in income in some future period accompanied by a decline in income now which leaves the present value of lifetime income unchanged (as would occur with a funded public pension scheme) will cause no change in lifetime consumption. However, saving will fall now to finance the same stream of consumption out of a smaller amount of income. Or, a transfer of income from a young person to an old person will cause a rise in total consumption because the propensity to consume out of wealth is higher for the old than for the young.

Changes in the interest rate have a somewhat more complicated effect

[3] If instead the increase in wealth is anticipated, consumption will rise in earlier periods and saving will fall to finance the increase in consumption.

on the consumption and asset accumulation profile. An increase in the interest rate will cause the consumption profile to become steeper so that over the life cycle more assets would have to be accumulated to finance future consumption. However, in the short run, savings could rise or fall, since the propensity to consume out of current wealth could increase or decrease with the interest rate. Note that the effect of an interest rate change on saving is likely to differ with age. The short-run interest elasticity of savings should be higher for younger persons than for older ones, because the human wealth effect is greater.

Finally, in the multi-period model, desired savings and wealth holdings may well be negative in the early part of the life cycle when earnings are relatively low. However, liquidity constraints may prevent an individual from holding negative wealth, so that consumption cannot exceed earnings when young. Later in the life cycle, earnings will be high enough for the individual to become a saver. From then on, the consumption stream follows the standard increasing pattern. With liquidity constraints, fluctuations in income in the constrained part of the life cycle result in one-for-one changes in consumption. Policies which change the timing of tax liabilities across the life cycle will thus have quite different effects when the household is liquidity-constrained. Moreover, a decrease in the interest rate which would ordinarily cause the individual to increase consumption early in the life cycle can no longer do so. It simply causes the individual's constraint to become tighter.

2.2. Aggregate savings

Determining aggregate savings involves more than simply aggregating the savings of households. One should also account for corporate savings (retained earnings). As well, public sector savings should be included if the government budget is not balanced.

2.2.1. Corporate savings

With perfect capital markets and no capital income taxes, corporate and personal savings would be perfect substitutes. If capital markets are characterised by imperfect information, corporate savings may have some advantages to shareholders. For example, internal financing may be less costly to a firm if its managers have better information about the profitability of the firm than do outsiders. There is a large literature on the implications of imperfect information on the financial structure of the firm, much of which has only limited relevance for tax issues. The structure of capital taxes (corporate and personal) typically introduces advantages to saving within the corporation as well. Unless the corporate tax is fully integrated with the personal tax and all corporate-source income imputed to shareholders as it accrues, there will be a tax advantage from retaining funds within the corporation rather than paying them out as dividends (Boadway and Bruce, 1992). This is referred to as the *trapped equity effect*, and can be used to explain not only the preference firms will have for retained earnings versus outside finance but also the incentives for the takeover of immature firms by mature ones (or their merging).

In taking account of corporate savings, the issue is whether or not households 'see through the corporate veil' and treat saving done on their behalf by corporations as part of their own saving (as they should). Assuming they do, then one should be able to think of individual saving as including retained earnings on their shares. This means that the tax applicable on these savings should include both personal and corporate taxes. In this chapter, we ignore the complications introduced by the corporate tax and corporate savings.

2.2.2. The consequences of public sector savings

To see the implications of public sector saving (or dissaving) in the determination of aggregate savings and its changes, consider a simple closed economy consisting of overlapping generations of identical individuals who leave no bequests. At a given time, individual behaviour differs only by age: younger cohorts will be saving and older ones dissaving. The sum of individual savings plus government saving will equal aggregate investment; equivalently, the capital stock will be the sum of household wealth holdings less government debt. Most of the issues involved in aggregation can be seen by concentrating on policies which involve income changes alone.

Revenue-neutral income changes for each household. Consider first the hypothetical case of a policy which changes the after-tax income stream of a given cohort but keeps its present value the same. For example, each member of the cohort might pay lower taxes (receive transfers) early in life and higher taxes later, such that the present value of the changes is zero. The typical individual in this cohort will save more when young to spread the income change over the life cycle to keep the consumption stream unchanged. In the absence of any other changes, aggregate saving and the demand for assets would increase temporarily while that cohort was young, then fall temporarily while it was old, but remain unchanged after that cohort had passed away. However, from the point of view of the government, net revenue would be lower while the cohort was young and higher when it was old. To make good the tax-transfer change without affecting other households in the economy, the government would have to borrow money. The amount of the public dis-saving would exactly offset the increased private saving, and total saving would remain unchanged. More generally, the same principle would apply to a permanent tax reform which took increased taxes from the old and reduced them for the young. In order that the present value of taxes of *all* cohorts remain the same, this would have to be accompanied by an increase in government debt. The demand for assets by households would have permanently increased, but so would the supply of assets from the government by an equal amount. The economy would remain unchanged in real terms and all households would be equally as well off.[4]

Revenue neutrality at each point of time. The picture is somewhat different if changes in government debt are ruled out. Consider a scheme in which transfer are made permanently from young persons to old persons, and the scheme is self-financing at each point in time. Examples of such policies include tax reforms which move tax liabilities earlier in the life cycle, unfunded public pensions, and in-kind transfers of public services to the elderly financed by taxes on the young. When the scheme is first introduced, all members of the older cohorts obtain an increase in their income and are better off. The incomes of individuals born after the policy change will be lower when young and higher when old; they will save less for retirement. Thus, the demand for assets will decrease and private investment will be lower. Whether such individuals are better or worse off depends upon the characteristics of the economy. The money they contributed to the scheme when young would have earned a return equal to the rate of interest r (neglecting capital income taxes). On the other hand, a continual scheme of transfers from the young to the old will earn an implicit rate of return equal to the rate of growth of the economy g.[5] If $g = r$, the net present value of the intergenerational trans-

---

[4] In this example, the same result would apply if households were altruistic towards their heirs. Since no intergenerational transfers are involved, there is no need for bequest behaviour to change in response to the tax transfer scheme.

[5] To see this, suppose population grows at the rate n and that there is no technical progress, so $g = n$. In the two-period life-cycle case, if T is the tax per worker, the transfer per retiree will be $T(1 + n)$. The present value of the scheme over the life cycle will be

fer is zero, so that individual welfare is unaffected in the long run, even though the level of private capital will be lower. The economy is said to be on the *Golden Rule* growth path. If $g > r$, the scheme will increase not only the welfare of the current older cohort, but also that of all future cohorts. In this case, the stock of capital is above the Golden Rule level; the economy is said to be *over-capitalised*. The intergenerational transfer scheme is Pareto-improving. And if $r > g$, the scheme will make young and future cohorts worse off while it makes the older better off. In this case, a scheme of intergenerational transfers from the young to the old will make the better off at the expense of future generations. Of course, the reverse is true as well.

The above effects of intergenerational income transfers depend upon the assumptions of the model being used. If, instead of being selfish, individuals are altruistic towards future generations, at least part of the effects of intergenerational transfers will be offset by changes in bequest behaviour. Thus, a scheme which transfers from the younger to the older will induce the older cohorts to increase their bequests. Changes in bequests will fully offset the effects of the transfer if Ricardian equivalence applies (Barro, 1974). The effects will also differ from the above model if there are capital market imperfections. If very young workers face liquidity constraints, an increase in the tax on them will serve to reduce their consumption rather than their saving, and the adverse effect of the scheme on aggregate saving will be lessened (Hubbard and Judd, 1987). Similarly, if annuity markets are imperfect or absent, an intergenerational transfer from the young to the old will provide a sort of annuity. This will reduce the demand for precautionary saving and will cause aggregate saving to fall by even more than described above (Abel, 1985).

3. The Effects of Taxes on Saving

The effect of taxes can be inferred readily from the above discussion. Taxes influence saving through two main mechanisms. First, they may affect the rate of return to saving and, second, they may affect the income stream which is converted into a stream of consumption (and possibly

$-T + T(1 + n)/(1 + r)$, which will be positive or negative according to whether n is greater or less than r. More generally, the same result would hold if cohorts live for several periods and if technical progress occurs. The implicit rate of return on the intergenerational transfer scheme would be g, which now equals the sum of n plus the rate of technical progress.

bequests) through saving. These effects can be seen by concentrating on three forms of taxation—wage taxation, consumption taxation, and capital income taxation. (Income taxation is equivalent to capital income taxation combined with wage taxation.) For simplicity, we assume that taxes are at proportional rates.

3.1. The effect of taxes on individual saving

Consider an individual who obtains an earnings stream for a given number of working periods, and then is retired for a given number of periods. Capital markets are perfect so the individual is able to borrow freely against future earnings. As well, annuities are available to insure against uncertainty in the length of life, so that we can proceed as if the age of death is fixed and known. There are no bequests, so saving is for life cycle smoothing purposes alone. The consumer maximises the discounted sum of utilities of consumption in each period subject to a budget constraint which says that the present value of lifetime consumption expenditures equals the present value of lifetime earnings after tax. All taxes are incorporated into the budget constraint. Consumption expenditures include taxes on consumption; the earnings stream is net of wage taxes; and earnings are discounted by the interest rate net of capital income taxes. In these circumstances, the effect on saving of each of the three taxes is straightforward.

Wage taxation. A tax on wages reduces lifetime wealth and leaves the after-tax interest rate unchanged. The time profile of consumption over the life cycle will shift downwards, though its shape will remain the same. Similarly, the time profile of earnings will shift downwards during working periods. Saving will fall during the working years, since less consumption during retirement needs to be financed and fewer assets will be demanded. The earlier in the life cycle earnings are obtained, the greater will be the decrease in saving. Equivalently, the later in the working part of the life cycle a wage tax is imposed, the higher the proportion of the tax will go to reduced savings.

Consumption taxation. A consumption tax causes the consumption stream to fall in exactly the same way as for a wage tax. It does so not by lowering the earnings stream, but by increasing the cost of consumption. However, because the tax liability occurs later in the life cycle, saving will not fall as much. In fact, in the case of a lifetime utility function which is the discounted sum of identical per-period utility functions of the constant elasticity form ($U(C) = C^{\alpha}$), saving and asset accumulation will be unchanged by a consumption tax (Beach, Boadway, and Bruce, 1988). The rise in the cost of consumption with given lifetime wealth causes consumption to fall in the same proportion in each period. Since the consumption tax also applies proportionately in each period, consumption expenditures inclusive of the tax remain unchanged; so the same amount of saving is required in order to finance them (since earnings are unchanged). The fact that a consumption tax leaves saving unchanged makes tax substitutions involving consumption taxes easy to analyse.

Capital-income taxation. A capital-income tax is equivalent to a reduction in the after-tax interest rate. In the short run, it will have an ambiguous effect on saving depending on the relative sizes of the substitution, income, and human-wealth effects. The magnitude of the human-wealth effect will be larger the later in the remaining life cycle earnings are obtained (for example, the younger the person is when the tax is imposed). Over the longer run, the reduction in the after-tax interest rate causes the entire consumption profile to become flatter, so that, over the life cycle, the saving needed for life cycle smoothing will be reduced.

3.2. Tax substitutions with individual revenue neutrality

From these individual tax effects, it is straightforward to infer the effect of substituting one tax for another. First, consider tax substitutions which raise the same amount of revenue in present value terms from the individual. Since a consumption tax does not affect saving, substituting a wage tax or a capital-income tax for a consumption tax will have the same effects as imposing those taxes alone, as just discussed. The wage tax substitution will cause individual savings to all, while the capital tax substitution will have an ambiguous effect on savings in the short run, but will reduce the demand for assets over the life cycle. Substituting a capital income tax for a wage tax will also have an ambiguous effect, since both are likely to reduce the demand for assets in the long run.

These ambiguities disappear once we take public sector savings into account. If the present value of tax liabilities of all cohorts is to be kept constant, the time pattern of government tax receipts will change; it will need to borrow or lend. For example, when a wage tax is substituted for a consumption tax, the entire amount of the fall in private savings comes about from the change in timing of tax liabilities, since the consumption stream remains unchanged. In this case, the fall in private savings will be exactly offset by an increase in public savings as a result of the fact that tax revenues are received earlier. Thus, total savings will remain unchanged, along with the path of consumption and capital accumulation for the economy as a whole and the welfare of all cohorts. In fact, when tax changes are revenue-neutral for all households, all changes in private savings which originate in changes in the timing of tax liabilities will be offset by changes in public savings in the opposite direction.

Only those sources of change resulting from the relative price effect of a change in the after-tax interest rate will cause saving to change. Thus, in the case of the replacement of a capital income tax for a wage tax, the substitution effect which causes saving to fall will remain. The fact that taxes are collected earlier in the life cycle under the wage tax will be of no consequence for aggregate saving; the increase in private saving this generates will be offset by a decrease in public saving. Moreover, given the changes in public saving, the substitution of a tax on capital income for a wage tax will have exactly the same aggregate effect as the substitution of the same tax for a consumption tax. That is, saving will fall in both cases by the substitution effect. The tax on capital income will represent a distortion in the capital markets; all individuals will be worse off as a result of substituting a capital income tax for either a wage tax or a consumption tax.

3.3. Tax substitutions with aggregate revenue neutrality in each period

The above exercises require the government to collect the same amount of revenue in present value terms from each cohort. They should be viewed as illustrative only since it is difficult to imagine the government being able to institute tax changes which are revenue-neutral for every cohort, even if public saving is allowed. It is more likely to be the case that some cohorts will gain and others lose. (Indeed, this is often the objective of tax reforms.) Suppose instead that we consider the same three sorts of tax substitutions when the same amount of total tax revenue is generated in each time period so total public saving remains unchanged. Again, capital markets are assumed to be perfect and households leave no bequests.

Suppose the economy is in steady-state equilibrium with a consumption tax used to finance an exogenous stream of government expenditures. The government then switches to a wage tax which generates the same stream of revenues per period. In the period in which the tax substitution occurs, members of the older cohort (the retired plus the workers part way through their working life) obtain a windfall gain since they no longer have to pay taxes on their consumption and escape bearing the full burden of the wage tax. Younger workers and future generations face a wage tax rather than a consumption tax. They will reduce their savings, since their tax liabilities occur earlier in the life cycle. Thus, the total stock of capital in the economy will fall. In the new wage-tax steady state, individuals will be worse off if $r > g$, as is normally the case. The tax substitution will be equivalent to a pure intergenerational redistribution, with older cohorts gaining at the expense of all future cohorts. It is purely redistributional, in the sense that there is no efficiency gain; the economy simply moves from one point to another on its intertemporal utility possibility frontier, though the process of transition can take several periods.

Next, suppose the consumption tax is replaced by a capital income tax. If the lifetime utility function is homothetic (e.g. the discounted sum of constant-elasticity-of-consumption utility functions), the reduction in consumption tax will have no effect on saving. The capital income tax will cause the consumption profile to flatten out, so asset accumulation over the life cycle will fall, even though saving early in the life cycle could rise or fall. Thus, the capital stock should decline with the tax change. Long-run welfare will unambiguously decline if $r > g$, both due to the distortion imposed by the capital income tax and due to the further reduction in the capital stock. During the transition, however, older cohorts are made better off. For them, consumption tax liabilities will be higher later in life than capital income tax liabilities.

Finally, suppose a capital income tax is substituted for a wage tax. As with the previous case, this one will have a relative price effect and a timing effect. The relative price effect will be the same as for the previous case. The timing effect will be stronger in favour of increasing saving, since the wage tax is collected earlier in the life cycle than was the case for the consumption tax. Thus, in the long run, aggregate saving could rise or fall, and households could become better or worse off. However, in the short run, since taxes are collected earlier in the life cycle under the wage tax, older cohorts are made worse off during the transition to the new long-run equilibrium.

These results rely on the assumptions we have made about individual behaviour and capital markets. Suppose that individuals are altruistic towards their heirs and that bequests fully reflect that, so Ricardian equivalence applies. Any purely redistributive transfer between cohorts resulting from tax reform will be undone by a change in bequests. In the case of substituting a wage tax for a consumption tax, which is exactly equivalent to a lump-sum transfer from younger to older cohorts, bequests will rise by the full amount of the transfer with no real changes in the economy. For the other two tax substitutions, the intergenerational transfer component will be offset by changes in bequests, leaving only the relative price effect. Since the relative price effect amounts to introducing an inefficiency in the economy, utilities of all cohorts along the growth path will be reduced when the capital income tax is introduced.

If capital markets are imperfect, the effects will differ as well. For example, if individuals are liquidity-constrained, substituting a wage tax for a consumption tax cannot be expected to reduce saving for the youngest cohorts. Since they cannot dissave, the additional tax liability they face must be met by a fall in consumption rather than an increase in borrowing. Thus, the adverse effects of the tax substitution on saving will be lessened. The same applies for the substitution of a wage tax for the capital income tax. Similarly, if lifetimes are uncertain and annuity markets are imperfect, the substitution of a wage tax for a consumption tax will implicitly affect the amount of insurance implemented through the tax system. The consumption tax system increases the need for precautionary saving relative to the wage tax because consumption tax liabilities are incurred as long as the household is alive. Thus, the substitution of a wage tax will reduce saving more than it otherwise would.

3.4. Summary

One way to summarise this section is to review the ways in which tax policy could be used to increase aggregate saving. These will depend upon the appropriate model of the economy. For simplicity, consider only tax reforms that are revenue-neutral in each period, ruling out changes in government debt. In the absence of bequests and liquidity constraints, saving is increased by the substitution of a consumption tax for a wage tax or by any other tax reforms that redistribute from older to younger generations (that is, which collect taxes later in the life cycle). A tax reform that changes the net rate of return on saving may increase or decrease the rate of saving depending on the relative magnitudes of the income and substitution effects. If annuity markets are incomplete, so that unintentional bequests exist, a tax reform that substitutes tax liabilities later in life for those earlier will reduce the effect on saving since this will be equivalent to providing annuities to the household (since the payment of the tax later in life is contingent on being alive). As well, if the household is liquidity-constrained early in life, the effect of the reform on saving will be further blunted, since the household will want to consume more of the additional income obtained early in life.

By comparison, in an economy in which Ricardian equivalence applies, pure intergenerational transfers are completely undone by bequest changes and leave aggregate saving unchanged. On the other hand, increases in the after-tax rate of return on savings should unambiguously increase saving. Since the income effects of tax reforms are offset by bequests, all that is left is the substitution effect which is unambiguous in direction. The effects arising out of liquidity constraints and incomplete annuity markets should also apply here. However, in a world of Ricardian equivalence, these market imperfections are much less likely to occur. Transfers within the family ought to be able to overcome liquidity constraints, and family dynasties should be able to self-insure against the uncertainties of length of life.

4. Empirical Analysis of Savings

As we have seen, a number of different theories of consumption and saving behaviour have been put forward. In order to deal with practical problems of public policy, one would like to know what theory has the best ability to explain observed behaviour; beyond this, it would be desirable to have a good predictive model that would provide quantitative estimates of the behavioural responses of households to different policy initiatives. Broadly speaking, empirical research on savings can help us to test competing theories and to estimate the values of crucial parameters; simulation analyses, discussed in the next section, can be used to explore, in a more predictive spirit, the implications of different policies in models of the economy that build on the tests and estimates derived from empirical research.

Much of the empirical research on savings is not directed specifically to the analysis of the effects of taxation; rather, it is concerned with understanding the basic nature of household decision-making. As is clear from our previous discussion, however, the effects of taxes can depend sensitively on the nature of savings behaviour, so this empirical research carries important implications for the analysis of tax policy. A detailed review of the vast empirical literature on saving is beyond the scope of this chapter, but it is useful to review the main lines of empirical research from the perspective of potential applications to tax analysis.

4.1. Studies of aggregate savings behaviour

For the purposes of tax analysis, the effect of interest rates on consumption and savings is of particular importance, but early empirical research on aggregate consumption functions had not found interest rates to be important explanatory variables. Indeed, according to 'Denison's Law', the proportion of national income devoted to saving is more or less constant over long periods. If this were true, the interest elasticity of the savings rate would be approximately zero, since interest rates are observed to fluctuate substantially over time. Boskin (1978), however, casts doubt on the validity of Denison's Law, arguing that the stability of the gross savings rate masks considerable variation in the rate of savings *net* of depreciation. Boskin regresses the aggregate net savings rate on an estimate of the real after-tax rate of return on saving and concludes that the interest elasticity of savings is in the range of 0.2–0.4. Subsequent research has yielded mixed results; Howrey and Hymans (1978) conclude that interest rates have little effect on savings, while Blinder and Deaton (1985) find that *nominal* interest rates tend to depress consumption but *real* interest rates do not, a result not readily reconciled with theoretical models that suggest that consumers make decisions based on real trade-offs.

Instead of estimating traditional aggregate consumption functions, a number of studies follow Hall (1978) in attempting to estimate a model built on the assumption that aggregate consumption is the outcome of intertemporal optimising behaviour by a representative household. Here the objective is to recover underlying structural parameters of the preference structure of the representative agent which could then be used, among other things, to estimate the interest elasticity of savings. In one such study, Mankiw, Rotemberg, and Summers (1985) conclude that the data reject the testable implications of the underlying hypothesis of intertemporal optimising behaviour by a representative agent. Hall (1988) finds that consumers are not very willing to substitute between present and future consumption, implying a low interest-elasticity of saving.

Overall, it would be fair to say that empirical analysis of aggregate consumption data has been inconclusive in its findings about the effects of interest rates on savings. In part, at least, the divergent findings of the literature on aggregate consumption and savings can be traced to differences in the data used, as different investigators choose somewhat different concepts of savings, income, and other key variables. Another perennial source of controversy concerns the choice of variables to include in an aggregate consumption function. In addition to tax policy *per se*, it has been suggested in various contexts (Bosworth, Burtless, and Sabelhaus, 1991) that aggregate savings may be sensitive to fluctuations in stock market prices and real estate values, changes in capital market institutions (new types of borrowing arrangements, for example), increases in government deficits or demographic shifts (for example, changes in age structure, increases in the number of single-parent families). Carroll and Summers (1987) identify government borrowing and differences in the tax treatment of capital income (especially through tax-sheltered savings arrangements) and interest expense as probable contributors to recent divergences in savings rates in the USA and Canada. A failure to incorporate these sorts of factors in an estimated aggregate consumption function not only harms the overall explanatory power of a model but may also result in misleading estimates of the effects of other variables such as interest rates and income. The correct specification of a macro-level consumption function to incorporate detailed institutional factors is usually far from clear, however. Undoubtedly this helps to explain the increased interest in the use of micro-level data in consumption analysis, as discussed further below.

As explained in earlier sections, tax policy affects not only the net rate of return on saving but the distribution of tax burdens over time. Many empirical studies use macro-level data to assess the impact on aggregate consumption of effects of changes in tax timing resulting from public pension or debt policy. In one well-known analysis of the effect of the US social security system on aggregate consumption, Feldstein (1974) calculates (net) *social security wealth*, i.e. the present value of benefits less taxes, aggregated across all age cohorts in a given year. Aggregate social security wealth in each year then becomes an explanatory variable in a time-series aggregate consumption regression equation. Feldstein estimates that social security wealth has a large positive effect on aggregate consumption, reducing savings rates and thus depressing wealth accumulation. (Beach, Boadway, and Gibbons (1984), however, distinguish between impact and long-run effects of social security policy and note that the long-run effects are likely to be quantitatively much smaller than the Feldstein impact estimates; for instance, social security is estimated to depress the stock of wealth by only about 5 per cent instead of the 30 per cent that Feldstein estimates.)

Exercises of this sort raise not only many aggregation and other econometric issues, but serious measurement problems. For example, the calculation of social security wealth requires a determination of households' expectations of future taxes and benefits, which are not directly observable (Leimer and Lesnoy, 1982). A second major measurement problem concerns the effects of other policies that redistribute income across generations, such as explicit government borrowing, public investment in both non-human and human capital, changes in the structure of taxation, and a host of other policies (Boadway and Wildasin, 1993). Recent efforts to develop more comprehensive measures of intergenerational flows through the public sector (Kotlikoff, 1992) may, however, prove useful in overcoming some of these problems for aggregate consumption function studies.

4.2. Micro-level analysis of savings

The tax systems of many countries provide preferential treatment for retirement savings, for owner-occupied housing, and for human capital investment. The taxation of households and firms is often not very well integrated and the tax treatment of gifts and bequests can be quite complex. Furthermore, different forms of wealth accumulation have differing degrees of liquidity, ranging from highly liquid cash-balance savings in financial institutions to rather illiquid capital tied up in equity on owner-occupied housing. The increasing availability of micro-data sets has encouraged researchers to attempt to take these complexities into account in the study of savings behaviour, as described in the following paragraphs.

4.2.1. Retirement savings

Many tax systems shelter pension and other retirement savings from taxation. Typically, contributions to pension plans, both by companies and by employees, are tax-deductible, and the returns to these contributions (whether they take the form of dividends, interest, or capital gains) can accumulate free of tax. When benefits are paid out to retirees, however, they are included in the taxable income of recipients and subject to personal tax. Since the returns to pension savings are not taxed on accrual, savings in pension programmes earn the before-tax rate of return, and therefore enjoy significant tax preferences relative to other forms of capital accumulation. A number of other special retirement savings vehicles in various countries provide individual-level tax-sheltered savings opportunities; these include Registered Retirement Savings Plans in Canada, Individual Retirement Accounts (IRAs), and, more recently, 401(k) plans in the USA, and personal pensions in the UK.

Retirement saving is empirically very important. In the USA, it accounts for more than half of national savings, but its composition has varied widely. Over the 1980s, pension contributions fell from being most of retirement savings to about half of the total; of pension savings, the proportion in defined-benefit plans fell relative to defined-contribution plans. Higher rates of return on pension fund assets (including appreciation of equity holdings) during the 1980s, making it easier for firms to maintain adequate funding for defined-benefit plans, may have contributed to this relative decline of defined-benefit contributions (Bernheim and Shoven, 1988); changes in the regulations governing defined-benefit pensions, such as rules concerning vesting of benefits, higher premiums to support government insurance of pension fund solvency, and increased taxes on employers who attempt to withdraw 'excess' pension fund contributions, may be another factor (Papke, Petersen, and Poterba, 1993). IRA contributions grew to about one-quarter of retirement savings before dropping off towards the end of the decade; 401(k) contributions rose from a trivial amount in 1980 to about one-third of retirement savings by the end of the 1980s (Poterba, Venti, and Wise, 1993). Retirement saving has also varied in magnitude and composition in the UK; for instance, the take-up of defined-contribution and personal pensions has increased markedly since the 1988 Social Security Act made these available as contracting-out options from the State Earnings-Related Pension Scheme (SERPS) (Banks and Blundell, 1995a; Dilnot, Disney, Johnson, and Whitehouse, 1994).

A number of studies have investigated the relationship between retirement savings and other forms of wealth accumulation. Poterba (1987) estimates that an increase in corporate saving is accompanied by a reduction in household saving of about 50–75 per cent. Households seem to 'see through the corporate veil' to some degree but do not regard corporate saving as a perfect substitute for personal saving. IRAs would not necessarily be expected a priori to have very significant effects on aggregate savings (Gravelle, 1991), since IRA contribution limits are relatively small. Further, IRAs might substitute for employer-provided pension contributions, or otherwise change the *form* of household saving without changing its *level*. However, in a series of studies based on surveys of individual households, Venti and Wise (1992 and references therein) present evidence that IRA participation is higher for higher-income households and that households that make IRA contributions have not reduced their accumulation of other forms of financial assets. They find that households covered by pension plans do not appear to have levels of IRA contributions different from those that are not covered. Households appear to regard IRA savings as a distinct type of asset that is only imperfectly substitutable for other savings. Venti and Wise conclude that most IRA savings represent a net increase in total household savings. Evidence on the effect of personal pensions on savings in the UK is not yet available (Banks and Blundell, 1995b), but participation rates are high; as more UK data accumulate, it will be of interest to compare results with US research on IRAs. A challenge for future work on retirement savings is to develop models that can integrate the crucial but complex institutional details of tax-sheltered retirement savings vehicles within an overall framework for the analysis of total household savings.

4.2.2. Savings and housing

The accumulation of housing equity over time due to mortgage repayment and appreciation in house value increases a household's net worth and is thus a component of household saving, comprehensively defined. Indeed, housing equity can be a major component of personal saving for most households, who often retire with very little saving in the form of financial assets. The illiquidity of housing equity could significantly affect life cycle savings behaviour. Pre-retirement households whose housing increases in value would presumably wish to consume more but might find it difficult to translate appreciation in the price of a house into liquid resources that can be used for (non-housing) consumption. Older households usually experience large reductions in cash-flow income at retirement and might wish to liquidate some of their housing wealth, but doing so typically involves various transactions costs, so that their (non-housing) consumption might be cash-constrained.

Skinner (1989) studies this issue by regressing the consumption of a sample of home-owners on a measure of housing wealth. It appears that increases in housing value have little effect on consumption, which Skinner interprets as evidence of altruistically motivated bequests to subsequent generations. Manchester and Poterba (1989) find that households that take out second mortgages have lower overall net worth positions, which could mean that second mortgages permit homeowners to liquidate housing equity to finance consumption. Alternatively, it could be that some households experience unexpected reductions in cash flow or increases in desired consumption (for example, due to unemployment or medical emergencies) and that these households disproportionately seek out second mortgages. A negative correlation between second-mortgage borrowing and household net worth could then simply reflect the impact of a sudden need to increase consumption rather than any independent effect of the availability of second mortgages on consumption and savings. The link between savings and housing decisions for the elderly is discussed further below.

4.2.3. Savings behaviour of the elderly

Since the life cycle savings model emphasises the importance of savings for retirement, the behaviour of elderly households is of particular interest. If most saving is motivated by a desire to provide for one's old-age consumption, and if capital and insurance markets function perfectly, then one would expect older households to engage in substantial dissaving. In the absence of bequest motives for saving, the ideal life cycle consumption path is one that totally exhausts household wealth at the time of death. Hence, the life cycle theory would lead one to expect a negative wealth–age relationship in old age. As explained previously, however, this prediction must be qualified if insurance and capital markets are imperfect; uninsured risks concerning health and the age of death may give rise to precautionary motives for preserving wealth in old age, and to 'unintended' or 'accidental' bequests.

A substantial amount of empirical research has focused on understanding patterns of saving and dissaving in old age and on the purchase of annuities and insurance by the elderly. Conflicting evidence has emerged. Bernheim (1987), for instance, finds that 'bequeathable' wealth, i.e. non-annuitised wealth, including housing wealth as well as financial and other assets, tends to decrease after retirement, as suggested by the life cycle theory. A more comprehensive measure of wealth that includes both private pension benefits and social security benefits, however, seems to remain approximately constant over time. Hurd (1992) concludes that households do generally draw down their wealth at rates consistent with the pure life cycle theory; he also observes that parents and non-parents tend to dissave at approximately equal rates, casting doubt on the importance of bequest motives for wealth accumulation. Friedman and Warshawsky (1989) analyse retirement annuity contracts and find 'load factors' (mark-ups above actuarially fair prices) of 20–40 per cent. Though substantial, these are similar to the load factors on other commonly purchased types of insurance, suggesting that the low level of wealth annuitisation reflects a desire to preserve wealth for bequest purposes rather than a serious market imperfection.

Much of the wealth of the elderly takes the form of somewhat illiquid housing equity. Venti and Wise (1990 and references therein) examine the housing wealth of older households, comparing those who stay in their existing dwellings with those who move. If the consumption of older households is generally liquidity-constrained, movers would presumably choose less-costly housing, freeing up liquid wealth with which to sustain current consumption. Instead, it appears that aged movers acquire new housing that is just about as costly as their previous dwellings, so that housing equity remains relatively constant. The underlying motivation for the preservation of housing wealth is not entirely clear, but to the extent that it occurs, it casts doubt on the hypothesis that consumption of the elderly is liquidity-constrained. Such behaviour also suggests that the relatively limited use of reverse-annuity mortgages may be attributable more to a simple lack of demand rather than to any institutional barriers on the supply side.

Bernheim (1991) observes that many older households purchase term life insurance which, in terms of its effects on the household's budget constraint, is basically equivalent to the *sale* of an annuity, with the proceeds of the sale accruing to the insurance policy beneficiaries. Such insurance increases the level of bequests at the expense of current own consumption, suggesting that the elderly do value planned bequests and that pure life cycle consumption motives cannot, by themselves, explain observed savings behaviour.

4.2.4. *Heterogeneous savings behaviour and liquidity constraints*

There is no compelling a priori reason why all households should necessarily follow the same behavioural rules in their consumption and savings decisions. Several authors (Diamond, 1977; Diamond and Hausman, 1984; King and Dicks-Mireaux, 1982) use household-level data to examine the pattern of wealth-holding by age and permanent income level. Households with low lifetime incomes frequently save so little that they cannot sustain a level of post-retirement consumption close to that achieved during the working lifetime, indicating that a significant fraction of the population acts more myopically than the life cycle model of consumption smoothing would suggest. On the other hand, a relatively small but important fraction of households save a great deal, as evidenced by the fact that mean levels of wealth, by component and in total, are frequently far higher than median levels. The behaviour of these households also cannot easily be explained in terms of consumption smoothing over the life cycle, but for the opposite reason: the savings of these households appear to be based on much longer-term objectives, involving perhaps the transfer of wealth to their children or to others.

Further evidence of the heterogeneity of household consumption behaviour, if not of underlying savings motives, comes from studies that suggest that a significant proportion of consumers are credit-constrained (Hall and Mishkin, 1982; Hayashi, 1985; Mariger, 1986; Zeldes, 1989b; Wilcox, 1989; Japelli, 1990). The data and empirical tests differ among these studies, but indicate variously that consumption may be more sensitive to fluctuations in current income than is consistent with intertemporal optimising behaviour, that younger households with small amounts of liquid assets save less and have more difficulty obtaining credit than other consumers, and that the behaviour of households with significant asset holdings does conform to the restrictions implied by intertemporal optimising whereas this is not true for households with few assets. An international comparison by Japelli and Pagano (1989) suggests that the proportion of income accruing to credit-constrained households may be as low as 12 per cent in Sweden and as high as 50–60 per cent in Spain, Italy, and Greece, with estimates of about 21 per cent for the USA and 40 per cent for the UK. Evidently, liquidity constraints do not interfere with the consumption of all households, but they are not trivial in extent either.

4.2.5. *Intergenerational transfers*

There is considerable controversy in the literature about the magnitude of intergenerational transfers. Data on bequests—the amount of bequests, their disposition, and the attributes of households that make them—are quite limited. A few authors (Menchik, 1988; Tomes, 1988) have analysed court records pertaining to individual estates, but such data are not easily obtained and often lack important information on other household attributes. Aggregate-level data on the magnitude of bequests are generally unavailable. Furthermore, bequests are only one form of intra-family transfers. Parental nurturing of children begins at infancy and involves the expenditure of both parental time and pecuniary resources at least until young adulthood. Parents may provide financial support for their children's higher education or for purchases of housing or durable goods, while older children may support their parents in times of financial need and may spend significant amounts of time caring for their parents. Few data sources are available that measure these sorts of intergenerational transfers.

In the absence of direct observations on the magnitude of intergenerational transfers, Kotlikoff and Summers (1981) attempt to infer how important they may be by estimating the extent of aggregate savings that might be reasonably attributed to pure life cycle motives. The residual—all savings other than for life cycle purposes—they attribute to intergenerational transfers, whether accidental, altruistic, or strategic in nature. They estimate that as much as 50–80 per cent of wealth accumulation in the USA arises from intergenerational transfers, though this estimate is sensitive to the resolution of some subtle conceptual questions (Modigliani, 1988; Kotlikoff, 1988).

What motives underlie the intergenerational transfers that do occur? Altonji, Hayashi, and Kotlikoff (1992) examine the consumption response of related households to changes in the resources of any one household. If parents and their adult children are altruistically linked, the resources of each should be effectively merged in an extended-family budget constraint, such that the consumption of each household unit depends on the resources of the extended family but not on the separate contributions of each to the family's resources. The evidence indicates that most households are not strongly altruistically linked, in the sense that own resources do influence own consumption, but that the households are still somewhat linked in the sense that own consumption does depend on the resources of other related households. Cox (1990) and Cox and Japelli (1990) find that parents and children are linked through *inter vivos* transfers that offset liquidity constraints facing the latter. Other studies (Bernheim, Shleifer, and Summers, 1985) favour the strategic bequest motive. Additional work is needed to sort out these competing hypotheses.

In summary, empirical research does indicate that tax policy can significantly affect savings decisions; this much at least is apparent from the studies of retirement savings through tax-sheltered accounts. There can be little doubt that the extent of pension-fund savings is attributable in significant part to the fact that pensions are tax sheltered, but available evidence does not strongly support the notion that total private (personal and corporate) saving can be treated as a meaningful aggregate. Some but not all households seem to be subject to liquidity constraints; some but not all households may be linked through intergenerational transfers; some but not all savings behaviour seems consistent with a precautionary savings motive; annuities markets do exist but are not heavily utilised, either because the annuities are too expensive or because households wish to leave bequests; and some households appear to make very little provision at all for retirement. The availability of new data, especially new micro-data, has greatly facilitated empirical research, but data limitations continue to plague researchers and to spawn conflicting interpretations. In the face of all this uncertainty, convincing empirically based quantitative analyses of the effects of tax policy on savings are difficult. Simulation methods provide one means by which the effects of policy can be assessed quantitatively, conditional on the assumed structure of a simulation model. We turn to simulation analysis next.

5. Simulation Analysis of Tax Policy

Economic models of the savings behaviour of individual households can become rather complex. Even simple life cycle models with fixed labour supply and perfect capital markets involve analysis of optimal consumer choice over as many commodities as the number of periods in the life cycle. Adding such plausible complications as bequests and other intergenerational transfers, human capital formation, liquidity constraints, or uncertainty about earnings or mortality makes it very difficult to obtain much detailed insight from the theoretical analysis of general models. Understanding the effect of taxation on individual savings behaviour alone does not reveal the effect of taxes on relative factor supplies, factor prices, and the dynamic evolution of the economy—the effects which are often of greatest interest in policy evaluation. To examine these effects, it is necessary to analyse tax policies in a general equilibrium framework. The development of tractable dynamic general equilibrium models for tax analysis is a most challenging undertaking, however.

In the face of these complexities, researchers have come to rely increasingly on simulation methods. Simulation analysis is now an important adjunct to empirical research, enabling investigators to 'test' whether particular hypotheses about savings behaviour are consistent with empirical regularities, to gauge the likely empirical importance of certain types of savings behaviour or to guide econometric analysis. Simulation models make it possible to study more complex and realistic policy questions, and to gain more insight into the relative practical importance of key parameters, than would otherwise be the case.

5.1. Precautionary savings

As an example of the use of simulation models of savings behaviour, consider the case of precautionary savings. Previous sections discussed the effects on savings of imperfections in the market for annuities and of liquidity constraints. Still a third type of market imperfection arises from the difficulties that consumers may have in insuring themselves against the risk of uncertain earnings. Earnings uncertainty can arise from the risk of unemployment, from industry or occupational shocks to wages, or from individual health and other risks. These earnings risks are not readily insurable, since such insurance creates obvious disincentives to labour supply. Thus, households must 'self-insure' using precautionary savings.

A number of authors have developed models of 'precautionary' savings in which households accumulate wealth as a form of insurance against earnings risk. In general, these models are technically complex, since they involve optimisation in a multi-period uncertainty setting. However, they can usefully be simulated, using data on observed earnings levels and risk and with plausible preference specifications. One use of such simulations is to determine how much saving households might undertake because of this precautionary motive. Zeldes (1989a) estimates that precautionary savings could account for roughly 10–20 per cent of observed savings in the USA. (Guiso, Japelli, and Terlizzese (1992) estimate that earnings risk in Italy is such that the precautionary motive can explain only a very small fraction of savings there, however.)

Simulation methods can also uncover qualitative properties of precautionary savings models that may be difficult to establish using general theoretical analysis. For example, models with precautionary savings generate 'excess sensitivity' of consumption to current income and low rates of wealth decumulation on the part of the elderly, both empirical observations that have been interpreted by some as inconsistent with standard life cycle/permanent income hypothesis models, and as possibly providing evidence of credit rationing or of a bequest motive for saving. If these simulations do not constitute formal empirical tests of the precautionary savings motive, they at least provide a convincing conjecture for what may lie behind some of the apparent anomalies in the empirical studies.

5.2. Dynamic tax analysis

The work of Auerbach, Kotlikoff, and Skinner (1983) and Auerbach and Kotlikoff (1987) illustrates well the potential policy applications of simulation models. These authors develop an overlapping-generations model in which each household engages in life cycle saving over a deterministic lifetime, choosing a consumption stream and labour supply to maximise lifetime utility subject to a lifetime budget constraint, taking factor prices (i.e. wage and interest rates) as given. Given a path of factor prices over the life cycle, it is possible to calculate the utility-maximising choices of each household. Making appropriate assumptions about the demographic trends in the economy, one can aggregate across households of different ages to determine aggregate consumption, savings, and labour supply conditional on factor prices; the supply of savings and the supply of labour determine the economy's capital/labour ratio. But the factor prices themselves depend on this ratio through its effect on the marginal productivity of each factor; the exact relationship depends on the production technology. A dynamic equilibrium in this model is a path of factor prices over time such that the factor supplies forthcoming, conditional on these prices, give rise to that factor-price path under marginal-productivity factor pricing. Of course, this means that factor prices and factor quantities are simultaneously determined. Since households are assumed to be forward-looking intertemporal optimisers, it also means that today's factor supplies, and thus today's factor prices, depend on tomorrow's factor prices. In equilibrium, the entire dynamic path of price and quantity decisions by all households must be consistent. One main task in a simulation analysis is to devise computational procedures that find these equilibrium prices and quantities.

A special case of a dynamic equilibrium in this model is the steady state, in which factor prices and factor proportions are unchanging over time. Steady states are typically used as starting-points for policy analysis. For example, the economy might be in a steady-state equilibrium with a proportional or progressive income tax. The tax system drives a wedge between gross and net factor prices, the former still being determined by marginal-productivity factor pricing and the later entering into household lifetime budget constraints. Since lifetime consumption/saving and labour/leisure paths are calculated explicitly, it is straightforward to determine the value of lifetime utility in the initial steady state, under the initially given tax policy. Having established a benchmark equilibrium, one can then change the tax structure for example—by imposing a switch from income to consumption or wage taxation.

A change in tax policy causes the equilibrium of the economy to change, eventually leading to a new steady state. Early simulation studies (e.g. Summers, 1981) compared the steady-state equilibrium under one tax structure with that under another. More recent work carries the analysis further by examining the transition path from an initial steady state to a new steady state, making it possible to trace out the effects of a change in tax policy over time. This turns out to be quite important for policy evaluation, as becomes apparent when analysing a switch from a comprehensive income tax to either a consumption tax or a wage tax. Both the consumption and the wage tax eliminate the income tax distortion of the consumption/savings decision, and both result in a significantly higher steady-state capital/labour ratio. The initial impact on households of different generations that results from a switch to one or the other of these taxes is quite different, however. A switch to a consumption tax effectively captures some of the previously accumulated wealth of those who are old at the time of the tax change, since their wealth buys fewer consumption goods than would have been the case under the income tax. The taxation of the stock of accumulated wealth is lump-sum in nature (assuming that the tax reform was not anticipated) and entails no efficiency loss. On the other hand, a switch to a tax on earnings eases the tax burden on the elderly, who would have had to pay some taxes on their interest income under the income tax, while the young, for whom earnings are a more important source of income, have to pay higher taxes.

Simulation analysis not only reveals these qualitative effects of tax policy, it allows one to quantify various effects. For instance, in Auerbach, Kotlikoff, and Skinner (1983), those who are 18 or more years into the life cycle at the time of the policy change are harmed by a switch to a consumption tax, while all younger households and future generations benefit. The converse is true when switching to an earnings tax. Steady-state welfare is higher under the consumption tax than under the income tax, but a move from an income tax to a tax on wage income alone lowers steady-state welfare; expressed in terms of welfare-equivalent changes in lifetime wealth, the consumption tax raises steady-state welfare by 6 per cent, while the wage income tax reduces it by 4 per cent. These results illustrate clearly the differences between the short- and long-run effects of tax substitutions, and the way that these policy issues raise the issue of intergenerational income distribution. Moreover, as is common in this literature, these numbers are relatively large, suggesting that issues surrounding the effect of taxation on savings can be quantitatively important.

To separate the efficiency and distributional effects of tax policy, Auerbach et al. introduce the fiction of a lump-sum intergenerational redistribution mechanism through which some generations can compensate others. If the cohorts alive at the time of a switch from an income to a consumption tax are compensated so that their welfare is unchanged, subsequent generations can still enjoy an increase in welfare equivalent to that which would result from an increase in lifetime wealth of 1.73 per cent. Evidently, the 'long-run' welfare gains from consumption taxation are more than adequate to compensate those who suffer during the transition. In moving from an income to an earnings tax, there are short-run gains but long-run losses. In this case, if the welfare of those alive at the time of the tax change is held constant, the welfare of succeeding generations fall, in wealth-equivalent terms, by 2.33 per cent. Those who gain from this policy do not gain enough to compensate the losers.

Simulation analysis of dynamic fiscal policy has been extended to incorporate multiple capital assets. Gahvari (1984) considers housing as a second type of capital good, and finds that a revenue-neutral tax reform that imposed a tax on housing would increase the capital intensity in the industrial sector. If the pre-tax of return on industrial capital exceeds the growth rate of the economy, this will enhance steady-state welfare. Lord (1989) analyses the revenue-neutral substitution of consumption taxation for wage taxation in an economy with both human and non-human capital. As before, wealth accumulation increases, but the magnitude of the effect is dampened, and much of the increase goes to human capital rather than physical capital.

5.3. Policy analysis with imperfect markets

When capital markets are imperfect, the welfare analysis of taxation and savings is likely to change substantially. However, there are few routes open to the analyst who wishes to understand the implications of tax policy in such an environment. Market imperfections interact with tax policy in complex ways that make purely theoretical analysis extremely difficult. A number of studies have shown how simulation models can offer a tractable framework for the study of tax policy while incorporating capital market imperfections such as liquidity constraints or incomplete annuities markets.

Abel (1985) studies the introduction of a public pension system in an overlapping-generations model where households have uncertain lifetimes and where private annuities markets do not exist, so that accidental bequests occur. The introduction of a fully funded (actuarially fair) social security system reduces risk and thus the need for private precautionary saving, which is welfare-improving. If the capital stock is below the Golden Rule level, however, steady-state consumption levels fall, so the effect on social welfare is ambiguous. The transitional impact of a fully funded scheme is to benefit the first generations (since accidental bequests are still high), but subsequent generations could be made better or worse off.

Hubbard and Judd (1987) investigate the simultaneous impact of both liquidity constraints and an absence of annuities markets. A funded public pension programme in this model exacerbates liquidity constraints that limit the consumption of the young, even though it provides valuable insurance; liquidity constraints thus reduce any welfare gains from such a policy, or may result in welfare losses. This problem is even greater if the scheme is unfunded; one way around it is to make contributions age-dependent, with higher contributions later in the working life when the liquidity constraint is not binding.

Altig and Davis (1992) have developed simulation models incorporating both capital market imperfections and altruistically motivated intergenerational transfers. Altig and Davis consider various forms of liquidity constraints that might face young households, such as a complete inability to borrow or interest rates on loans that exceed the interest obtainable on savings, for instance, because of asymmetric tax treatment of interest income and interest expense. They emphasise that young workers are likely to face rising earnings profiles and that they would therefore wish to borrow in order to smooth consumption over time; altruistic parents might therefore wish to make *inter vivos* transfers in order to help their children overcome the losses that they suffer from capital market imperfections. (Altruistic parents can get a larger psychic return from a given wealth transfer to their children if they provide the transfer at a time when the marginal utility of consumption of the children is unusually high, which is the case when they are credit-constrained.)

These models are naturally more complex than those with perfect capital markets and no transfers, because there are many possible equilibrium regimes: depending on the parameters of the model, the young may or may not be liquidity-constrained, and parents may or may not make transfers to them. Altig and Davis examine the effects of changes in implicit tax subsidies to borrowing and taxes on interest income for different possible equilibrium scenarios. If the young do not receive transfers from their parents and are not liquidity-constrained (essentially a traditional life cycle environment), a reduction in the implicit subsidy to borrowing from 11 per cent to zero raises the steady-state capital/labour ratio by about 10 per cent. If instead the children are liquidity-constrained and receive transfers, the estimated response is closer to 12–14 per cent; if the children are not liquidity-constrained and receive transfers (a situation close to the Barro model), the policy has no effect at all. By comparison, a reduction in the tax rate on interest income from 22 per cent to 11 per cent raises the capital/labour ratio by 4–8 per cent, 0–1 per cent, and 16–18 per cent in each of these cases. Notice that the magnitudes differ by type of policy change within each regime, even though the policy change in each case is a tax reform that raises the rate of return on net saving. Notice also that the magnitudes differ by type of regime for each policy change.

As a final example of an interesting policy application of simulation analysis, it is instructive to consider the evaluation of debt and tax policy in a model where households face uninsurable income risk and therefore have an incentive to engage in precautionary saving. Barsky, Mankiw, and Zeldes (1986) and others analyse the effect of a reduction in an earnings tax that results in a temporary increase in government borrowing; this tax cut is made up by subsequent increases in taxation. In Barsky et al., the experiment is structured so that the burden of debt repayment falls on the households which enjoyed the initial reduction in taxes. In a certainty environment with life cycle or dynastic savers, such a policy change would be neutral because it would not change the lifetime budget constraint of any household. In a world with uncertain earnings, however, a certain tax cut now coupled with an increase in future tax rates changes the distribution of income not only across time periods but across states of nature. As a result, changes in the intertemporal structure of taxation are not neutral in their impacts on consumption and savings; the marginal propensity of households to consume out of the higher disposable income resulting from a current tax cut, coupled with a future tax increase, can well be much closer to the values that characterise myopic Keynesian consumption behaviour rather than to the value of zero predicted by the Barro model. The magnitude of the marginal propensity to consume is calculated for tax changes that extend over one or more periods into the future, and for varying degrees of earnings risk. For example, a current tax cut coupled with a tax increase five periods later may generate additional consumption equal to around 20 per cent of the tax reduction if the level of uncertainty is in a range that corresponds approximately to the variability found in observed earnings distributions. However, the marginal propensity to consume approaches zero as the duration of the fiscal policy diminishes and as the amount of risk in the economy falls.

6. Normative Issues in the Analysis of Taxation and Saving

In this section, we focus on three normative issues that have arisen in the context of taxing saving. The first looks at what can be learned for the tax treatment of saving from applying the theory of optimal taxation to a dynamic setting. The second concerns the optimal rate of saving and the role of taxation in achieving it. Finally, we look at what has been the main tax policy issue in this context—the choice between income and consumption as a tax base.

6.1. Optimal taxation in a dynamic setting

Optimal taxation involves the selection of a welfare-maximising tax system in a world in which non-distorting taxes are either not feasible or do not satisfy the desired equity properties. As such, it is an exercise in applied second-best theory. It is now well known that in a second-best world, where prices are distorted and no longer reflect social marginal values, welfare analysis becomes very complicated. We adopt the strategy of restricting ourselves to simple cases and searching for sufficient conditions for appealing and understandable results. Since the analysis in the literature is fairly technical, we do little more than summarise the main results in words. In most cases, intuitive explanations are not possible. Much of our discussion will be in terms of present and future consumption; the consequences for saving can be inferred readily.

The benchmark case is that of a single household in a two-period setting with variable labour supply and no bequests. The individual chooses present and future consumption (C_1 and C_2) and labour supply (L) to maximise lifetime utility subject to a lifetime wealth constraint. Assume initially that labour is supplied in the first period only, so that all income is earned then. The government must raise a given amount of lifetime revenue from the household, fixed in present value terms, using taxes on C_1, C_2, and L. This encompasses all of the taxes considered above, or combinations thereof.[6] Moreover, given that there are only two relative prices in the economy, we can arbitrarily set one of the three taxes equal to zero and rely on the other two to achieve all feasible equal-revenue outcomes. Assuming that the tax on labour is zero, we can focus on taxing C_1 and C_2, alone. (In other words, any tax on labour is equivalent to an equal-rate tax on C_1 and C_2, so can be incorporated into the taxes on the latter.)

The problem is like a standard three-good optimal commodity tax problem. According to the 'Ramsey rule' (Heady, 1993), optimal taxation implies that the demands for all three goods should fall by approximately equal proportions. An alternative characterisation of the three-good optimal tax structure asserts that the tax rate should be higher on the good which is more complementary with (or less substitutable for) leisure (Harberger, 1964). Thus, in the two-period context, if C_2 is more complementary with leisure than C_1, it should be taxed at a higher rate; in other words, there should be a tax on capital income, though not likely at the same rate as the tax on labour income. If both are equally complementary with leisure, so that a change in the price of leisure leaves the ratio C_1/C_2 unchanged, the tax rate should be the same for both goods. Either a proportional tax on consumption or a wage tax would be optimal; there should be no tax on capital income. It might be argued that these conditions are especially unlikely to be satisfied in an intertemporal context in which the variability of leisure occurs in period 1, while consumption is spread over two periods.

These results depend on several strong assumptions concerning household and government behaviour and the nature of the economy. Various extensions to the simple model have been studied in varying degrees of detail, and we summarise the results obtained for each.

6.1.1. Steady-state utility maximisation

As a first attempt to introduce elements of a dynamic economy, suppose the above household is put into the context of an economy of overlapping generations, and the government is assumed to maximise per capita utility in the steady state. The level of steady-state utility now depends not only on tax distortions, but on how much capital households choose to accumulate relative to the Golden Rule level. If the government is allowed to borrow or lend, variations in the stock of debt can control the

---

[6] A general consumption tax is a uniform tax on C_1 and C_2. A wage tax is a tax on L, or, equivalently by the budget constraint, a uniform tax on C_1 and C_2. A capital income tax is a tax on C_2. An income tax is a system of taxes on C_1 and C_2, with that on C_2 being higher. And C_1 and C_2 can be selectively taxed by excise taxes.

stock of capital in the economy. In this case, taxation can be directed solely at revenue-raising and the tax structure will be given by the standard Ramsey rule, as above. On the other hand, if the government is unable to deploy debt to achieve the desired steady-state capital stock, its choice of tax structure will have to address two objectives—minimising the dead-weight loss and influencing the amount of capital accumulated. For example, if private saving generates a level of capital such that $r > g$, the tax structure should be altered so as to encourage more saving. King (1980) shows that, when the government is restricted to using taxes on wage and capital income only, it is optimal to tax capital income more heavily. The reason is that capital income taxes are incurred in the second period, so households must save to pay for them. However, if taxes on consumption are used as well, the need for capital income taxes is reduced, since (as discussed above) consumption taxes generate more steady-state saving than wage taxes.

This steady-state analysis ignores transitional problems. To get to the optimal steady state by increasing the capital stock (if that is required), the older generations will have initially to forgo some consumption. The time path of adjustment will then depend upon the relative weights given to the lifetime utility of different generations. We return later to the issue of choosing the time path of taxes to maximise an intertemporal social welfare function.

6.1.2. Many goods

If there are many goods in each period, the analysis becomes quite complicated, especially if the government is constrained to levy the same tax rate on each good independent of the age of the household, as would be the case when taxes are indirect. The effect of this is to introduce as many second-best pricing constraints as there are types of goods. As is well known from the theory of second best, very few general results can be obtained, and none has been obtained in this context. In the absence of these pricing constraints, the problem would be a standard optimal tax one.[7] However, even in this case, there are conditions under which wage (or proportional consumption) taxation would be optimal. That will be the case if the utility function is such that increases in income cause

---

[7] One would expect some further results could be obtained in the case in which lifetime utility was a separable function of the first-period consumption bundle, the second-period consumption bundle and leisure. Then per-period consumption could be treated as a composite commodity, and one could rely on wage and capital income taxes alone.

equal proportionate increases in the demand for all goods, and changes in the wage rate do not affect the proportion in which goods are consumed.[8]

6.1.3. Variable leisure in both periods

Alvarez, Burbidge, Ferrall, and Palmer (1992) have analysed the taxation of labour and capital income in the two-period case where utility in each period depends upon leisure and a consumption good. They show that, if wage rates and the interest rate are constant over the life cycle, optimal wage tax rates decline with age if the interest rate exceeds the utility discount factor (and vice versa). More generally, the ability to condition wage and consumption taxes on age eliminates the need to tax interest income. On the other hand, if the wage tax (or consumption tax) cannot be conditioned on age, interest income becomes optimal if the interest rate exceeds the utility rate of discount; this is because an interest income tax is like a declining wage tax, though imperfectly so.

6.1.4. Many consumers per cohort

The presence of many consumers in each cohort raises issues of redistributive equity if the consumers have differing incomes. In standard models of optimal income taxation, income differences arise from both different levels of 'ability' across households and different amounts of labour supply.[9] The government is assumed to be able to observe incomes, but not underlying abilities, and can levy a non-linear income tax as well as indirect taxes at different rates on different commodities. In a static context, Atkinson and Stiglitz (1976) have shown that, if the consumption bundle is separable from leisure in the utility function (i.e. if changes in the amount of leisure taken do not affect the marginal rate of substitution among the various pairs of commodities), non-linear wage taxation will suffice; differential commodity taxes are not needed. In the absence of separability, the government should combine the non-linear wage tax with an indirect tax system which imposes a higher tax rate on goods which are complementary with leisure (Edwards, Keen, and Tuomala, 1994). By extension, in a dynamic context, if the government is able to tax present and future consumption differentially, the latter

---

[8] Technically, this is so if utility is homothetic in goods, and if the marginal rate of substitution between all pairs of goods is independent of the level of leisure (i.e. goods are separable from leisure in the utility function).

[9] See Heady (1993) for a non-technical survey of this literature.

would be taxed more heavily if it is more complementary with leisure.[10] Stiglitz (1987) has extended the results of Atkinson and Stiglitz (1976) to an overlapping-generations setting in which households consume a vector of goods in each of two periods and supply labour only in the first. If debt policy can be used to control the level of capital stock, and if the relative wages between skilled and unskilled workers are independent of the capital stock, progressive wage (or lifetime expenditure) taxation is the most efficient redistributive instrument if consumption and leisure are separable in the utility function. However, if relative wages vary with the capital stock or if the government cannot use debt policy, interest taxation or subsidisation becomes a useful supplementary instrument. If it wishes to encourage saving either to increase the capital stock towards its optimum or to induce a fall in the relative wage of the high-ability persons, an interest subsidy is called for, and vice versa.

6.1.5. Altruistic preferences

If altruism is such that Ricardian equivalence applies, the representative household can be viewed as being infinitely lived. Chamley (1986) has investigated the optimal tax problem in this context assuming that leisure and consumption are variable in each period and the government must collect a given stream of revenue through a combination of taxes on wages and capital income. Given an initial stock of previously accumulated capital, the optimal tax plan will be one in which the government initially imposes a relatively high tax on capital income, but gradually replaces it by a wage tax; in the long run, only a wage tax is used. The latter result reflects the fact that, given the additive intertemporal utility function, the steady-state optimal tax structure involves only a wage tax. The initial use of capital taxation occurs because, at the time the tax problem is solved, some capital has already been accumulated, so it yields a fixed stream of income which can be taxed with no dead-weight loss. However, the government cannot distinguish 'old' from 'new' capital and must tax the return to all capital identically. As time goes by, the proportion of old to new capital rises, so that the distorting effect of capital income taxation increases, so the taxation of capital income has to be gradually phased out and replaced by wage taxation.

Not that the structure of this problem gives rise to a time-

---

[10] One way to do this would be to combine a tax on income with one on consumption. By varying the rates on the two, any combination of a tax on present and future consumption could be attained. It is interesting to note that many countries' income tax systems are essentially of this sort, given that they shelter part of capital income.

inconsistency. If the government were to redo its optimal tax problem in any future period, given the stock of capital that had then been accumulated, it would renege on its previous plan and impose a high capital income tax once again rather than abiding by the previously announced lower and falling rate.

6.1.6. Time-consistent taxation

The notion of the time-inconsistency of capital income taxation in dynamic models was eloquently stated by Fischer (1980). He considers a two-period model in which a single household receives an endowment of wealth, saves some of it for second-period consumption, and supplies labour in the second period. The government has to raise revenue in the second period through a combination of labour and capital income taxation. Viewed from the beginning of the first period, the optimal tax plan is one which uses a wage tax and, depending on the utility function, perhaps a capital income tax. However, if the government could re-optimise at the beginning of period 2, after the saving decision had been taken, it would opt to get as much revenue as possible from capital income taxes and as little as possible from wage taxes. The government's announced optimal tax plan is therefore not credible. A *time-consistent policy* outcome will be one in which the household behaves according to an expected tax structure that is the same as the one that is actually chosen. It will have the highest capital income tax rate and the lowest wage tax rate consistent with government budget balance. Household saving and welfare will be lower than in the optimal tax solution.

Given the excessive capital income taxation resulting from the time–inconsistency of optimal taxation, it is natural to consider whether alternative policies might be used to mitigate its effects. One obvious policy is to provide savings incentives 'up front', knowing that the income from those savings will be taxed too heavily. An alternative is to constrain the government in its use of policy instruments. In an extension of the Fischer model to allow for variable labour supply in both periods, Rodgers (1987) has argued that, given a particular set of household preferences, consumption taxation might be preferable to wage taxation in a time-consistent equilibrium, even though the opposite is true in the optimal tax equilibrium. Mitigating the consequences of time-inconsistency by constraining the instruments available to the government seems an attractive alternative, though it is not at all clear how such a commitment could be made binding.

6.2. Is the saving rate too low?

The importance of the saving rate has been at the forefront of policy debates in recent years, and has been responsible for many policy recommendations, such as instituting full funding of public pensions, retiring the public debt, and replacing the income tax with a consumption tax. Is the saving rate too low? Feldstein (1977) argued for the USA that, because $r > g$, it was. (Recall that r is the rate of return on capital, while g, the rate of growth in the economy, is the implicit return on intergenerational transfers.) He argued that, in these circumstances, the loss to the current old from increasing saving (reducing intergenerational transfers) is more than offset by the discounted gain to future generations. His argument involved not only the difference between r and g, but also capital market inefficiency and intergenerational discounting.[11] To evaluate it, we investigate what we can infer about the optimality of the saving rate from the fact that $r \neq g$. Three main aspects of the optimality of the saving rate can be identified—dynamic inefficiency, capital market inefficiency, and intergenerational equity.

6.2.1. Dynamic inefficiency

An economy is dynamically inefficient if it is possible to increase the welfare of a member of at least one generation without decreasing the welfare of any person in any generation. The circumstances in which the economy is dynamically inefficient are quite limited. Basically, g must exceed r now or at some time in the future and continue that way indefinitely (Starrett, 1972). Dynamic efficiency does not occur if r eventually becomes greater than g and stays that way indefinitely, even though $g > r$ now and for some time into the future. Also, dynamic inefficiency cannot occur in any economy with altruistic bequests in which Richardian equivalence applies; if there were dynamic inefficiency, bequests would adjust so as to increase dynastic utility.

Implications for saving policy cannot be derived from the dynamic inefficiency argument, since it is virtually impossible to know whether the economy is on a dynamically inefficient growth path; that would involve seeing into the indefinite future. For example, we cannot infer

---

[11] Specifically, he derived that the present value to society of an increase in saving by £1 was given by $(r - g)(1 + \delta)/((\delta - g)(1 + d))$, where δ is society's discount rate between present and future consumption (reflecting differences in the marginal utility of consumption caused by growth in consumption) and d is the individual's discount rate (which is less than r because of capital income taxation).

from the fact that $r > g$ now that the economy is dynamically efficient, since it is possible that $g > r$ eventually.

6.2.2. Capital market inefficiencies

Inefficiencies on capital markets can arise either from distortions, such as capital income taxes, or from externalities. Evaluating the inefficiencies caused by capital income taxes involves studying the optimal tax system as outlined above. If capital income taxes are set 'optimally', the existence of positive taxes does not reflect under-saving. One obvious reason why capital income taxes might be set non-optimally in practice is that tax systems treat different types of assets differently. Imputed income on consumer durables is typically untaxed, mainly because of measurement problems. The same is true for capital income on human capital investment. Saving for retirement is usually treated preferentially as a matter of policy (for example, to encourage persons to save for their own retirement so as to reduce the need for future state support). Moreover, different types of capital income generated by investment in capital goods are treated differentially by the business tax system: corporations are taxed differently from unincorporated businesses, tangible assets from intangibles, manufacturing from resources and so on. In these circumstances, capital is likely to be allocated inefficiently among uses in the economy. Moreover, given the preferential treatment given to durables and human capital, there is too little investment in capital goods. Given the difficulty of taxing these other forms of investment, a case can be made for encouraging physical capital investment.

Externalities can arise on the saving side or on the investment side. In the former case, the argument is that, if saving for bequests is motivated by intergenerational altruism, it may be like a public good in the sense that all members of the current generation benefit from the amount that each person saves for future generations (e.g. Sen, 1967).[12] The social return to saving will therefore exceed the private return, so that we might expect the rate of saving to be too low; indeed, given the extent of the free-rider problem involved, persons may well leave no bequests even though they are altruistic towards future generations. The implication is

---

[12] In an ingenious argument, Bernheim and Bagwell (1988) have argued that saving for bequests becomes a public good even in a Ricardian world in which each person cares only about their own direct heirs. In this world, people care indirectly about all their future descendants. But, by the natural process of intermarriage among persons of different family lines, all persons become interrelated in the long run and care about each other's heirs.

that government redistribution from current to future generations would be Pareto-improving.

The argument about investment externalities has been given prominence recently with the advent of the 'new growth theory' (Romer, 1986), though it goes back to the growth theory of the 1960s. Investment is said to embody technical progress (for example, new knowledge, learning by doing), the returns of which are not fully appropriated by the firms undertaking it. This implies that social returns are higher than private returns, so that investment is too low. This constitutes an argument for intervention on the investment side of the market rather than the saving side, at least in an open economy. For both saving and investment externalities, there exists a difficult measurement problem of verifying the extent to which external effects are present.

6.2.3. Intergenerational equity

If the economy is dynamically efficient, if capital-income taxes are set optimally, and if externalities are corrected, gains to future cohorts from higher saving can be attained only by redistributing from current cohorts. Naturally, this involves making a value judgement involving the comparison of utilities of different generations. The conventional way to analyse such policies is by the use of an intergenerational social-welfare function which explicitly incorporates the trade-off between the welfare of different generations. A convenient form to use is the weighted utilitarian form:

$$W(u_1, u_2, \ldots) = \sum_{t=0}^{\infty} \frac{u_t}{(1 + \alpha)^t} \qquad (1)$$

where u_t is the per capita lifetime utility of generation t and α is the utility discount rate. Two sorts of value judgements are involved in $W(.)$. One concerns the way in which the utility function u_t varies with the lifetime consumption of cohort t. The more rapidly the marginal utility diminishes with consumption, the more *inequality-averse* is the social-welfare function and the greater the tendency to equalise consumption across generations. The second involves the utility discount factor which determines the weight to be given to future generations. For $\alpha=-\infty$, only the welfare of the first generation matters. In the other extreme, $\alpha = 0$ and equal weights are given to the welfare of all generations.

Suppose that there is no technical progress, that population grows at the rate n, and that a planner wishes to maximise $W(.)$. The optimal path of capital accumulation can be characterised as follows. If the optimal capital/labour ratio is sufficiently low, so that $r - n > \alpha$, the level of consumption per capital and the capital/labour ratio (saving rate) should be increasing over time, and vice versa. (Note the difference with Feldstein (1977).) The economy approaches a long-run optimum in which $r - n = \alpha$; because of the discounting of future generations' utilities, the long-run optimum involves a smaller capital/labour ratio and a smaller level of consumption than is true of the Golden Rule optimum. The higher the discount rate α, the lower are the long-run optimal levels of the capital/labour ratio and of consumption.[13] The speed of adjustment of the economy to the long-run optimum depends upon the extent of inequality aversion in the social-welfare function. The more rapidly does the marginal utility of consumption diminish, the more quickly is the capital stock adjusted for a given difference between $r - n$ and α. This analysis thus implies that the savings rate is too low if $r - n > \alpha$, and it should be increased more rapidly the greater is the rate at which the marginal utility of consumption diminishes as consumption rises.

6.3. The consumption versus income-tax debate

From a tax-policy point of view, a key issue concerning taxation and savings is whether the base of the direct tax system should include capital or not. This section addresses that issue.

There are two polar forms of personal tax bases which have been advocated in the literature: *comprehensive income* and *consumption*, or their equivalents. Comprehensive income (Y) is defined to include two components—current consumption (C) plus all net accruals to wealth (ΔW, or real saving, S). Using the single-period budget constraint of the household, comprehensive income can be written:

$$Y = C + \Delta W = E + rW + A \tag{2}$$

where E represents labour earnings, r is the real rate of return on wealth, and A includes autonomous receipts, such as inheritances, gifts received, and windfall gains received during the period.[14]

---

[13] The weighting of welfare levels in different generations could reflect their population. For example, if the intergenerational social welfare function is the population-weighted sum of total (rather than per capita) utilities and if total utilities are discounted at the rate $\hat{\alpha}$, then per capita utilities will be discounted at $\alpha = \hat{\alpha} - n$. The economy converges to an optimum in which $r = \hat{\alpha}$.

[14] There is an issue as to whether bequests and gifts given ought to be deducted from the right-hand side of the equation. If the giving of gifts and bequests is considered an act of consumption, they should not be deducted. Of course, the gift will then be

There are some problems involved in applying a comprehensive income base. Not all sources of consumption are included in (2), such as consumption from household production and leisure. Moreover, there are several difficulties encountered in measuring capital income, rW. In principle, this should include all forms of returns to assets including interest, dividends, accrued capital gains, capital income from unincorporated business, imputed rent on consumer durables (especially housing), and the imputed return of assets such as transaction balances and insurance. These should all be indexed for inflation and should include an appropriate risk premium. Unfortunately, the measurement of these items is difficult and impractical. Perhaps even more problematic is the fact that, in principle, the return to human capital investment ought to be included as capital income. Including all earnings in E is equivalent to treating investment in human capital on a *cash-flow* accounting basis rather than capitalising such expenditures, as is the case with other forms of capital investment. Needless to say, it would be extremely difficult correctly to impute a rate of return to human capital investment. To do so would require, for example, that forgone earnings be capitalised rather than being deducted on a cash-flow basis. This would require information on the depreciation of human capital. Thus, a truly comprehensive income tax is not feasible from a purely administrative point of view.

The alternative, a personal consumption (expenditure) tax, first advocated by Kaldor (1955), avoids some of these problems. The consumption tax base can be obtained from rearranging (2) to give:

$$C = E + rW - \Delta W + A. \tag{3}$$

Thus, consumption is simply income less saving. From this, it would appear that all the problems of measuring income reappear in (3). However, except for the difficulty in measuring consumption, this is not the case. It is no longer imperative to measure capital income on an accrual basis or to index capital income for the effect of inflation on asset values. Capital gains which accrue, but are not spent, add both to rW and to ΔW so cancel out. Similarly, inflationary losses in the value of wealth will be offset by the fact that nominal capital income is included in the base. Thus, all accounting for tax purposes can be done on a cash-flow basis, which is relatively easy to administer.

Furthermore, unlike with a comprehensive income tax, returns to capital which take an imputed form, such as imputed rent on housing,

double-counted to the extent that it gives rise to consumption by the recipient. However, this may be reasonable in that the gift gave rise to two acts of consumption. This issue need not concern us here since precisely the same problem arises under consumption taxation as under income taxation.

need not be measured under a consumption tax. To see this, note that the present value of $rW - \Delta W$ is simply zero, so omitting both the deduction for saving and the capital income on a given asset from the tax base will not change its present value. This is referred to in the literature as treating assets on a *tax-prepaid* basis, as opposed to that of equation (3), which is the *designated asset* basis (US Treasury, 1977; Meade, 1978). The tax-prepaid method eliminates the need to measure capital income.

In implementing a consumption tax, some assets could be treated on a designated basis and others on a tax-prepaid basis. Those assets whose returns take the imputed form, such as consumer durables, are natural candidates for the tax-prepaid method. For others, the designated method is more suitable. For example, unincorporated business earnings are best treated on a designated, or cash-flow, basis, because of the difficulty of differentiating capital income from labour income within the firm, and because of the fact that pure rents would go untaxed under the tax-prepaid method. Similarly, investment in human capital is best treated on a cash-flow basis to avoid the problem of having to include forgone income in the tax base. For other assets, such as financial assets, either method would be suitable. In fact, there are advantages in allowing households to decide which assets to treat on a tax-prepaid basis and which to designate. Combining the two bases allows them to arrange their time stream of tax liabilities as they choose, thereby allowing the smoothing of their tax base over time for averaging purposes (i.e. self-averaging). At the same time, since records must be kept of designated assets to ensure that they are taxed when run down, there is an administrative cost involved in designating assets, which households will want to minimise.

In practice, direct tax systems do not tend to conform to either a consumption or a comprehensive income tax, but contain elements of both. While financial asset income tends to be taxed (though not always uniformly), many forms of capital income escape taxation. Housing and other consumer durables tend to be treated as tax-prepaid assets, if not even more generously through mortgage interest deductibility. Pension saving is treated on a cash-flow or designated basis, as is human capital investment. It can be argued that most income tax systems are actually closer to a consumption tax system in the sense that a larger proportion of assets are non-taxable than are taxable.

While the administrative arguments favour consumption taxation, what of the economic arguments? Since the difference between the two concerns the taxability of capital income, the issue revolves around the efficiency and equity arguments for taxing capital income.[15]

[15] It should be noted that the choice between an income tax and a personal

6.3.1. Efficiency arguments for a consumption tax

The choice between a consumption and an income tax concerns whether or not to tax future consumption more heavily than current consumption. Since neither tax applies to leisure, we are in a second-best world in which the outcome is not easily predictable. In the simple case in which there are two periods and labour is supplied in the first only, the optimal tax results discussed earlier for the single-household case apply. If first- and second-period consumption are equally substitutable for leisure, a consumption tax would be efficient. If second-period consumption is more complementary with leisure, it should bear a higher tax. In the latter case, this does not necessarily imply that an income tax should be used rather than a consumption tax—that is, that capital and labour incomes be taxed at exactly the same rates; that would require a particular degree of complementarity. Generally, if second-period consumption is complementary with leisure, the optimal tax would require some combination of an income and a consumption tax to ensure that the ideal differential tax on second-period consumption is attained. Things get more complicated once one takes account of the fact that under income taxation it will be impossible to tax all capital income on a par; there will be inter-asset distortions implying that capital is allocated inefficiently among alternative uses. This presumably weakens the case for income taxation. More generally, there has been no optimal tax model developed to date that gives a comprehensive income tax as the preferred outcome. Thus, the case for income taxation must be based on other considerations, such as the ease with which labour income may be converted into capital income by taxpayers.

6.3.2. Equity arguments for a consumption tax

The original proponent of consumption taxation, Kaldor (1955), used essentially an equity argument to make his case. He suggested that persons should be taxed according to what they take out of the 'social pot' rather than what they contribute to it. In utilitarian terms, the notion is that one's well-being is determined by consumption rather than by income. However, as with efficiency considerations, variability of leisure complicates matters as well. Given that neither tax base includes leisure, it is not obvious whether consumption is a better indicator of utility than is income. One might expect by analogy with the efficiency case that

consumption tax revolves around the base only. In principle, virtually any degree of progressivity can be attained for a given base by the choice of a suitable rate structure.

income may be a better index of utility if future consumption is sufficiently more complementary with leisure than is current consumption. This turns out to be the case. As we have seen earlier, in a multi-consumer world with non-linear taxation, if the consumption bundle (including both present and future consumption) is separable from leisure, a non-linear consumption tax will be optimal. In the absence of separability, the analysis is more complicated and results have yet to be derived for the multi-period setting. We have seen earlier that, with non-linear consumption taxation and linear commodity taxation, the linear tax rate will be higher on goods which are more complementary with leisure. One might expect that with non-linear taxation possible on future consumption, as with a progressive income tax, if future consumption is more complementary with leisure than current consumption is, the optimal redistributive tax system will involve a progressive income tax, generally alongside a progressive consumption tax. One complicating feature of income taxation is that it does not satisfy horizontal equity. Persons with the same lifetime wealth but with different time profiles of earnings will be treated differently under an income tax. Those whose earnings occur earlier in the life cycle will pay higher taxes.

Thus, the choice between a consumption and an income base involves many considerations, some of which are difficult to verify. Administrative considerations favour consumption taxation, while efficiency and equity arguments can go either way. However, in order to justify income taxation, complementarity of future consumption with leisure is required for both equity and efficiency criteria to be satisfied. Even if such complementarity exists, it is likely that income taxation alone will not be optimal. Given the imperfections of an income base, and the administrative costs of running a joint consumption and income tax system, it is not surprising that the US Treasury *Blueprints* (1977), the Meade Report (Meade, 1978), and the Economic Council of Canada (1987) all opted for progressive consumption tax. Of course, there are various hybrids of consumption and income taxation that are used in practice. An interesting one is that used in Nordic countries combining flat taxes on capital income with a progressive labour income tax. This avoids many of the administrative difficulties of taxing capital income on a par with labour income while at the same time retaining some capital income taxation for distributive or revenue-raising reasons (Sørensen, 1994).

References

Abel, A. B. (1985), 'Precautionary saving and accidental bequests', *American Economic Review*, vol. 75, pp. 777–91.

Altig, D., and Davis, S. J. (1992), 'The timing of intergenerational transfers, tax policy, and aggregate savings', *American Economic Review*, vol. 82, pp. 1199–220.

Altonji, J. G., Hayashi, F., and Kotlikoff, L. J. (1992), 'Is the extended family altruistically linked? Direct tests using microdata', *American Economic Review*, vol. 82, pp. 1177–98.

Alvarez, Y., Burbidge, J., Ferrall, T., and Palmer, L. (1992), 'Optimal taxation in a life-cycle model', *Canadian Journal of Economics*, vol. 25, pp. 111–22.

Atkinson, A. B., and Stiglitz, J. E. (1976), 'The design of the tax structure: direct versus indirect taxation', *Journal of Public Economics*, vol. 6, pp. 55–75.

Auerbach, A. J., and Kotlikoff, L. J. (1987), *Dynamic Fiscal Policy*, Cambridge University Press.

—— —— and Skinner, J. (1983), 'The efficiency gains from dynamic tax reform', *International Economic Review*, vol. 24, pp. 81–100.

Banks, J., and Blundell, R. (1995a), 'Taxation and personal saving incentives in the UK', in J. Poterba (ed.) *Public Policies and Household Saving*, Chicago: University of Chicago Press.

—— —— (1995b), 'Household saving behaviour in the UK', in J. Poterba (ed.) *International Comparisons of Household Saving*, Chicago: University of Chicago Press.

Barro, R. J. (1974), 'Are government bonds net wealth?', *Journal of Political Economy*, vol. 82, pp. 1095–117.

Barsky, R. B., Mankiw, N. G., and Zeldes, S. P. (1986), 'Ricardian consumers with Keynesian propensities', *American Economic Review*, vol. 76, pp. 676–91.

Beach, C. M., Boadway, R. W., and Bruce, N. (1988), *Taxation and Savings in Canada*, Ottawa: Minister of Supply and Services Canada.

—— and Gibbons, J. O. (1984), 'Social security and aggregate wealth accumulation revisited: dynamic simultaneous estimates in a wealth-generation model', *Economic Inquiry*, vol. 22, pp. 58–79.

Bernheim, B. D. (1987), 'Dissaving after retirement: testing the pure life cycle hypothesis', in Z. Bodie, J. B. Shoven, and D. A. Wise (eds.), *Issues in Pension Economics*, Chicago: University of Chicago Press.

—— (1991), 'How strong are bequest motives? Evidence based on estimates of the demand for life insurance and annuities', *Journal of Political Economy*, vol. 99, pp. 899–927.

—— and Bagwell, K. (1988), 'Is everything neutral?', *Journal of Political Economy*, vol. 96, pp. 308–38.

—— and Shoven, J. B. (1988), 'Pension funding and saving', in Z. Bodie, J. B. Shoven, and D. A. Wise (eds.), *Pensions in the US Economy*, Chicago: University of Chicago Press.

—— Shleifer, A., and Summers, L. H. (1985), 'The strategic bequest motive', *Journal of Political Economy*, vol. 93, pp. 1045–76.

Blinder, A. S., and Deaton, A. (1985), 'The time series consumption function revisited', *Brookings Papers on Economic Activity*, pp. 465–511.

Boadway, R. W., and Bruce, N. (1992), 'Problems with integrating corporate and personal income taxes in an open economy', *Journal of Public Economics*, vol. 48, pp. 39–66.

—— and Wildasin, D. E. (1993), 'Long-term debt strategy: a survey', in F. van Winden and H. A. A. Verbon (eds.), *The Political Economy of Government Debt*, Amsterdam: North-Holland.

Boskin, M. J. (1978), 'Taxation, saving, and the rate of interest', *Journal of Political Economy*, vol. 86, pp. S3–S27.

Bosworth, B., Burtless, G., and Sabelhaus, J. (1991), 'The decline in savings: evidence from household surveys', *Brookings Papers on Economic Activity*, pp. 183–256.

Carroll, C., and Summers, L. H. (1987), 'Why have private savings rates in the United States and Canada diverged?', *Journal of Monetary Economics*, vol. 20, pp. 249–79.

Chamley, C. P. (1986), 'Optimal taxation of capital income in general equilibrium with infinite lives', *Econometrica*, vol. 54, pp. 607–22.

Cox, D. W. (1990), 'Intergenerational transfers and liquidity constraints', *Quarterly Journal of Economics*, vol. 105, pp. 187–218.

—— and Japelli, T. (1990), 'Credit rationing and private transfers: evidence from survey data', *Review of Economics and Statistics*, vol. 72, pp. 445–54.

Davies, J. B., and St-Hilaire, F. (1987), *Reforming Capital Income Taxation in Canada*, Ottawa: Minister of Supply and Services Canada.

Diamond, P. A. (1977), 'A framework for social security analysis', *Journal of Public Economics*, vol. 8, pp. 275–98.

—— and Hausman, J. A. (1984), 'Individual retirement and savings behavior', *Journal of Public Economics*, vol. 23, pp. 81–114.

Dilnot, A., Disney, R., Johnson, P., and Whitehouse, E. (1994), *Pensions Policy in the UK: An Economic Analysis*, London: Institute for Fiscal Studies.

Economic Council of Canada (1987), *Road Map for Tax Reform*, Ottawa: Minister of Supply and Services Canada.

Edwards, J., Keen, M., and Tuomala, M. (1994), 'Income tax commodity taxes and public good provision: a brief guide', *Finanzarchiv*, vol. 51, pp. 472–87.

Feldstein, M. S. (1974), 'Social security, induced retirement and aggregate capital accumulation', *Journal of Political Economy*, vol. 82, pp. 905–26.

—— (1977), 'Does the United States save too little?', *American Economic Review*, vol. 67, pp. 162–81.

Fischer, S. (1980), 'Dynamic inconsistency, cooperation and the benevolent disembling government', *Journal of Economic Dynamics and Control*, vol. 2, pp. 93–107.

Friedman, B. M., and Warshawsky, M. (1989), 'The cost of annuities: implications for savings behavior and bequests', *Quarterly Journal of Economics*, vol. 105, pp. 135–54.

Gahvari, F. (1984), 'Incidence and efficiency aspects of differential taxation of residential and industrial capital in a growing economy', *Journal of Public Economics*, vol. 25, pp. 211–33.

Gravelle, J. G. (1991), 'Do individual retirement accounts increase savings?', *Journal of Economic Perspectives*, vol. 5, pp. 133–48.

Guiso, L., Japelli, T., and Terlizzese, D. (1992), 'Earnings uncertainty and precautionary saving', *Journal of Monetary Economics*, vol. 30, pp. 307–37.

Hall, R. E. (1978), 'Stochastic implications of the life cycle–permanent income hypothesis: theory and evidence', *Journal of Political Economy*, vol. 86, pp. 971–87.

—— (1988), 'Intertemporal substitution in consumption', *Journal of Political Economy*, vol. 96, pp. 339–57.

—— and Mishkin, F. S. (1982), 'The sensitivity of consumption to transitory income: estimates from panel data on households', *Econometrica*, vol. 50, pp. 461–81.

Harberger, A. C. (1964), 'Taxation, resource allocation, and welfare', in J. Due (ed.), *The Role of Direct and Indirect Taxes in the Federal Revenue System*, Princeton: princeton University Press.

Hayashi, F. (1985), 'The effect of liquidity constraints on consumption: a cross-sectional analysis', *Quarterly Journal of Economics*, vol. 100, pp. 183–206.

Heady, C. (1993), 'Optimal taxation as a guide to policy: a survey', *Fiscal Studies*, vol. 14, no. 1, pp. 14–41; repr. as Chapter 2 of this volume.

Howrey, E. P., and Hymans, S. H. (1978), 'The measurement and determination of loanable-funds savings', *Brookings Papers on Economic Activity*, pp. 655–85.

Hubbard, R. G., and Judd, K. L. (1987), 'Social security and individual welfare: precautionary saving, liquidity constraints, and the payroll tax', *American Economic Review*, vol. 77, pp. 630–46.

Hurd, M. D. (1992), 'Wealth depletion and life-cycle consumption by the elderly', in D. A. Wise (ed.), *Topics in the Economics of Aging*, Chicago: University of Chicago Press.

Japelli, T. (1990), 'Who is credit-constrained in the US economy?', *Quarterly Journal of Economics*, vol. 105, pp. 219–34.

—— and Pagano, M. (1989), 'Consumption and capital market imperfections', *American Economic Review*, vol. 79, pp. 1089–105.

Kaldor, N. (1955), *An Expenditure Tax*, London: Allen & Unwin.

King, M. A. (1980), 'Savings and taxation', in G. M. Heal and G. A. Hughes (eds), *Public Policy and the Tax System*, London: Allen & Unwin.

—— and Dicks-Mireaux, L.-D. L. (1982), 'Asset holdings and the life-cycle', *Economic Journal*, vol. 92, pp. 247–67.

Kotlikoff, L. J. (1988), 'Intergenerational transfers and savings', *Journal of Economic Perspectives*, vol. 2, pp. 41–58.

—— (1992), *Generational Accounting*, New York: Free Press.

—— and Summers, L. H. (1981), 'The role of intergenerational transfers in aggregate capital accumulation', *Journal of Political Economy*, vol. 89, pp. 706–32.

Leimer, D. R., and Lesnoy, S. D. (1982), 'Social security and private saving: new time-series evidence', *Journal of Political Economy*, vol. 90, pp. 606–29.

Lord, W. (1989), 'The transition from payroll to consumption receipts with endogenous human capital', *Journal of Public Economics*, vol. 38, pp. 53–74.

Manchester, J. M., and Poterba, J. M. (1989), 'Second mortgages and household savings', *Regional Science and Urban Economics*, vol. 19, pp. 325–46.

Mankiw, N. G., Rotemberg, J. J., and Summers, L. H. (1985), 'Intertemporal substitution in macroeconomics', *Quarterly Journal of Economics*, vol. 1010, pp. 225–51.

Mariger, R. P. (1986), *Consumption Behavior and the Effects of Government Fiscal Policies*, Cambridge: Harvard University Press.

Meade, J. E. (1978), *The Structure and Reform of Direct Taxation: Report of a Committee Chaired by Professor J. E. Meade*, London: Allen & Unwin.

Menchik, P. L. (1988), 'Unequal estate division: is it altruism, reverse bequest, or simply noise?', in D. Kessler and A. Masson (eds.), *Modelling the Accumulation and Distribution of Wealth*, Oxford: Clarendon Press.

Modigliani, F. (1988), 'The role of intergenerational transfers and life cycle saving in the accumulation of wealth', *Journal of Economic Perspectives*, vol. 2, pp. 15–40.

Papke, L. E., Petersen, M., and Poterba, J. M. (1993), 'Did 401(k) plans replace other employer provided pensions?', National Bureau of Economic Research, Working Paper no. 4501.

Poterba, J. M. (1987), 'Tax policy and corporate saving', *Brookings Papers on Economic Activity*, pp. 455–503.

—— Venti, S. F., and Wise, D. A. (1993), 'Do 401(k) contributions crowd out other personal saving?', *Journal of Public Economics*, vol. 58, pp. 1–32.

Rogers, C. A. (1987), 'Expenditure taxes, income taxes and time-inconsistency', *Journal of Public Economics*, vol. 32, pp. 215–30.

Romer, P. M. (1986), 'Increasing returns and long-run growth', *Journal of Political Economy*, vol. 94, pp. 1002–37.

Sen, A. K. (1967), 'Isolation, assurance and the social rate of discount', *Quarterly Journal of Economics*, vol. 81, pp. 112–24.

Skinner, J. (1989), 'Housing wealth and aggregate saving', *Regional Science and Urban Economics*, vol. 19, pp. 305–24.

Sørensen, P. B. (1994), 'From the global income tax to the dual income tax: recent tax reforms in the Nordic countries', *International Tax and Public Finance*, vol. 1, pp. 57–79.

Starrett, D. (1972), 'On golden rules, the "biological theory of interest", and competitive inefficiency', *Journal of Political Economy*, vol. 80, pp. 276–91.

Stiglitz, J. E. (1987), 'Pareto efficient and optimal taxation and the new new welfare economics', in A. J. Auerbach and M. Feldstein (eds.), *Handbook of Public Economics*, vol. 2, Amsterdam: North-Holland.

Summers, L. H. (1981), 'Capital taxation and accumulation in a life cycle growth model', *American Economic Review*, vol. 71, pp. 533–44.

Tomes, N. (1988), 'Inheritance and inequality within the family: equal division among unequals, or do the poor get more?', in D. Kessler and A. Masson (eds.), *Modelling the Accumulation and Distribution of Wealth*, Oxford: Clarendon Press.

US Treasury (1977), *Blueprints for Basic Tax Reform*, Washington DC: Government Printing Office.

Venti, S. F., and Wise, D. A. (1990), 'But they don't want to reduce housing equity', in D. A. Wise (ed.), *Issues in the Economics of Aging*, Chicago: University of Chicago Press.

—— —— (1992), 'Government policy and personal retirement saving', *Tax Policy and the Economy*, vol. 6, pp. 1–41.

Wilcox, D. W. (1989), 'Social security benefits, consumption expenditure, and the life-cycle hypothesis', *Journal of Political Economy*, vol. 97, pp. 288–304.

Zeldes, S. P. (1989a), 'Optimal consumption with stochastic income', *Quarterly Journal of Economics*, vol. 104, pp. 275–98.

—— (1989b), 'Consumption and liquidity constraints: an empirical investigation', *Journal of Political Economy*, vol. 97, pp. 305–46.

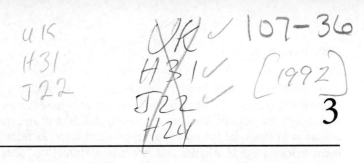

3

LABOUR SUPPLY AND TAXATION

RICHARD BLUNDELL

1. Introduction

There are many margins on which the tax system may be thought to influence labour supply. Indeed, it was the perceived disincentives on work effort induced by the tax and benefit system that provided much of the justification for the extensive tax and benefit reforms of the 1980s. In the UK over the 1980s, direct tax rates faced by individuals at the top end of the earnings distribution fell from over 80 per cent to around 40 per cent, with less dramatic, but well-publicised, reductions for basic-rate payers. The 1986 tax reform in the USA contained similar reductions in high rates and a move towards simplification of the tax structure. The more recent policy experiments elsewhere in Europe and Scandinavia have tended to mirror those in the UK and the USA. In Sweden, for example, the 1991 reforms have taken the top tax rates from over 80 per cent to around 50 per cent, with the consequent reduction in the large number of tax bands to just two, at 30 per cent and 50 per cent. Following the pattern of reforms in the USA and the UK, revenue neutrality was achieved in Sweden by broadening the tax base through a reduction in the amount of deductions and an increase in indirect taxation. It is clear that these policy experiments and those in other industrialised countries provide an ideal opportunity to assess our understanding of labour supply responses.

The author would like to thank Michael Devereux, Alan Duncan, Paul Johnson, Costas Meghir, Graham Stark, Steven Webb, and Ian Walker for helpful discussions and comments. The financial support of the Economic and Social Research Council (ESRC) is gratefully acknowledged. The work was carried out as part of the programme of the ESRC Research Centre for the Microeconomic Analysis of Fiscal Policy at IFS. All errors are the author's alone.

First published in *Fiscal Studies* (1992) vol. 13, no. 3, pp. 15–40.

So what of the likely impact of such reforms on labour supply? As economists, our usual framework for analysis of behavioural responses is through the supply elasticity. However, this is not an appropriate means of analysis for labour supply responses, since, as we will document below, wage elasticities and effective marginal tax rates diverge substantially across individuals. In particular, there are the well-documented differences in elasticities between married men and married women, and between part-time and full-time workers. Such differences are pervasive in many other dimensions and, in sum, there is no single representative elasticity. Moreover, most tax systems, even after the reforms of the 1980s, leave different individuals facing significantly different effective marginal tax rates. The task in tax reform analysis, therefore, is appropriately to associate individual labour supply responses with corresponding marginal tax rates. This is the objective of micro-simulation models, to which we will turn increasingly throughout this survey. It is difficult to believe that a reliable guide to the impact of tax reform on labour supply can be achieved without such micro-simulation analysis.

Labour supply itself is difficult to define. Typically we use the term to refer to both hours of work and labour market participation, although, as we shall argue below, these are likely to respond to tax reform in rather different ways. In addition, should we account for effort or just hours? Should we take a life cycle view or is a static single-period analysis sufficient? Does the choice of occupation or human capital dominate individual choices?

Despite these difficulties, labour supply responses are commonly attributed a prominent role in the analysis of tax reform. For example, Hausman and Poterba (1987) and Bosworth and Burtless (1992) in their evaluation of the US tax reforms emphasise the importance of labour supply responses, especially those by married women. As we shall see below, this reflects a general view that labour supply responses—at least as measured by hours of work—are likely to be largest for married women. This conjecture is supported by the early work of Rosen (1976a and 1979b), suggesting that the perception of marginal tax rates among this group is good, and by the numerous empirical studies that have recovered relatively large elasticities from both experimental and sample survey data sources for married women. It should be added, however, that the divergence in predicted responses across these studies, even for married women, remains large. Indeed, as is well known, economic theory alone—even the simplest neoclassical framework—does not hold clear-cut predictions of the direction of responses, let alone their magnitude.

Although the appearance of a large number of potentially contradictory empirical measures of labour supply responses may be cause for despair, recent attention to the robustness of such empirical analyses has pointed to a high degree of sensitivity with regard to statistical methods adopted and treatment of the after-tax income schedule facing workers. Given that reliable estimates from a representative sample will probably involve several thousand individual data points, for each of which a detailed analysis of the tax and benefit constraint is required, it is perhaps less surprising that progress in this area is slow and subject to error. Our starting-point, therefore, is a description of the reforms to the tax system in the UK of the 1980s as they have changed the level and distribution of effective marginal tax rates—most especially their incidence on married women.

2. A Picture of UK Tax Reform and Labour Supply in the 1980s

2.1. Tax and benefit reform

Over the 1980s, the main benefits and tax allowances were maintained in real value, with the exception of the lump-sum child benefit, which by 1989 had lost 10 per cent of its value in real terms. Basic income tax allowances showed a real increase over this period, despite the real cut in 1981. These are the allowances above which the basic rate of income tax is collected and their real increase has taken a significant number of taxpayers out of the tax system. Table 3.1 summarises some of the main features of the UK tax and benefit system over the 1980s. It details the monotonic decline in basic and higher income tax rates. This is countered, to some degree, by the increase in the rate of National Insurance contributions (NICs), which is incident on all earnings above a lower earnings limit that is close to the basic tax allowance, and below an upper earnings limit that is somewhat lower than the point at which the higher income tax bracket begins. Indeed, the structure of NICs changed twice, in 1985 and 1989, in an attempt to iron out kinks faced by the lower-paid. Added to this is the rise in the VAT rates which displays the shift towards indirect taxation.

As Johnson and Stark (1989) note, many of the gains and losses that occurred over this period were as a result of reforms to the system of

TABLE 3.1. *Tax and benefit changes, 1979–1988*

	1979	1980	1981	1982	1983	1984	1985	1986	1987	1988
Basic rate income tax	33→30	30	30	30	30	30	30	29	27	25
Top rate	83→60	60	60	60	60	60	60	60	60	40
Real increase in basic tax allowance	2	2	–9	6	8	6	3	2	0	2
NIC	6.5	6.75	7.75	8.75	9	9	9	9	9	9
VAT	9→15	15	15	15	15	15	15	15	15	15

Source: Johnson and Stark (1989).

means-tested benefits. Overall, it is clear from Table 3.2 that by 1988 the gains resulting from the cumulated effects of these changes were spread reasonably far down the income distribution even though, for the majority of working individuals, the marginal tax reductions were mitigated by increases in indirect taxes and increases in the level of National Insurance contributions. Nevertheless, for many earners, reductions in the marginal rates were significant. At the bottom end, high rates of benefit withdrawal in excess of 100 per cent were largely removed, although this often occurred at the cost of extending the range of earned income over which the lower withdrawal rates were effective. Moreover, reforms to family credit may also have increased the number of low earners facing high marginal tax rates.

TABLE 3.2. *Average gains, 1979–1988*

Income decile	Percentage losing	Percentage gaining	Household type	Average gain (£ per week)
1	22	59	Single unemployed	–2.16
2	26	56	Single employed	7.02
3	32	53	Single parent	7.08
4	32	53	Single-earner couples:	
5	22	60	no children	13.25
6	18	69	with children	5.50
7	14	73	Two-earner couples:	
8	15	73	no children	9.80
9	10	80	with children	8.50
10	12	78	Single pensioner	2.31
			Couple pensioner	2.04
Overall	20	65		
			Overall	7.18

Source: Johnson and Stark (1989).

2.2. Hours of work and earnings in the 1980s

Since empirical evidence on labour supply responses suggests that they differ depending on hours worked, gross earnings, and a number of other characteristics that also determine marginal tax rates, it is important to note how changes in the effective marginal tax rates, noted above, affected individuals according to their position in the income and hours distribution. For example, Table 3.3 presents the average marginal rates faced by women married to employed men sampled from the UK Family Expenditure Survey broken down by hours ranges. The reductions in marginal tax rates were clearly not restricted to women on higher hours but were present throughout the range of hours worked. It is also interesting to note that there are significant proportions of married women in each of these hours ranges, except the very lowest, throughout the period. This contrasts quite strongly with the distribution of working hours in other European countries—see, for example, the case for France in Bourguignon and Magnac (1990).

TABLE 3.3. *Tax rates and weekly hours of work for working women married to employed men, 1981–1988 (%)*

Hours	Percentage of sample	Average marginal tax rates							
		1981	1982	1983	1984	1985	1986	1987	1988
≤5	9	2	0	4	5	0	0	7	3
6–10	10	4	10	5	7	3	8	8	2
11–15	12	14	10	9	8	8	10	12	9
16–20	15	31	27	26	25	20	22	22	21
21–25	8	36	36	36	37	36	29	29	28
26–30	8	38	38	38	37	38	35	31	33
31–35	11	39	40	39	38	39	38	36	35
36–40	28	39	39	39	40	40	38	36	39
41–45	2	36	39	39	35	43	37	38	32
>45	1	39	39	39	40	40	38	33	31
Total		30	29	29	28	28	28	27	25

Source: Blundell, Duncan, and Meghir (1995).

For such married women, the debate over hours of work responses seems most relevant. Their hours of work are spread over a wide range and this is prevalent over most occupations, as is displayed in Table 3.4. Although the bunching in certain skilled and administrative occupations is suggestive of collective agreement on labour supply rather than pure

TABLE **3.4.** *Hours of work for working women married to employed men, by occupation group, 1981–1986 (%)*

Hours	Professional	Administrative	Teaching	Clerical	Shop worker	Skilled	Semi-skilled	Unskilled
≤5	2.42	0.94	8.76	2.48	1.75	2.21	3.42	9.68
6–10	4.83	1.25	7.63	5.30	9.75	5.65	16.52	23.65
11–15	5.43	1.57	7.81	5.70	21.44	7.37	14.13	30.00
16–20	15.46	4.08	6.48	12.30	27.49	10.32	16.39	16.83
21–25	8.09	2.51	9.14	6.07	11.31	7.62	9.16	8.41
26–30	8.70	5.64	28.57	5.17	5.46	5.65	7.74	3.33
31–35	13.04	13.17	13.52	18.90	2.53	8.60	4.32	1.43
36–40	38.53	58.62	9.71	39.84	16.96	47.17	23.61	5.24
41–45	0.97	5.33	2.86	1.26	0.58	1.72	0.90	0.32
>45	0.72	3.76	3.24	0.29	0.19	0.25	0.77	0.00

Note: Armed Forces were excluded throughout.
Source: Author's own calculations.

individual choice, the wide spread of hours is also quite striking and appears to warrant a labour supply interpretation.

Finally, it is worth noting that the distribution of pre-tax earnings has changed significantly over this period. Table 3.5 shows the significant growth in inequality of full-time gross earnings. However, as Johnson and Webb (1992) have shown, the largest part of the growth in inequality over the 1980s can be attributed to tax and benefit reforms.

TABLE **3.5.** *Average decile earnings of full-time employees, 1979–1988*

Decile	1979 (£ per week)	1988 (£ per week)	Percentage increase, 1979–88
1	33.50	71.65	114
2	47.55	106.95	125
3	57.50	130.25	127
4	66.50	151.45	128
5	74.95	173.50	131
6	84.30	197.95	135
7	94.85	224.90	137
8	107.10	258.25	141
9	123.95	309.65	150
10	176.75	503.45	185
Population	86.80	212.75	145

Source: Johnson and Webb (1992).

3. Evaluating Welfare Gains and Labour Supply Responses

In the standard model of labour supply, tax reform enters individual choices through two response parameters—those on the hourly wage and the unearned income variables, the latter variable being the income available for consumption that is independent of the labour supply decision itself. A reduction in the marginal tax rate increases the pay-off to an extra hour of work and, by tilting the budget constraint, simultaneously increases the effective level of unearned income. These two effects may work against each other and point to why in the presence of non-proportional taxes the wage response coefficient alone is not sufficient to make predictions.

Labour supply increases themselves do not automatically imply welfare gains, since, although income and therefore consumption are increased, leisure time is reduced. As a result, wage responses need compensating for the loss in leisure time. These compensated responses are the pure substitution effects that are used to measure welfare or efficiency gains. Welfare losses from taxation therefore involve an income compensation for the consequent loss in utility and, as was the case for predicting behavioural responses, such money metric measures of welfare losses or gains again require an estimate of both the income and the wage response parameters.

Although there have existed brief periods of agreement among economists on the size of these response parameters, they have turned out to be short-lived—especially for male labour supply. For example, in his exhaustive survey of male labour supply, Pencavel (1986) points to the small and negative responses by prime-aged men recovered in the early microeconometric analyses especially in the USA. These results were subsequently challenged in the more coherent and elegant 'second-generation' studies developed in Burtless and Hausman (1978) and Hausman (1981). These studies pointed to positive wage effects and negative income effects resulting in non-trivial welfare losses due to taxation, hinting at some overall expansion in labour supply from the proposed reforms.

However, although elegant and internally self-consistent, the results from studies using the Hausman procedure have been shown to be rather fragile to misspecification and measurement error. More robust estimation techniques for the USA appear to point to smaller elasticities (see MaCurdy, Green, and Paarsch (1990)) or at least indicate sensitivity to the measurement of marginal tax rates and non-taxable other income. This conclusion is also reflected in the work on other countries; see, for example, the studies by Flood and MaCurdy (1992) and Blomquist (1992) for Sweden.

For married women, these sensitivity issues are potentially more critical once it is recognised how influential, and yet unreliable, the estimated wage effect on participation can be (see Mroz (1987) for the USA and Blundell, Ham, and Meghir (1987) for the UK). In the standard model, a simple reservation wage condition is used to determine participation in which an individual moves into employment if the market (after-tax) wage exceeds his or her reservation wage. It is easy to show that many of the large elasticities for female labour supply are simply an extrapolation of the wage effect on participation. Yet, since we cannot know the true market wage for non-participants or correctly measure the size of fixed and search costs, such an extrapolation must be unreliable.

This distinction between participation and hours of work is an example of the potentially important features of the labour market that are often ignored in simulation models. They relate to fixed costs of work for women with children and the cyclical nature of demand-side constraints on job offers which makes the participation decision so hard to analyse. They should also include the pay-off to on-the-job human capital investment and the impact on life cycle wealth of taxation which focus attention on the importance of future after-tax wage changes for *current* labour supply responses.

3.1. Budget constraints and the distribution of hours

If individuals can exert some degree of choice over their labour supply, the characteristics of a tax and benefit system should have implications for observed labour supply behaviour. For example, if the tax and benefit system does not lead to a proportional tax, in which the effective marginal tax rate is constant, we should observe bunching in the hours distribution. As indicated in Section 2, the UK system of National Insurance contributions leads to such a situation, since at the lower earnings limit (LEL) or 'notch', the point at which NI payments begin to be made, there is an infinite effective marginal tax rate. As a result, we might expect part-time workers to attempt to locate themselves just before the LEL notch and relatively few to be found just above. Figure 3.1, which focuses on a sample of part-time working women from the 1984 UK

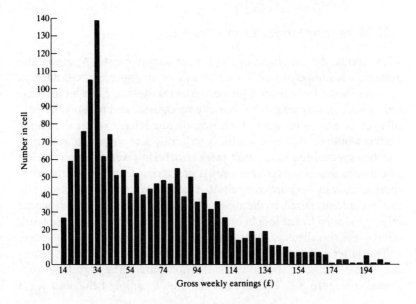

FIGURE **3.1**. Married women's earnings and the NI kink
Source: Blundell, Duncan, and Meghir (1995), 1984 FES data.

Family Expenditure Survey (FES), appears to confirm this prediction, with the LEL notch falling at around £34 per week for this sample.

Clearly, choice theory would suggest that, if the LEL notch was lowered (raised), the bunching of hours would tend to move down (up). For similar reasons, choice theory predicts that bunching will also tend to occur where the marginal tax rate increases—say from zero to 25 per cent. However, for those individuals actually paying the 25 per cent band, a cut in the tax rate may induce an increase or decrease in work effort. For those with taxable earnings just above the tax allowance, the effect can only be positive, but for those on higher income, the response can go either way. A decrease in work effort in this case is commonly referred to as 'backward bending' labour supply and is explained by the income effect (from the extra income) working against the positive incentive effect of the marginal tax reduction. Of course, even with backward-bending supply, direct tax increases would still induce an individual welfare loss in comparison with the lower-tax situation, although the supply of effort or hours is increased. In this case, a more redistributive tax can also raise hours of work.

3.2. Measuring labour supply responses

What should be the shape of the labour supply curve? Whatever the answer, it is unlikely to be linear. By way of an argument, consider an increase in the tax rate in a proportional tax system. Such an increase reduces the hourly wage for those in employment and reduces the pay-off to every extra hour worked. Those individuals free to enter the labour market would therefore be less likely to join. Those already in work may also be expected to reduce their work effort. However, from our earlier discussion, this latter result is only a prediction from choice theory if those already in work are compensated for the loss in utility generated by the loss in leisure time. In the absence of such compensation, the income effect generated by the loss in earned income may increase desired work effort—the so-called backward-bending supply curve referred to above.

This latter effect is likely to be more important for individuals working longer hours, as is evident in the non-parametric regression presented in Figure 3.2. This depicts the labour supply behaviour for a

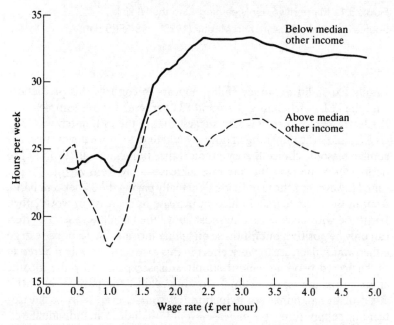

FIGURE 3.2. A picture of labour supply (lone mothers): kernel regression, 1981–1986 data.

Source: Blundell, Duncan, and Meghir (1992).

sample of single working mothers above and below other median income from the UK FES data source. This regression analysis places no restriction on the slope of the labour supply curve at any point but displays a negative slope with hours worked. It also displays a strong income effect, with the labour supply curve for mothers with above median other income nearly everywhere below that for the group with below median other income.

This picture of labour supply also provides a compelling example of the estimation methodology for tax reform simulation. By looking at individuals facing different hourly wages and other incomes, as in Figure 3.2, we would hope to learn about the size of hourly wage and other effects and then be able to infer how particular individuals might change their behaviour in the face of reforms to the tax system.[1]

When tax and benefit systems are complex, the budget constraint facing individuals in the labour market can be highly non-linear. As a result, the effective hourly wage rate facing individuals as they change their hours is far from constant. In order to evaluate elasticities or responses to tax changes, we need to know how labour supply adjusts to wage changes induced by tax changes. However, in any survey we will see individuals with the same gross wage choosing very different labour supplies. This could happen because their preferences differ but it may also reflect differences in their marginal tax rates. Separating these two influences is highly problematic.

An advantage of the move to simplification of the tax system of the 1980s has been the possibility to select large groups of workers for whom the tax rate is essentially constant. Indeed, Figures 3.3 and 3.4 show the proportion of lone mothers and married women respectively in the UK FES who pay tax at the basic rate—the 'tax sample'. Selecting workers in these samples (and correcting for selection bias) allows the potential for a more robust evaluation of labour supply responses. This is the approach adopted in Blundell, Duncan and Meghir (1992 and 1995).

Another disadvantage of systems with many different tax rates is the problem of grouping at (or near) kink points. As argued above, choice theory suggests that grouping should occur, and, moreover, for

---

[1] Reforms to the system of means-tested benefits may also be treated in the same framework, since they usually combine an hourly wage change, through the movements in benefit withdrawal rates, with a change in the level of unearned income. However, since benefit systems often act to support family income, withdrawal rates will often be effective on all workers in the household. This can produce quite complex interactions in household labour supply, most notably in the UK for the labour supply of women married to unemployed men, a group which displayed persistently lower rates of labour market participation during the 1980s (see Kell and Wright (1990)).

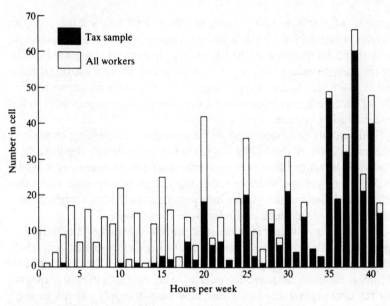

FIGURE **3.3.** Hours distributions (lone mothers)
Source: Blundell, Duncan, and Meghir (1992).

individuals at these points, desired labour supply should be below the tax kink when evaluated at the after-kink tax rate and above the kink when evaluated at the before-kink tax rate. Only in this case will those individuals bunched near the kink point be following rational choice behaviour. However, this can also be shown to imply that the compensated wage elasticity is positive. In other words, optimisation theory holds at these points. If there are lots of such tax kinks, as in the complex budget constraint case, empirical results can be misleading in so far as the data are not given a free hand in determining the labour supply relationship.

To illustrate this point briefly and to stress its significance in the debate over tax policy and labour supply, let us consider the linear labour supply model, popular in tax reform analysis (see Hausman (1981) and Blomquist (1983)). In the context of the model for hours of work, we may write this model as

$$h = a + bw + cy$$

where h, w, and y represent measures of hours, hourly wages, and other income respectively, while a, b, and c are the unknown constants, the latter two of which represent the response coefficients for the wage and

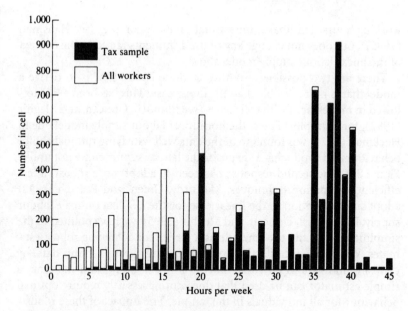

FIGURE **3.4.** Hours distributions (married women)
Source: Blundell, Duncan, and Meghir (1992).

other income variables. Together they determine desired labour supply for any wage and income combination.

When marginal tax rates increase, an individual will decide to remain at a tax kink if his or her desired hours at the higher tax rate would be below the tax kink. For this to be true, the parameters b and c have to be restricted. In particular, they must accord with choice theory which requires b–ch to be positive. Since, with many kink points, this must be true for a wide range of hours, b will have to be positive and c negative. However, with b positive there is *forward-sloping* labour supply everywhere. So restrictions from theory become a constraint on the empirical evidence. A negative b cannot be recovered even if for a large section of the data the slope is close to zero or negative! The MaCurdy, Green, and Paarsch (1990) results show that these restrictions appear to have been binding in the influential Hausman (1981) results and may explain the fragility of this model to small changes in specification.

Any realistic empirical model has to allow measurement error and optimisation error. When added to the model above, this allows individuals who would like to locate at the tax kink (or notch) to be observed off this point and consequently 'smooths' out the resulting distribution of working hours. This makes the estimation more complex (see Hausman (1985)), but does not change any of the arguments raised in the context of the linear labour supply model above.

There are two possible responses to these issues. One is to derive a model that is more flexible than the linear case. This has been a line followed in my research with colleagues (see Blundell, Duncan, and Meghir (1992), for example). There, the non-linear labour supply model due to Heckman (1974) was found to fit the data well, satisfying rational choice behaviour and producing a shape for the labour supply curve not unlike Figure 3.2. The second response has been to adopt more robust, if less efficient, estimation techniques. MaCurdy, Green, and Paarsch (1990) adopt such an option in the linear case for the US data on male labour supply. In Blundell, Duncan, and Meghir (1995), we have pointed to the simplification of the tax schedule as a device for achieving robust estimates. With only one effective tax kink for large groups in our data, by choosing individuals on either side of and well away from the kink, a simple estimator can be used that does not necessarily require optimal behaviour for all individuals in the sample. The impact of these robustness results on our understanding of labour supply responses is discussed below in the context of the literature on labour supply estimates.

3.3. Some labour supply estimates

As has already been noted, the size of income and wage responses is still the subject of some debate among empirical economists, even after more than twenty years of detailed statistical analysis. By far the most reliable picture of labour supply responses concerns married women, although, as can be inferred from Table 3.6, the range of estimated elasticities is large. Table 3.6 provides a comparison across a number of empirical studies. It is not exhaustive but it is representative. In general, the results point to a positive uncompensated wage elasticity and to a negative income effect, as choice theory would suggest. This results in reasonably large compensated wage effects and indicates that efficiency gains from lowering tax rates on these women would be non-negligible.

As mentioned earlier, there is still some debate as to the sensitivity of these estimated labour supply models to small changes in specification, and it is clear that studies adopting more robust procedures tend to find slightly smaller elasticities. For example, Mroz (1987) suggests the wage elasticity on hours for women in work in the USA is as small as 0.10, while the results from Blundell, Duncan, and Meghir (1995) place this

TABLE **3.6.** *Some elasticities for married women's labour supply*

Author	Sample	Uncompensated wage	Compensated wage	Income
Cogan (1981)	US	0.65	0.68	–0.03
Hausman (1981)	US	0.45	0.9	–0.45
Arrufat and Zabalza (1986)	UK	0.62	0.68	–0.06
Blundell and Walker (1982)	UK			
	No children	0.43	0.65	–0.22
	One child	0.10	0.32	–0.22
Arellano and Meghir (1992)	UK			
	No children	0.37	0.44	–0.13
	Young children	0.29	0.50	–0.40
	Old children	0.71	0.82	–0.21

Source: Killingsworth (1983) and author's own calculations.

estimate at around 0.2 for married women in the UK. However, the latter study deliberately utilises a non-linear labour supply curve following the discussion of Figure 3.2 above. As a result, the wage response depends critically on the hours of work at which it is evaluated. For some women there are large positive responses, while for others the response to an increase in the hourly wage is very small or even negative. This can also be seen in the work of Arrufat and Zabalza (1986) in their study of married women's labour supply in the UK. Again the elasticity falls significantly with hours worked, highlighting the importance of micro-stimulation in the evaluation of tax reforms, since different tax reforms will impact differently on individuals depending on their wage and hours of work.

There is much less variation in the labour supply of married men, and generally empirical studies have avoided a separate analysis of non-participation, partly due to the relatively high participation rates (in comparison with those of married women). It is also reasonable to suppose that the majority of prime-aged men are likely to be found in occupations/industries in which labour supply is determined by collective agreement of some kind. As a result, there are many fewer believable studies of male labour supply, and those that have been made find smaller and often negative wage elasticities. Table 3.7 documents some illustrations from the literature. The first point to note is that, because men are generally found in full-time employment, these results are not completely out of line with the results for women, especially those in full-time employment. However, the lack of variation generally leads to a lack

TABLE 3.7.   *Men's labour supply elasticities*

Author	Sample	Uncompensated wage	Compensated wage	Income
Hausman (1981)	US	0.03	0.95	–0.98
Ashworth and Ulph (1981)	UK	–0.33	0.29	–0.62
Blundell and Walker (1982)	UK	–0.23	0.13	–0.36

Source: as Table 3.6.

of precision. It should also be pointed out that the larger income effects in Table 3.7, especially in the case of Hausman (1981) for the USA, imply large compensated effects and therefore correspondingly sizeable efficiency losses from taxation. However, the results of MaCurdy, Green, and Paarsch (1990) suggest this income effect is probably overestimated.

In sum it is usually felt that the response to tax reductions in terms of working hours by prime-aged men is small and possibly negative, with working hours probably determined in some collective manner. This coincides with the idea put forward in Lazear (1983) that unions/collective agreements are more likely to be found where there are small supply elasticities and more homogeneous groups of workers. Moreover, there is evidence from Ham (1986a and 1986b) that men, especially non-participants, are off their labour supply curve.

For lone parents, the position is somewhat different. In the UK, these are mainly women who face childcare costs and a benefit system that makes part-time work, at least for those on low wages, unattractive. As a result, many fewer of these women work part-time, especially in comparison with women married to employed men. However, they are a group whose importance in the labour market and to the benefit system is growing rapidly (see Dilnot and Duncan (1992)). Empirical results for this group tend to be more recent and in Table 3.8 some elasticities are presented. Since fewer of these women work part-time, the elasticities tend to be dominated by the participation effect, and the large elasticities in the studies by Bingley, Symons, and Walker (1992) and Jenkins (1992) for the UK certainly reflect the strong wage effect on participation. Once working hours alone are considered, as is the case in Blundell, Duncan, and Meghir (1992), we find the characteristic fall in the wage elasticity, with values for the uncompensated elasticity around 0.2 or less. Again this probably reflects an underlying labour supply curve much like that

TABLE **3.8.** *Lone mothers' labour supply elasticities*

Author	Sample	Uncompensated wage	Compensated wage	Income
Hausman (1980)	US	0.53	0.65	–0.18
Bingley, Symons, and Walker (1992)	UK	0.76	1.28	–0.52
Jenkins (1992)	UK	1.44	—	–0.24

Source: as Table 3.6.

depicted in Figure 3.2 in which elasticities around the point of participation are large but fall off rapidly with increases in working hours.

4. Characteristics of the 'Real World'

Before turning to a practical micro-simulation of tax reforms, we focus our attention on certain caveats in the above approach to the measurement of labour supply responses which reflect features of the 'real world' that are likely to interfere to a lesser or greater extent with predictions from the choice theoretic framework outlined above. Some of these are well researched but others are still part of the research agenda.

4.1. Fixed costs of work

These have already been the focus of some discussion above in the context of the participation decision for women with children. In general, fixed costs take the form of time or money costs and may even arise as part of the tax and benefit system itself. For example, benefit systems seeking to keep family income above a minimum level can severely reduce the incentive to accept a job offering less than the amount of income that takes family income over the minimum threshold. For women on low hourly wages, part-time jobs become less attractive and choice is restricted to non-participation or jobs with full-time earnings. Childcare is often felt to fall into this category and as a result makes part-time employment less attractive.[2] These effects are not restricted to

---

[2] Although there is clear evidence that childcare availability positively affects participation of women with young children, it is often available on a daily or hourly basis and as a result may often act like a proportionate tax (or subsidy) on earnings.

young children; the presence of older dependent relatives in the household is also found to be negatively correlated with participation.

The presence of fixed costs influences the trade-off between work and non-work and reduces the effectiveness of marginal wage increases at the point of participation as an encouragement to work. For example, earnings disregards which in effect raise the marginal wage for those with very low weekly earnings, although still encouraging work through an income effect, would be far less effective in the presence of fixed costs.

All this suggests that labour market participation is likely to be decided on in a rather different way from the way in which choices are made about increasing or decreasing labour supply for those in work, for whom the fixed cost is a sunk cost—simply reducing income whatever hours are chosen. Empirically, we should model the wage (and tax) effects on participation separately. It is interesting to note that almost all studies of tax reform *do not* do this despite the clear empirical evidence—Mroz (1987), for example—that wage and income effects are highly sensitive to this separation.

The Cogan (1981) study for the USA showed the elasticity falling from almost 2 to around 0.5, once fixed costs were included, for the married women in his sample, whose fixed costs averaged some 28 per cent of annual earnings. Similarly, the Blundell, Ham, and Meghir (1987) study of married women in the UK showed a significant downward shift in the wage response after fixed costs were allowed for. As mentioned above, this distinction does not tend to be made in models used in tax reform simulation.[3] As a result, they extrapolate a strong wage effect on participation across the whole hours distribution. This is further exacerbated in a linear model where a strong wage effect at low hours, as in Figure 3.2, for example, would produce highly misleading predictions at higher hours.

4.2. Life cycle savings, demographics, and wealth

In a life cycle model, individuals may supply labour in order to save for future periods where the relative value of non-work activity is higher. In general this will cover retirement, periods of ill health, and periods of unemployment. For women (and men to some extent), this will also

---

[3] The reason for this is simple but not convincing—unless fixed costs can actually be measured, the effects of tax reform on *participation* in these models is more difficult to predict. Nevertheless, it is critical in our understanding of participation effects of tax and benefit reforms.

cover periods of family formation. As a result, two otherwise identical individuals may supply very different levels of labour reflecting their different expectations of future needs and uncertainties. The individual with higher future needs or a more uncertain future income stream is correspondingly less well-off and will supply more labour. To allow for this, a life cycle consistent labour supply model has been introduced into the literature (MaCurdy, 1983; Blundell and Walker, 1986) in which *consumption* expenditures are used to correct unearned income for savings. The UK FES data are ideal for this, as they include consumers' expenditure records for all households as well as their weekly labour supplies. The general effect of this adjustment to income is to increase the size and precision of the income effect on labour supply, the former *increasing* the compensated elasticity and the welfare costs of tax distortions.

It is clear that a change in marginal tax rates will have an impact on future earned income and therefore on expected wealth. Savings will adjust to reflect this. When a tax reform occurs, it is usually considered permanent and is often unexpected. As a result, it can have a large wealth effect. For example, if a marginal tax reduction reduced the need for saving, the wealth effect may add to the usual income effect initially reducing the effectiveness of the incentive to supply more effort. On the other hand, if this is coupled with an expected decline in the real value of state pensions and unemployment benefit, it may encourage the supply of effort by workers.

Most empirical analyses of intertemporal labour supply focus on the intertemporal elasticity of substitution, which measures the response to an *anticipated* change in the real wage in one period holding all future real wages constant and maintaining the marginal utility of income (see Altonji (1986) and Browning, Deaton, and Irish (1985)). It is not surprising, at least in a world without uncertainty, that a fall in the *real* wage for one period would reduce labour supply during that period in the knowledge that it is a once-off change. Uncertainty and risk aversion reduce this effect, but elasticities for women are often large and can be in excess of one (see Heckman and MaCurdy (1980)). However, a tax change is usually neither temporary nor anticipated. Moreover, marginal utility cannot be maintained, since tax increases (decreases) reduce (increase) wealth and therefore increase (reduce) marginal utility. The upshot is that this large intertemporal elasticity can be significantly reduced once unexpected wealth effects are acknowledged. Card (1995) finds the intertemporal substitution elasticity reduced by more than 50 per cent once wealth effects are accounted for. It is likely that the standard life cycle consistent elasticity provides an inflated view of responses after wealth effects are accounted for (see Bover (1989) for a useful presentation of elasticities for the USA). It may well be the case that the standard uncompensated wage elasticities provide a more accurate guide to responses.

4.3. On-the-job human capital and seniority

It is well documented that for some groups of individuals there is a significant pay-off to participation in terms of wage growth. In other words, interrupted labour market histories reduce wages (see Eckstein and Wolpin (1989) and Shaw (1989), for example). This can occur in a neoclassical model with on-the-job human capital or in a collective bargaining model with seniority-related pay. In either case, the pay-off to continuing in employment may induce participation where 'simple' choice theory would suggest otherwise. Short-run (temporary) fluctuations in income or marginal wages are less likely to result in movements into and out of the labour market, thereby reducing the impact of short-run changes to taxes and benefits.

In terms of encouraging investment in human capital, a linear proportional tax is clearly preferred to a system with an increasing marginal rate (see Heckman (1976)). In terms of the impact on labour supply elasticities, the evidence for married women seems to point to a larger experience effect for professionals and those with high educational qualifications. It is unlikely, therefore, that the 'simple' labour supply model would provide reasonable predictions for such groups.

4.4. Job queues, unions, and collective bargaining

If unions bargain over employment and wages, then there will be unfulfilled supply at the going wage and not all individuals who would like to supply work will receive a job offer. More generally, with information asymmetries and a continuously changing environment, there will be individuals who would like to work but who do not receive job offers. This again suggests that the participation effects of wage changes will not simply reflect individuals who would like to work but who do not receive job offers. This again suggests that the participation effects of wage changes will not simply reflect individual choice.

For groups of workers in industries or occupations where unions negotiate over hours of work, as well as employment and wages, the consequence of bargaining will in general be a restriction on supply. This may well result in a spurious negative correlation between hours of work and real marginal wages. For this reason, researchers have often been reluctant to fit standard labour supply models to data on men (or women) in highly unionised sectors and is yet another reason why the focus has often been on female labour supply, particularly in non-professional occupations.

4.5. Benefit take-up and effective tax rates

Although means-tested benefits induce a 'tax rate' on earned income through the withdrawal mechanism, they are also invariably subject to a lower than 100 per cent take-up among eligible households. Housing benefit (see Blundell, Fry, and Walker (1988)) and family credit (see Dorsett and Heady (1991)) are two examples. As Fraker and Moffitt (1988) point out, an increase in the withdrawal rate can exhibit two opposing responses. The increase in the rate will induce a higher tax rate for those continuing to take up, but, as the benefit is now worth less, some eligible individuals may decide to stop taking up and for them the effective tax rate on earned income is reduced. Indeed, in their study of Food Stamps in the USA, Fraker and Moffitt find these effects almost completely cancelling out in aggregate. In the UK, take-up is responsive to the *value* of the benefits (see Blundell, Fry, and Walker (1988)) and this observation can be expected to reduce the impact of withdrawal-rates changes on overall labour supply.

5. Tax Reform and Micro-Simulation

5.1. The attraction of micro-simulation

As an illustration of the power of micro-simulation in enhancing our understanding of tax reform, I will draw on two reforms to the tax and benefit structure facing married couples considered in Blundell et al. (1988). The two reforms are designed to distinguish between reforms that induce largely income effects and those that induce marginal tax rate changes. They are both approximately revenue-neutral. The first reform reduces the married man's tax allowance (MMA) to that of a single adult and uses the extra revenue to increase child benefit—almost doubling the lump-sum amount per child. The second reform uses the tax revenue to allow the transfer of tax allowances between partners so as to minimise the household's tax liability. The second reform uses the tax revenue to allow the transfer of tax allowances between partners so as to minimise the household's tax liability. This effectively induces a marginal tax rate equal to the husband's rate on married women's earnings previously below the single allowance.

The transferable allowance reform has many features typical of popular tax reforms and illustrates clearly why single elasticities evaluated at sample means are not useful for much tax reform analysis. The reform generates both income changes and marginal wage changes. Moreover, it is only women on earnings below the single allowance (SA) who face the increase in marginal tax rates. There is a break-even point £B at which the increased income effects from the allowance transfer disappear.

Simulation of the reform takes place over a large sample of married couples drawn from the UK Family Expenditure Survey data. Each of the married women is assumed to have a desired labour supply which does not impose the simple reservation wage condition on participation and allows a non-linear shape to responses, much as is pictured in Figure 3.2 above. The labour supply can become backward-bending at high hours and differs with the age of the woman, the number (and age) of children in the household, and the level of other family income and saving.

Table 3.9 gives the results for the child benefit reform, decomposed according to the number of dependent children in the household. Column 1 presents the 'predicted' or 'simulated' average hours change. The changes reflect the negative impact of unearned income on labour supply. For households without children, income falls (by MMA−SA) and hours rise, while for households with more than one child, income

TABLE 3.9. *The child benefit reform*

Number of children	Percentage of sample	Change in number of hours	Change in income (at hours of $\bar{h}$)	Change in income (hours not fixed) (£)	Welfare loss (£)
		(1)	(2)	(3)	(4)
0	34.1	0.64	−4.13	−3.27	4.13
1	21.8	0.14	−0.89	−0.67	0.85
2	32.1	−0.29	2.48	2.06	−2.51
3+	11.9	−0.55	6.56	5.89	−6.57
All	—	0.09	−0.02	0.10	0.01

Note: The welfare loss is a money metric equivalent loss measure, as described in section 3.
Source: Blundell et al. (1988).

rises and hours fall. For households with a single child, the net effect is small. Notice that, on average, the hours change from this (approximately revenue-natural) reform is low, but the impact by *household type* is important. The hours responses clearly reduce the impact of the lump-sum transfer, as can be seen from the income changes given hours $\bar{h}$ and with labour supply allowed to respond. These responses also mean that the money metric welfare loss will differ from the income loss.

The transferable allowance reform similarly emphasises the importance of micro-simulation. For the first three groups of women in Table 3.10— the non-participants and those who were below the single allowance—the marginal tax rate jumps from zero (albeit for a small minority) to the basic rate. The results show an income effect, since for all those earning below the break-even point £B there is an income gain. (Notice—with some interest!—this is turned into a household income loss after the labour supply response is accounted for.) For those with earnings above £B but less than £SA, the income loss is reinforced by a fall in hours. Again, the final row points to the importance of disaggregating responses.

TABLE 3.10. *The transferable allowance reform*

Household type	Percentage of sample	Change in number of hours (1)	Change in income (at hours of $\bar{h}$) (£) (2)	Change in income (hours not fixed) (£) (3)	Welfare loss (£) (4)
Non-participants	41	0	4.10	4.10	−4.10
Earnings <£B	6	−2.59	1.31	−1.16	−1.72
Earnings >£B, <£SA	9	−1.09	−2.02	−3.14	1.68
Basic rate	40	0.74	−3.93	−2.97	3.93
All	—	0.07	0.01	0.18	−0.05

Note: as Table 3.9.
Source: Blundell et al. (1988).

5.2. Simulating the basic rate tax reforms of the 1980s

The 1980s saw a number of policy experiments that may be expected to have influenced labour supply behaviour. They provide an ideal opportunity for counterfactual simulation and in what follows we consider one aspect of these reforms in the UK. As was discussed in Section 2, the three main features were the cut in basic rates, the increase in the real value of the basic income allowance for tax, and the shift towards indirect taxation from the increase in VAT. We will focus on the basic rate changes.[4] In particular, taking one of our most recent year of FES data (1989), we consider the *increase* in the basic rate from the 25 per cent level to the 33 per cent level that existed prior to 1980. In exploring this counterfactual, the increase in the real value of tax allowances will be ignored. The pre-1980 levels of tax allowances would also have implied higher tax rates for many workers— especially women in part-time employment. Similarly, we ignore the offsetting change in VAT. This is not to say that the micro-simulation model used in this analysis cannot account for these changes, but, to understand the pattern and magnitude of likely reactions, it is useful to move systematically through the individual components of any tax reform.

To illustrate the issues involved, attention will be focused on the group of married women with employed husbands. Analysis of this group has two advantages. First, the tax and benefit system for them is relatively straightforward. Second, we can contrast the differential impact that occurs depending on whether the husband's income is held constant or allowed to be affected by the tax reform—as it indeed was. The latter point will emphasise the importance of modelling income effects within the household in addition to substitution/incentive effects for individual household members.

Table 3.11 provides a cross-tabulation of hours pre- and post-reform for our sample of married women. For the bulk of women, there are small decreases in their hours of work in response to the basic rate increase, as we might expect from the small but generally positive uncompensated wage effects estimated in our models. The backward-bending effects are also apparent for a few women, reflected in points above the leading diagonal in Table 3.11. These latter effects are magnified in Table 3.12 once the husband's income is reduced in line with the basic rate increase. There are now many more responses lying above the diagonal in Table 3.12. There are even non-working women who now want to work, given the reduction in household income.

6. Conclusions

The aim of this survey has been to highlight the central role played by labour supply in tax reform evaluation and to stress the importance of

---

[4] It could be argued that the introduction of independent taxation was a major feature of tax reform in this period. However, its impact on labour supply was probably rather limited.

TABLE 3.11. *The effects of an increase in the basic rate of income tax on hours worked by women married to employed men*

Pre-reform hours	Post-reform hours												
	0	1–4	5–8	9–12	13–16	17–20	21–24	25–28	29–32	33–36	37–40	41–44	>44
0	147	—	—	—	—	—	—	—	—	—	—	—	—
1–4	—	49	—	—	—	—	—	—	—	—	—	—	—
5–8	1	—	33	1	1	—	—	—	—	—	—	—	—
9–12	—	—	—	49	186	1	4	1	1	1	—	—	—
13–16	—	—	—	2	3	78	1	1	—	1	1	—	—
17–20	1	—	—	—	—	7	—	—	—	—	—	—	—
21–24	—	—	—	—	5	—	74	—	—	—	—	—	—
25–28	—	2	—	1	—	—	3	72	—	—	—	—	—
29–32	—	—	—	—	—	—	—	4	63	—	—	—	—
33–36	—	—	1	—	1	1	—	1	5	81	—	—	—
37–40	—	—	—	—	—	—	—	—	—	14	178	—	—
41–44	—	—	—	—	—	—	—	—	—	1	8	14	—
>44	—	—	—	—	—	—	—	—	—	1	—	—	21

Source: Author's own calculations.

TABLE 3.12. *The effects of an increase in the basic rate of income tax on hours worked by women married to employed men, allowing the husband's income to change*

Pre-reform hours	Post-reform hours												
	0	1–4	5–8	9–12	13–16	17–20	21–24	25–28	29–32	33–36	37–40	41–44	>44
0	118	1	2	—	11	10	3	1	—	—	1	—	—
1–4	1	48	—	—	—	—	—	—	—	—	—	—	—
5–8	—	1	28	5	—	—	—	—	—	1	—	—	—
9–12	—	—	5	45	5	5	—	—	1	—	—	—	—
13–16	—	—	—	2	181	72	7	10	—	—	1	—	—
17–20	—	—	—	1	1	4	1	1	—	1	1	—	—
21–24	—	—	—	—	6	1	73	1	—	1	1	—	—
25–28	—	—	—	1	—	—	3	72	65	1	—	—	—
29–32	—	—	—	—	—	—	—	2	2	—	—	—	—
33–36	—	—	—	—	—	—	—	—	—	85	183	—	—
37–40	—	—	—	—	—	—	—	—	—	8	6	2	—
41–44	—	—	—	—	—	—	—	—	—	—	—	17	—
>44	—	—	—	—	—	—	—	—	—	—	—	—	22

Source: Author's own calculations.

micro-simulation analysis. The illustrative reform simulations in Section 5.2 help to focus attention on the importance of correctly associating individuals with differing wage and income responses to appropriate points on the tax and benefit schedule. Micro-simulation allows the distinction between the many types of individuals supplying labour in the economy and the variety of economic and demographic circumstances they face. The large and wide-ranging tax reforms of the 1980s provide a sequence of important policy experiments with which to evaluate tax reform responses. From the standpoint of the usual framework for measuring labour supply responses, we have shown that married women appear to be the group that seems most responsive to such reforms. However, this is also the group for which tax reform usually brings significant family income effects as well as marginal wage changes. Our simulation results have shown that these income effects can go a long way in cancelling out labour supply increases from this group and stress the importance of analysing tax reform in a household context.

The labour supply results referred to in Section 3 have also stressed that care is needed in both estimating and interpreting labour supply parameters. The overall picture of labour supply responses, especially for married women, is now fairly well understood, but the importance of distinguishing between participation and hours of work, reflecting the importance of fixed costs and job opportunities, is much less well researched. This is also the case with regard to the precise shape of the labour supply curve over the range of hours worked. The micro-simulation examples illustrate how important these aspects of labour supply are when evaluating tax reform, as some reforms are designed to encourage participation (changes to the benefit structure, for example) while others appear to be designed to encourage more work from those already in employment (reductions in basic and higher rates of tax, for example).

That labour supply analysis continues to be such a flourishing topic in applied research may appear puzzling. However, as we have argued, the standard model can be quite sensitive to small changes in specification and is still the subject of much robustness analysis. Moreover, it may not be an appropriate modelling framework for many groups in the labour market. Fixed costs and an allowance for intertemporal decisions provide important extensions. More generally, the institutional characteristics of collective agreements over working hours and the constraints on an individual's short-run responses to tax reforms take much of the analysis outside the narrowly defined static neo classical paradigm.

134   *Richard Blundell*

References

Altonji, J. G. (1986), 'Intertemporal substitution in labour supply: evidence from micro-data', *Journal of Political Economy*, vol. 94, pp. S176–S215.

Arellano, M., and Meghir, C. (1992), 'Using complementary data sources: an application to labour supply and job search', *Review of Economic Studies*, vol. 59, pp. 537–57.

Arrufat, J. L., and Zabalza, A. (1986), 'Female labour supply with taxation, random preferences, and optimization errors', *Econometrica*, vol. 54, pp. 47–63.

Ashworth, J., and Ulph, D. (1981), 'Estimating labour supply with piecewise linear budget constraints', in C. V. Brown (ed.), *Taxation and Labour Supply*, London: Allen & Unwin.

Bingley, P., Symons, E., and Walker, I. (1992), 'The labour supply of UK lone mothers: the effects of maintenance, and the welfare system', paper presented at the Fiscal Incentives and Labour Supply Conference, Institute for Fiscal Studies, June.

Blomquist, N. S. (1983), 'The effect of income taxation on the labour supply of married men in Sweden', *Journal of Public Economics*, vol. 22, pp. 169–97.

—— (1992), 'Estimation methods for male labour supply functions: how to take account of taxes', paper presented at the Fiscal Incentives and Labour Supply Conference, Institute for Fiscal Studies, June.

Blundell, R. W. and Walker, I. (1982), 'Modelling the joint determination of household labour supplies and commodity demands', *Economic Journal*, vol. 92, pp. 351–64.

—— —— (1986), 'A life cycle consistent empirical model of labour supply using cross section data', *Review of Economic Studies*, vol. 53, pp. 539–58.

—— Duncan, A., and Meghir, C. (1992), 'Taxation and empirical labour supply models: lone parents in the UK', *Economic Journal*, vol. 102, pp. 265–78.

—— —— (1995), 'Estimating labour supply responses using tax reforms', Institute for Fiscal Studies Working Paper W95/7.

—— Fry, V., and Walker, I. (1988), 'Modelling the take-up of means-tested benefits: the case of housing benefit in the UK', *Economic Journal*, vol. 98, pp. 58–74.

—— Ham, J., and Meghir, C. (1987), 'Unemployment and female labour supply', *Economic Journal*, vol. 97, pp. 44–64.

—— Meghir, C., Symons, E., and Walker, I. (1988), 'Labour supply specification and the empirical evaluation of tax reforms', *Journal of Public Economics*, vol. 36, pp. 23–52.

Bosworth, B., and Burtless, G. (1992), 'Effects of tax reform on labor supply, investment and savings', *Journal of Economic Perspectives*, vol. 6, pp. 3–26.

Bourguignon, F., and Magnac, T. (1990), 'Labour supply and taxation in France', *Journal of Human Resources*, vol. 25, no. 3.

Bover, O. (1989), 'Estimating intertemporal labour supply elasticities using structural models', *Economic Journal*, vol. 99, pp. 1026–39.

Browning, M. J., Deaton, A., and Irish, M. (1985), 'A profitable approach to labour supply and commodity demands over the life-cycle', *Econometrica*, vol. 53.

Burtless, G., and Hausman, J. (1978), 'The effect of taxes on labour supply', *Journal of Political Economy*, vol. 86, pp. 1103–30.

Card, D. (1995), 'Intertemporal labour supply: an assessment', in C. Sims (ed.), *Advances in Econometrics*, Cambridge: Cambridge University Press, vol. ii.

Cogan, J. F. (1981), 'Fixed costs and labor supply', *Econometrica*, vol. 49, pp. 945–64.

Dilnot, A. W., and Duncan, A. (1992), 'Lone mothers, family credit and paid work', *Fiscal Studies*, vol. 13, no. 1, pp. 1–21.

Dorsett, R., and Heady, C. (1991), 'The take-up of means-tested benefits by working families with children', *Fiscal Studies*, vol. 12, no. 4, pp. 22–32.

Eckstein, Z., and Wolpin, K. (1989), 'Dynamic labour force participation of married women and endogenous work experience', *Review of Economic Studies*, vol. 56, pp. 375–90.

Flood, L., and MaCurdy, T. (1992), 'Work disincentive effects of taxes: an empirical analysis of Swedish men', paper presented at the Fiscal Incentives and Labour Supply Conference, Institute for Fiscal Studies, June.

Fraker, T., and Moffitt, R. (1988), 'The effect of Food Stamps on labour supply', *Journal of Public Economics*, vol. 35, pp. 25–56.

Ham, J. (1986a), 'Testing whether unemployment represents life-cycle labor supply behaviour', *Review of Economic Studies*, vol. 53, pp. 559–78.

—— (1986b), 'On the interpretation of unemployment in empirical labour supply analysis', in R. W. Blundell and I. Walker (eds.), *Unemployment, Search and Labour Supply*, Cambridge: Cambridge University Press.

Hausman, J. A. (1980), 'The effect of wages, taxes and fixed costs on women's labor force participation', *Journal of Public Economics*, vol. 14, pp. 161–94.

—— (1981), 'Labour supply', in H. J. Aaron and J. A. Pechman (eds.), *How Taxes Affect Economic Behaivour*, Washington DC: Brookings Institution.

—— (1985), 'The econometrics of nonlinear budget sets', *Econometrica*, vol. 53, 1255–82.

—— and Poterba, J. M. (1987), 'Household behaviour and the Tax Reform Act of 1986', *Journal of Economic Perspectives*, vol. 1, pp. 101–19.

Heckman, J. J. (1974), 'Effects of child-care programs on women's work effort', *Journal of Political Economy*, vol. 82, pp. S136–S163.

—— (1976), 'A life-cycle model of earnings, learning, and consumption', *Journal of Political Economy*, vol. 84, pp. S11–S44.

—— and MaCurdy, T. E. (1980), 'A life-cycle model of female labour supply', *Review of Economic Studies*, vol. 47, pp. 47–74.

Jenkins, S. P. (1992), 'Lone mothers, employment and full-time work probabilities', *Economic Journal*, vol. 102, pp. 310–20.

Johnson, P., and Stark, G. (1989), *Taxation and Social Security 1979–1989: The Impact on Household Incomes*, IFS Commentary no. 12, London: Institute for Fiscal Studies.

—— and Webb, S. (1992), 'Recent trends in UK income inequality: causes and policy responses', paper presented at the Royal Economic Society Conference, March.

Kell, M, and Wright, J. (1990), 'Benefits and the labour supply of women married to unemployed men', *Economic Journal*, vol. 100, pp. 119–29.

Killingsworth, M. R. (1983), *Labor Supply*, Cambridge: Cambridge University Press.

Lazear, E. P. (1983), 'A competitive theory of monopoly unionism', *American Economic Review*, vol. 73, pp. 631–43.

MaCurdy, T. E. (1983), 'A simple scheme for estimating an intertemporal model of labour supply and consumption in the presence of taxes and uncertainty', *International Economic Review*, vol. 24, pp. 265–89.

—— Green, D., and Paarsch, H. (1990), 'Assessing empirical approaches for analysing taxes and labour supply', *Journal of Human Resources*, vol. 25, pp. 415–90.

Mroz, T. A. (1987), 'The sensitivity of an empirical model of married women's hours of work to economic and statistical assumptions', *Econometrica*, vol. 55, pp. 765–800.

Pencavel, J. (1986), 'Labor supply of men: a survey', in O. Ashenfelter and R. Layard (eds.), *Handbook of Labor Economics*, Amsterdam: North-Holland.

Rosen, H. (1976a), 'Taxes in a labour supply model with joint wage–hours determination', *Econometrica*, vol. 44, pp. 485–507.

—— (1976b), 'Tax illusion and the labour supply of married women', *Review of Economics and Statistics*, vol. 58, pp. 167–72.

Shaw, K. (1989), 'Life cycle labour supply with human capital accumulation', *International Economic Review*, vol. 30, pp. 431–57.

4

THE CORPORATION TAX

JACK MINTZ

....

1. Introduction

The corporation tax is arguably the most well-studied tax found throughout the world. Countless numbers of professionals study the impact of corporate tax law on the affairs of the corporation. Yet, despite considerable resources that are expended on compliance, the tax in many countries raises only a small proportion of revenue for governments. For example, in the G7 countries, taxes paid by corporations account for less than 8 per cent of tax revenues raised by governments, except for Japan, where the corporation tax yields about 15 per cent of government revenue.[1] This low revenue yield and high compliance cost have resulted in some experts and politicians questioning the usefulness of the corporate income tax.

Those who question the need for the corporation tax take the normative view that taxes, in the interest of transparency, should be imposed on individuals, not legal entities. After all, as the argument goes, people, not corporations, pay taxes. Even though a corporation has the legal right to hold property and contract with buyers and sellers, and is subject to the criminal and civil law of the state, its activities benefit the owners who own its capital, consumers who purchase its products or services, and

The author wishes to thank Pierre-Pascal Gendron, Sanjit Dhami, and Tom Tsiopoulos for assisting with the preparation of the manuscript. He also wishes to thank the Social Sciences and Humanities Research Council for its financial support and Michael Devereux for very helpful comments.

First published in *Fiscal Studies* (1995), vol. 16, no. 4, pp. 23–68.

[1] These are arithmetic averages. In contrast, individual income and sales taxes raised almost 24% and 25% of total tax revenues respectively in 1993. See Canada: Department of Finance (1994: table 105). Many Pacific Rim and developing countries are similar to Japan in terms of their reliance on corporate taxes.

employees who provide their effort. Any tax paid by the corporation must be passed on through higher prices, lower wages, or lower returns on capital. Thus, if one were to *pierce the veil* behind the legal entity called the corporation, it is argued that the tax ultimately falls on people. So, in the interests of determining the impact of the tax system on the welfare of individuals in society it is argued, 'why not tax people directly rather than indirectly via the corporation?'.[2]

In Section 2, an answer will be given to the question 'why is there a corporation tax?'. It is useful to begin with a normative argument for the corporation tax to understand its basic role in the economy. Following that, incentive effects of the corporate tax are discussed with respect to investment (Section 3), financing (Section 4), and risk (Section 5). The incidence of the corporation tax is considered in Section 6 and conclusions are provided in Section 7.

Prior to turning to the above questions, one caveat should be borne in mind when reading this survey. It is important to point out that the legal terms 'corporations' and 'companies' are used in a more general sense than that conveyed by their strict definition. Much of the discussion below applies, at least in principle, to all forms of businesses: corporations, sole proprietorships and partnerships (the latter two forms are unincorporated businesses). The term 'corporation' applies to a legally constituted entity of its own person. In its strictest sense, the important distinction between the corporation and unincorporated business is related to the concept of 'limited liability'. With limited liability, the corporation is responsible for satisfying legal claims imposed on it; the owners of the corporation are not personally responsible for any losses or damage caused by the corporation. With unincorporated businesses, claims can be made on individual owners, who are personally liable for losses and damages.[3]

---

[2] Public finance theorists have acknowledged the superiority of taxing final goods and services rather than intermediate goods and services. See Diamond and Mirrlees (1971) and Diewert (1987).

[3] In recent years, this distinction between corporations and unincorporated businesses has become blurred. Corporations may own unincorporated businesses, such as partnerships. Moreover, unincorporated businesses have acquired attributes of corporations in the case of 'limited partnerships'. These entities are unincorporated in that no special securities are issued by the corporation to its owners. None the less, limited partnerships reduce the risk faced by partners, who are protected from using personal resources to satisfy any claims.

2. Why is there a Corporation Tax?

Why do most countries impose a corporate tax on corporations? There are a number of reasons given for corporate taxation but the most important rationales are the following:

- the corporate tax is a benefit tax to ensure that corporations pay for public goods and services that improve their profits;
- the corporate tax is a withholding tax that serves as a backstop to the personal tax;
- the corporate tax captures the rents earned by owners of fixed factors.

2.1. The corporate tax as a benefit tax

Taxes may be levied not only to raise revenue but also to capture the benefits that public expenditures may provide for the private sector. For an efficient allocation of resources between the public and private sectors, government may levy 'benefit' taxes so that consumers are aware of the public cost of goods that are supplied to them. In a similar vein, companies operating in many countries benefit from certain public sector activities. The Meade Report (Meade, 1978) identified the legal construct of limited liability as a special benefit that should be subject to taxation. Perhaps, as a more important concern, public expenditures on infrastructure such as roads, communication networks, and even education and training improve the productivity and profitability of businesses.

From the point of view of ensuring an efficient allocation of resources in the economy, one may justify the corporate tax as a user charge or benefit tax to discourage companies from over-using public services. Given this argument, it would seem that the best corporation tax would be assessed on a base that is correlated with the type of government activity that benefits the firm. If public education and training are valuable to the company, a payroll tax on the use of trained workers would be an appropriate benefit tax. Public expenditures on roads and highways justify the use of tolls, motor fuel taxes, and car licence fees. Airport and municipal infrastructure expenditures are best covered by airport taxes and development fees.

At times, however, it may be difficult for governments to assess special user charges for administrative reasons. As an alternative, rent or property taxes may be used, since infrastructure expenditures increase the value or profitability of the corporation. However, the value of the corporation depends on more than just infrastructure, so that the rent or property tax is an imperfect mechanism to capture the true benefits associated with public expenditures.

2.2. The withholding role of the corporate tax

The most important rationale given for corporate taxation is with respect to its role as a backstop for the personal tax. Governments may follow either of two basic principles for the purposes of taxing individuals: comprehensive income or consumption. Comprehensive income as defined by Simons (1938) is used for consumption and to increase wealth and is derived from labour earnings (wages, salaries, and benefits) and capital income (dividends, interest, and accrued capital gains). Consumption can be defined as the value of expenditures on goods and services; this is equal to earnings less savings, by definition. Each of these principles is discussed in turn.

2.2.1. Comprehensive income taxation

When governments impose taxes on comprehensive income, the most difficult source of income to tax is 'accrued capital gains'. In principle, individuals would report changes in the market value of assets and pay tax on the annual increment in the value of assets. However, there are a number of difficulties in trying to tax capital gains on this basis. For instance, assets such as private corporate shares have no periodic market value for assessment. Moreover, the taxation of accrued capital gains could force individuals to liquidate assets in order to cover tax liabilities. As a consequence of these problems, almost all governments throughout the world tax capital gains on a realised basis instead (when assets are sold).[4]

As a result of taxing only realised capital gains, investors can shelter their income from taxation by letting tax-free corporations hold their assets instead. For example, consider an individual who could earn income paid directly to him or to an untaxed corporation owned by him. If the income is paid directly to the individual, person income taxes are

---

[4] See Helliwell (1969) and also Auerbach (1991), who has developed a scheme for the retroactive taxation of capital gains. The basic concept is to calculate a tax penalty that captures the value of interest cost savings due to the postponement of capital gains taxes arising from realised rather than accrual methods.

paid in the year when the income is accrued. Alternatively, when the income is paid to the untaxed corporation, the accrued income is not subject to tax. The value of the corporate shares held by the investor increases by the amount of accumulated income retained by the corporation. Given that the government taxes capital gains only on a realised basis, rather than on an accrued basis, the investor postpones the payment of personal tax on accrued income by leaving it in the corporation. Only when the investor needs cash from the corporation will personal tax be paid on dividends or capital gains arising from the sale or repurchase of shares.[5] Thus, in principle, one could deduct dividends from the corporate income tax base since there is no need to withhold taxes on such income at the corporate level since it is fully taxed at the personal level. Only withholding at the corporate level is needed for retained earnings of corporations.[6]

Given this rationale for withholding tax on corporate retentions, the corporate tax base would be, in principle, the following:

$$Y^r = R - C - \text{Dep} - I - \text{Div} \tag{1}$$

where $R =$ accrued revenues;

$\quad C =$ current costs (salaries and material expenditures);

$\quad \text{Dep} =$ economic depreciation (and depletion) of assets;

$\quad I =$ interest paid for borrowed capital; and

$\quad \text{Div} =$ dividends paid out.

Note that for a comprehensive income tax, the corporate tax should permit companies to deduct the economic costs of depreciation,[7] interest expense, and other costs incurred in the production process. This requires the indexation of profits for inflation as well as the correct market valuation of assets to calculate economic depreciation. This issue will be further addressed in Section 3, when the incentive effects of the corporate tax are considered.

Although the above discussion argues for a corporate tax on retentions, governments rarely allow dividends to be deducted from the

---

[5] The treatment of income received when corporations repurchase shares varies considerably by country. Income may be treated as dividends (UK) or capital gains subject to certain restrictions (Canada) or be preferentially treated (France).

[6] In principle, if dividends are subject to personal taxation, the dividends could be deducted from the corporation tax. This proposal was considered in the US Treasury report on integration (1992).

[7] Economic depreciation is the loss in the value of assets from one period to the next. It is equal to the cost of replacing capital net of real capital earned by holding the asset. See Section 3 for further elaboration.

corporate income tax.[8] In large part, this is a result of historical legal developments that led to the notion that corporate and individual tax-payers are the same; both would be taxed on net income (interest expenses are deductible but not distributed profits that are paid to the owner of the business). Without dividend deductibility, the corporate tax base becomes the following:

$$Y' = R - C - \text{Dep} - I \tag{2}$$

(revenues net of current costs, depreciation and interest expenses).

Even though legal reasoning was important for the development of the corporate income tax base, there is, however, an important economic motivation for not allowing dividends to be deducted from the tax base. For many countries, the deduction of dividends would result in an erosion in the amount of taxes collected from foreign direct investment. This concern suggests another reason for governments to impose the corporate income tax on equity income: namely, a desire to withhold income accruing to foreigners.[9] The value of withholding income from foreigners is enhanced by international tax-crediting arrangements which result in the crediting of corporate income taxes being against the corporate income taxes of capital exporters. Thus the corporate income tax of a capital importer becomes a revenue-sharing device with foreign countries.

Under the withholding role of the corporate tax (without the dedica-tion of dividends from the tax base), the corporation pays a tax on income on behalf of the shareholders. To avoid double taxation of divi-dend and capital gain income earned by individuals, some adjustment is then necessary under the personal tax to ensure that individuals do not pay tax twice on the same income. Three types of systems are possible: (i) a refund of the corporation tax when the corporation distributes income; (ii) a refund of the corporation tax to the shareholders (for example, a tax credit) that reduces personal taxes (i.e. imputation or gross-up and credit system); and (iii) an exemption of dividends and capital gains on corporate shares from personal taxation.[10]

---

[8] In some countries, distributed profits may be taxed at a lower rate than undistrib-uted profits (Germany and Austria). This would be equivalent to a partial deduction for distributions. For example, suppose the corporate tax rate is 50% on undistributed profits and 25% of dividends paid from corporate taxable income, then the tax rate on distrib-uted profits would be reduced from 50% to 25%.

[9] The Royal Commission on Taxation in Canada (1966) (the Carter Report) explic-itly recognised this argument for the corporate income tax, since a large portion of Canadian industry is owned by US investors.

[10] The exemption of dividend and capital gain income at the individual level is pursued in a number of countries. For example, Canada allows a portion of capital gain income to

EXAMPLE

**A corporation earns £100 distributed as dividends to the owner.
The personal tax rate is 50 per cent and the corporate tax rate is 40 per cent.**

	Refundable tax	Gross up and credit	Exempt personal income
Profit	£100	£100	£100
Corporate tax (40% rate)	−£40	−£40	−£40
Dividend	£60	£60	£60
Refund of corporate tax (66% of dividend)	£40	£0	£0
Gross dividend (including refund)	£100	£60	£60
Personal tax (50% rate)	−£50	−£50[a]	£0
Dividend tax credit	£0	£40[a]	£0
After-tax income	£50	£50	£60

[a]Tax calculated on dividends grossed up by the corporate tax and the credit is based on grossed-up dividends.

In the accompanying example, we show the underlying amounts of tax owing on dividend income with each type of integration system.

The first system provides a refund of corporate tax to the firm when dividends are distributed. If dividends are not distributed, the corporate tax operates as a tax on retentions. Note, however, that there is an additional tax on retentions if capital gains taxes at the personal level are paid when the investor sells shares.

The second method integrates corporate and personal tax by allowing individuals to claim a credit against personal taxes equal to the amount of corporate income tax paid by the corporation. Each shareholder pays personal tax on the dividends and capital gains, grossed up by the credit.[11] However, most countries provide a credit at the personal level based on dividends received without any imputation given for capital gains.

be tax free to ensure integration at the corporate and personal levels. Mexico exempts dividends paid out of taxed profits (dividends paid from untaxed profits are subject to a withholding tax).

[11] Australia uses this system for the treatment of dividends. Each shareholder receives a form indicating the amount of dividends paid plus the credit equal to the individual's share of corporate income tax. However, most countries with systems of integration do not match the amount of corporate income tax paid by the corporation with the value of the credit received by the investor. Instead, many countries apply a corporate tax on dividend distributions (e.g. UK advance corporation tax) which is credited against the normal corporate income tax (excess amounts can be carried forward). This ensures that the corporations that pay little regular corporate income tax pay out dividends that are taxed as much as the credit given to shareholders.

The third method, the exemption of capital gains and dividends, achieves integration only if the corporate income tax rate is equal to the personal tax rate. With progressive personal tax rates, this condition is nearly impossible to fulfil for all types of investors. As most shareholders tend to be in the top tax bracket, governments often set the corporate tax rate equal to the top personal tax rate on income as a rough way of achieving integration.

The choice of the method used for integration depends on several factors (see more detailed discussion by McLure (1979) and Cnossen (1993)). The first is whether integration should include both dividends and capital gains. Under the refundable corporate tax and imputation systems, governments rarely provide full integration for capital gain income. The exemption method, therefore, provides a better method of integration for capital gains on shares, even though the system is unlikely to integrate personal and corporate income taxes properly, for the reasons given above.

A second issue is related to the rage of corporate tax on profits. Governments often provide tax incentives and preferential corporate tax rates for specific industrial activities. An integration system that ensures that the credit received by the firm or shareholders is equal to the amount of corporate income tax can undo the value of tax preferences given to the corporation.

A third issue is related to international flows of capital. An imputation system of integration of corporate and personal taxes for only domestic shareholders (tax credits given only at the personal level) leaves untouched the double taxation of income received by foreign shareholders (see OECD (1991)). In an open economy, the corporation may find that its international cost of funds is not affected by integration measures, so that integration may not undo the effects of the corporate tax on the cost of capital (Boadway and Bruce, 1992; Devereux and Freeman, 1995). One possible policy is to provide tax credits for foreign shareholders (as in the case of the UK, which provides a credit for US shareholders for advance corporation tax). This would result, however, in a loss of revenue for the capital-importing country. Alternatively, governments could choose not to integrate personal and corporate taxes. However, this would create financial planning opportunities for domestic investors, who can try to ensure that income paid from the closely held corporation is taxed at the lowest rate.

In summary, then, the corporate income tax base in most countries includes both distributed and undistributed profits. There is much variation in the type of tax base found in many countries. Table 4.1 provides a comparison of the corporate income tax for the G7 countries.

2.2.2. Consumption taxation

An alternative tax base is consumption, which is the difference between income and savings. Consumption can be taxed at the personal level by allowing individuals to deduct contributions made to registered savings plans, while withdrawals of accumulated interest and principal would be fully taxed. Capital income earned by the plan would be exempt from taxation, and no deduction for interest expenses would be permitted (this regime applies to Canadian Registered Retirement Savings Plans). Alternatively, the consumption tax can be equivalently levied in present value terms by not permitting a deduction for savings nor taxing the interest and sale of assets (UK Personal Equity Plans) which has been referred to as the non-registered asset treatment.[12]

The main principle is that the interest rate would be exempt from taxation so that the tax has no intertemporal distortion.[13] As the interest rate is the price at which current consumption is exchanged to purchase future consumption goods, taxing interest is equivalent to increasing the price of future consumption relative to current consumption.[14]

As soon as non-registered assets are permitted under a consumption-based personal tax, a problem arises with respect to tax avoidance. For

[12] The following example illustrates equivalency of registered and non-registered asset treatments. An individual pays taxes at the rate of 25% and holds an asset for one year. Suppose that the rate of return on the asset is 10%, which is equal to the alternative rate of return on bond assets. For the individual, the present value of taxes paid for registered savings can be shown to be equal to that for non-registered savings:

	Income	Savings	Tax base	Tax paid
Registered savings				
Year 1	£10,000	£2,000	£8,000	£2,000
Year 2	£10,000	–£2,200	£12,200	£3,050
Present value of taxes: £2,000 + £3,050/1.1 = £4,773				
Non-registered savings				
Year 1	£10,000	£2,000	£10,000	£2,500
Year 2	£10,000	–£2,200	£10,000	£2,500
Present value of taxes: £2,500 + £2,500/1.1 = £4,773				

[13] Bradford (1986) defines a consumption tax as any tax that does not affect the opportunity cost of savings.

[14] The treatment of inheritances and bequests is an important issue. Bradford (1986) suggests that bequests and inheritances can be ignored: bequests are not deductible from the tax nor inheritances included. However, if bequests are viewed as a form of consumption, it is desirable to include inheritances in the tax base. See the Meade Report (1978) for a comprehensive analysis.

TABLE 4.1. Corporate income tax provisions, 1994

	Canada	France	Germany	Italy	Japan	UK	USA
Income							
Revenues	Yes	Yes	Yes	Yes	Yes	Yes	Yes
Intercorporate dividends	No (except private)	Exempt except subject to minimum tax (see below)	Exempt except subject to minimum tax (see below)	Exempt except subject to minimum tax (see below)	Exempt with ownership >25%	Exempt except subject to minimum tax (see below)	80% tax-free with ownership >20%
Capital gains	Three-quarters of gain	Short term: as income Long term: 19% except for 33% for portfolio securities	Real property	Real property (full rate)	Yes—land with surtax	Yes	28%
Expenses							
Wages and salaries	Yes	Yes	Yes	Yes	Yes	Yes	Yes
Inventory costs[a]	FIFO	FIFO	LIFO	LIFO	LIFO or FIFO	FIFO	LIFO or FIFO
Depreciation	Historical cost	Historical cost	Historical cost	Historical cost	Historical cost	Historical cost	Historical cost
Interest expense	Yes	Yes	Yes	Yes	Yes	Yes	Yes
Losses (operating only)[b]	Three-year c.b., seven-year c.f.	Five-year c.f.; depreciation expenses have indefinite c.f.	Two-year c.b., indefinite c.f.	Five-year c.f.	One-year c.b., five-year c.f.	Three-year c.b., indefinite c.f.	Three-year c.b., 15-year c.f.

Corporate tax rate	Federal: 29.12% Provincial: 8.9–17%	33⅓%	Federal: 45% (undistributed profits), 30% (distributed) State: 5–15% (deductible)	Central: 36% Local: 16.2%	Central: 37.5% Prefecture: 13.2% (deductible) Corporate inhabitants: 6–14.7% (deductible) Total tax rate: 51.4%	33%	Federal: 35% State: up to 12% (deductible)
Foreign source income	Yes except dividends from foreign affiliate	Exempt except for pre-compte (see below)	Exempt dividends if ownership >10%, otherwise taxed with credit for foreign taxes	Yes with credit	Yes with global credit	Yes with credit per source	Yes with global credit
Minimum tax	Capital tax reduced by corporate income surcharge Dividends from term preferred shares	Pre-compte: 50% on dividends paid (or 33% of grossed-up dividends)	25% of dividends paid	10% of dividends paid	No	ACT of 25% on dividends paid (or 20% of grossed-up dividends)	20% on income
Consolidation	No	Yes for property transfer	Yes	No	No	No, but relief for source losses	Yes
Capital and property tax	Provincial capital tax: up to 0.5% of assets Property tax	Property tax Business licence tax	0.6–11% of trade capital	Property tax: 0.4–0.6% Transfer tax: 6–17% New equity tax: 0.75%	1.7% on structures 1–4% on depreciable assets	Property tax only	No property tax

example, suppose a manager chooses to hold shares in a closely held corporation. Instead of receiving a salary, the manager obtains dividends. Under the non-registered asset system, the manager will obtain tax-free dividends even though the payment is a reward for effort. Unless there is a withholding tax on the business to ensure that earnings are fully taxed, the individual can escape taxation of consumption.

What form of withholding tax would therefore be needed on a business to ensure that all forms of earnings available for consumption are taxed? One possibility would be a business tax on 'cash flow' (revenues from the sale of goods and services (R), net of wages and salaries and other current expenditures (C) and net capital expenditures (K), with no inclusion of financial income or deduction of interest expense):[15]

$$Y^{cf} = R - C - K. \tag{3}$$

Net capital expenditures would be capital purchases (net of disposal of assets). The deduction of net capital expenditures is similar to the expensing of capital (100 per cent depreciation). In principle, it is also similar to expensing of savings at the individual level for a personal tax on consumption. In other words, the business is able to expense savings on behalf of the individual. Below, the properties of the cash-flow tax as a rent tax will be discussed in more detail.[16]

If a business tax is imposed on cash flow it could withhold returns that would otherwise escape taxation for owners of non-registered assets. If the rate of tax is equivalent to the (top) personal tax rate on consumption, the rents will be withheld on non-registered assets.[17]

No country in the world has attempted to impose a direct personal tax on consumption. However, most countries rely on some form of consumption taxation. The consumption treatment is available in many

---

[15] See the Meade Report (Meade, 1978), Capital Taxes Group (1991), US Treasury (1977), Bradford (1986), Boadway, Bruce, and Mintz (1987), and Devereux and Freeman (1991). For a discussion on implementation problems with the cash-flow tax, see Mintz and Seade (1991) and Shome and Schutte (1993).

[16] The above cash-flow tax base has been referred to as the R base (i.e. real transactions). There are other alternative bases used for cash-flow taxes. For example, as the Meade Report (Meade, 1978) points out, there is an equivalent tax base called the R + F base which includes financial transactions. Under the R + F base, net debt (debt liabilities less loans) would be added to the tax base and net interest expense and repayment of debt would be deducted from the base. Another alternative is the S base, which would tax distributions of profits net of new equity issues.

[17] Given the example in footnote 12 of a 10% rate of return, note that a taxpayer would pay, with non-registered assets, £4,773 in personal taxes. It is assumed capital does not depreciate. The business will pay cash-flow taxes on the difference between revenues and the cost of investment in each year. In the example, the business tax paid at a 25% rate would be equal to the following:

countries for retirement savings (for example, pension plans) and sometimes housing (imputed rental income may not be taxed and expenses such as mortgage interest are not deductible).[18] What is most interesting is that over fifty countries now use only a withholding tax on business as a tax on personal consumption (without taxing individuals directly). This is the value added tax (VAT), which applies to sales of firms with a deduction for (or credit for tax on) purchases from other businesses. The only difference between the tax base in equation (3) above and the VAT is that wages and salaries are not deductible from the VAT base.[19] However, this is not surprising, since there is no tax on wages and salaries at the personal level under the VAT system.[20] Thus we can think of the VAT as a withholding tax for the purposes of taxing consumption on a non-registered asset basis.

2.3. The corporate tax as a rent tax

A third justification for the corporate tax is that it could be an efficient method of taxing the rents earned from non-reproducible factors of

	Revenues	Net capital expenditure	Tax base	Tax owing
Year 1	£0	£2,000	−£2,000	−£500[a]
Year 2	£400	−£2,000	£2,400	£600

Present value of taxes: −£500 + £600/1.1 = £45

Total personal and business taxes = £4,773 + £45 = £4,818

[a]The firm would claim a refund equal to £500 or carry forward loss at 10% to claim against future profits.

Note that a non-registered asset treatment with the cash-flow tax yields the equivalent amount of tax paid as the registered asset case (£4,818) without a cash-flow tax.

[18] For example, Canada treats owner-occupied housing in this manner.

[19] Only the origin-based VAT can be equivalent to a payroll and rent tax on a corporation. A payroll and rent tax on corporations is an origin-based tax: it applies to production consumed by residents or non-residents (consumption of foreign goods and services by consumers is exempt from taxation). A VAT that exempts export sales and taxes imports is a destination-based tax that falls on consumption of residents only. If the consumption tax applies to all goods and services, there is no difference between the origin and destination bases, since the exchange rate will adjust for the tax (Lockwood, de Meza, and Myles, 1994). However, with exempt goods and services, the two taxes will not be equivalent.

[20] VATs are used in many developing countries where it may be difficult to tax individuals on their wages and salaries except by withholding at the firm level.

production such as entrepreneurship, land, and natural resources.[21] Taxing rents, which are the return to factors over and above that needed to compensate them for their use, is efficient, since investment and financing decisions of business are not distorted. In some countries, the government may be the landowner; a tax on rents accruing to land would serve as a royalty payment for the use of land. Even if the government did not own the property, it may find that taxation of rents is an efficient tax (this point was initially made by George (1879) and subsequently shown in the optimal tax literature (Atkinson and Stiglitz, 1980)).

On a periodic basis, rents are measured as the revenues earned by the corporation net of the imputed costs of production. Imputed costs include current expenditure (C) on labour compensation and material costs as well as the costs of holding capital. Capital costs in turn are economic depreciation (Dep) and the financing costs of both debt (interest, I) and equity financing (the opportunity cost of equity, OCE). The tax base for annual rent tax is therefore:

$$Y^R = R - C - \text{Dep} - I - \text{OCE}. \tag{4}$$

The difference between the rent tax and the corporate income tax (equation (2) above) is imputation of the cost of equity financing (OCE), which makes the rent base smaller than the income tax base.

It is difficult to measure the periodic rent base correctly. It requires the proper imputation of the cost of depreciation and the real cost of debt and equity. The measurement of cost of depreciation is based on the replacement cost of capital, correcting for any real capital gains earned by holding assets. The real cost of financing requires a correction for inflation that erodes the value of assets that are fixed in nominal terms. Moreover, to ensure that government shares both gains and losses in income (risk), it is necessary to allow for the refundability of losses by providing the equivalent of a tax credit equal to the rate of tax times the loss.[22]

An alternative to the periodic rent tax is the cash-flow tax as described above (equation (3)). The difference between the cash-flow base and the periodic rent base is that the former allows for the expensing of capital while the latter allows for the deductibility of the imputed costs of capi-

---

[21] The concept of using the corporate tax to tax rents is originally discussed by the Meade Report (Meade, 1978).

[22] Examples of refundability include carrying back losses (providing an immediate credit to the firm) carrying forward losses at a rate of interest. Refundability is discussed further in Section 5.

tal for depreciation and financing.[23] Since expensing is simple compared with measuring depreciation and financing costs, the cash-flow tax is arguably much easier to implement. There would remain a need to allow for the refundability of losses, since it is likely that the firm would have a negative cash flow in early years. Moreover, there are complications with international transactions (for example, transfer price issues) when other countries do not rely on a cash-flow tax (Mintz and Seade, 1991). None the less, there are some jurisdictions that have implemented forms of cash-flow taxes as rent taxes on resource companies (British Columbia and Australia) or as a general tax on corporations (Croatia). Under these regimes, capital is expensed and losses are carried forward at a rate of interest. Perhaps more experimentation with cash-flow taxes will be attempted in the future.

3. Taxes and Investment

Most research has concentrated on the impact of corporate taxes on the investment behaviour of firms. A typical analysis of the effect of taxation on capital stock (the corresponding flow is investment) is to consider a neoclassical firm that is perfectly competitive in product and input markets. The firm adjusts its capital stock, perhaps subject to adjustment costs or completely irreversibly. Given that capital decisions affect profitability over many years, the firm must formulate expectations about future economic variables (for example, input and output prices) and tax regimes (corporate tax rates, depreciation rates, and so on). The usual model treats tax variables as unchanging over time, although some analyses may try to incorporate changes in tax policy regimes. The taxes considered for analysis include the corporate income tax, capital tax, property tax, an resource tax. Specific tax incentives for capital may also be modelled, such as investment tax credits and allowances, accelerated depreciation, and tax holidays.

The firm maximises the value of its equity or, alternatively, the present

---

[23] Boadway and Bruce (1984) show that any combination of depreciation and financing costs that satisfies the condition that the capital costs are fully deductible in present value terms results in a corporate tax on rents. For example, one could allow depreciation to be deducted based on any rate applied to the undepreciated capital cost of an asset that is indexed each period at the rate of interest. See Capital Taxes Group (1991) and Devereux and Freeman (1991), which provide for an alternative but equivalent tax base that allows for the opportunity cost of equity to be deducted.

value of cash flow which is equal to its value of equity and debt. The firm thus chooses the optimal path of investment, taking into account relevant economic and tax variables. The firm invests in capital until the value of marginal product (less adjustment costs) is equal to the *user cost of capital* (Jorgenson, 1963). The user cost of capital can be thought of as the 'rental or lease price' of capital, which is equal to depreciation, risk, and financing costs, adjusted for taxes. The cost of risk is discussed in Section 5. At this point, it would be useful to explain, in detail, the cost of depreciation and financing.

The cost of depreciation. The cost of depreciation, in economic terms, is the reduction in the value of the asset over a given period. Suppose a firm purchases a machine for q_0. Over the period, the machine physically deteriorates by an amount δ so that only $1-\delta$ units of the machine are left at the end of the period. Suppose, further, that identical new machines can be sold for, in real terms, q_1 per unit at the end of the period. The reduction in the value of the machine over the period is thus equal to $q_0 - (1 - \delta)q_1 = (\delta - x)q_1$, where $x = (q_1 - q_0)/q_1$. The term $\delta - x$ is the 'economic depreciation rate', which is equal to the rate of physical wear and tear less the rate of real capital gains accrued from holding an asset (evaluated at the cost of replacement). Note that even land 'depreciates' in economic terms; even though physical depreciation may be zero ($\delta = 0$), there may be real capital gains or losses from the holding of land.

The cost of finance. The cost of finance is the imputed cost of borrowing money from financial markets. Given the absence of risk, the cost of finance, denoted as r, is equal to the net-of-corporate-tax cost of issuing debt and equity. If ρ is the nominal opportunity cost of investing equity in the firm (before the payment of personal taxes) and π is the rate of inflation, the real cost of equity finance is $\rho - \pi$. For example, if equity owners require a 10 per cent nominal return on investments, prior to the payment of personal taxes, and inflation is 5 per cent, then the real cost of equity finance is 5 per cent.[24] If i is the nominal bond interest rate, which is deductible from corporate taxable income at the corporate tax rate, u, then the real cost of debt finance is therefore $i(1 - u) - \pi$. For example, if 10 per cent is the payable interest rate on corporate bonds, the corporate tax rate is 40 per cent and the inflation rate is 5 per cent, then the real cost of debt finance to the firm is only 1 per cent. How actual financing costs of equity and bonds relate to each other is discussed in the next section, since the cost of finance depends on arbitrage in financial markets.

As will be discussed in Section 4, the optimal choice of financing will depend on both tax and non-tax considerations. Using the formulation of Auerbach (1979), the firm can be characterised as minimising its cost of finance by choosing its optimal debt/equity ratio prior to making its investment decision.[25] Thus the firm would have a discount rate that would be a weighted average of the cost of debt and equity finance. Letting the proportion of investment to be financed by debt be β (therefore $1 - \beta$ is the proportion financed by equity), the cost of finance is equal to

$$r = R - \pi = \beta i(1 - u) + (1 - \beta)\rho - \pi \tag{5}$$

where R is the nominal cost of finance.

3.1. The user cost of capital

Taking into account these depreciation and financing costs, one can derive the user cost of capital which is the minimum return needed for investment to take place. Note, first, that the cost of buying a capital good is £q per unit. If the government provides an investment tax credit which reduces corporate income tax payments by an amount equal to a percentage of gross investment, φ, the cost of each purchased capital good is reduced to £$q(1 - \varphi)$. In addition, when a capital good is purchased, the government provides tax depreciation deductions that are of value to the firm. Let £Aq be the present value of tax depreciation allowances.[26] Thus the effective cost of buying an asset is equal to £$q(1 - \varphi - uA)$.

[25] The weighted cost of finance would be used to discount tax depreciation allowances. Not all of the literature uses this approach. In King and Fullerton (1984), for example, there is no presumption that firms would use a weighted cost of finance.

[26] There are a number of schemes permitted for tax depreciation. The most common ones are initial (or investment) allowances (with an immediate write-off of a percentage of the asset) and annual allowances usually provided on a declining balance or straight-line basis. The tax value of depreciation allowances is equal to the corporate tax rate, u, multiplied by the depreciation deduction given in each period and discounted by the firm's nominal cost of finance (R in equation (5)). Initial allowances may or may not be used to reduce the cost basis of assets that are depreciated. Under declining balance depreciation given at the rate α as a percentage of the cost of the asset, the write-off, per pound of the cost base, in each period is $u\alpha(1 - \alpha)^t$, discounted by $(1 + R)t^{-1}$. The present value

Under the assumption that the firm optimally chooses its capital stock, the user cost of capital can be easily derived. The return earned on the last pound of investment equals gross income[27] net of corporate taxes and is given by $F'(1 - u)$. The cost of holding capital is equal to the annual cost of depreciation and financing costs multiplied by the effective purchase price of capital, $(r + \delta - x)q(1 - \varphi - uA)$. For the optimal investment decision, the marginal return is equal to the marginal cost of holding capital, so this implies

$$(1 - u)F' = (\delta - x + r) q (1 - \varphi - uA). \tag{6}$$

Under steady-state conditions, the firm holds capital stock so that the return per pound of investment is constant over time and this can be obtained by rearranging the above expression:

$$P = \frac{F'}{q} = \left(\frac{\delta - x + r}{1 - u} \right)(1 - \varphi - uA), \tag{7}$$

The right-hand side equation (7) multiplied by the price of capital, q, has been interpreted as the user cost of capital for a firm that invests in depreciable assets such as machinery, structures, and land. Other formulas, more complicated than shown here, have been derived for inventories (King, 1977; Boadway, Bruce, and Mintz, 1982) and natural resources (Boadway, Bruce, McKenzie, and Mintz, 1987).[28]

Expression (7) suggests that the corporate tax system affects the user cost of capital in three ways:

- the corporate tax reduces gross income thereby increasing the user cost of capital in three ways:
- the corporate tax reduces the effective purchase price of capital through depreciation allowances and investment tax credits;

of tax depreciation on a declining balance basis in $A = u\alpha/(\alpha + R)$. Thus if the firm's discount rate is $R = 10\%$, the tax depreciation rate is 20% and the corporate tax rate is 50%, then $A = 0.33$. Under straightline depreciation (a percentage constantly written off each year based on the life of the asset), the tax value of the write-off is equal to $\zeta = uq/T$ in each period, with T being the life of the asset. The present value of tax depreciation under straightline depreciation is equal to $PV = u[1 - (1 + R)^{-T+1}]/TR$. If the life of the asset is 10 years, then $PV = 0.29$.

[27] Adjustment costs can be included by subtracting them from the net revenues earned by the firm as current expenses or by adding them to depreciation costs if adjustment costs are capital in nature.

[28] The user cost of capital for inventories held for less than one year is equal to $F' = (r + \sigma\pi)/(1 - u)$, with $\sigma = 0$ if governments allow inventories to be expensed or valued according to LIFO (last-in-first-out implies that the price of the latest inventory is used to assess cost), or $\sigma + 1$ if inventories are valued according to FIFO (first-in-first-out implies that the price of the oldest inventory is used to assess cost).

- the corporate tax reduces financing costs by allowing companies to write off nominal interest expenses.

The above discussion is based on a model that considers capital as a stock that yields a flow of income over time (point input and flow of output process). However, some types of industries require capital to be built from ongoing expenditures on current inputs to produce a stock (flow of input and point output process). This particularly applies to research and development, exploration and development by resource companies, and construction projects.

3.2. Neutrality of the corporate tax

One can show that the corporate tax would be neutral with respect to investment decisions of a firm under a rent or cash-flow tax, investment is expensed ($A = 1$), there is no investment tax credit ($\varphi = 0$) and interest is not deductible ($r = \beta i + (1 - \beta)\rho - \pi$). Under these conditions, the user cost of capital, which becomes $q(r + \delta - x)$, is independent of the corporate tax.[29]

Governments, however, rarely try to achieve neutrality by taxing only rents. They purposely try to influence investment behaviour by giving special exemptions or deductions such as accelerated depreciation allowances for manufacturing investments, investment tax credits for machinery, and lower corporate tax rates for specific industries. Table 4.2 provides a list of special concessions provided by the G7 countries under the corporate tax.

Governments may also provide tax holidays for firms, although the above expression (equation (7)) is inappropriate. Under a tax holiday, the qualifying company (usually a new company) is exempt from paying taxes for several years. Once the holiday is completed, the firm begins paying corporate income taxes. Thus, when a firm invests in long-lived assets, such as structures, the government taxes the income after the holiday is over and this can affect the cost of capital during the holiday. As Mintz (1990) shows, the holiday investment will bear taxes if the tax depreciation allowances after the holiday are of less value than the economic depreciation cost. This will happen when tax depreciation

---

[29] Similarly, if the real cost of equity and debt financing is deductible, $r = [\beta i + (1 - \beta)\rho - \pi][1 - u]$, and depreciation deductions are equal to economic depreciation based on the replacement cost, the user cost will be independent of the corporate income tax (e.g. under declining balance methods, $\alpha = \delta - x$ and undepreciated cost is increased by inflation each period so that tax depreciation is equal to $u\alpha(1 - \alpha)^t(1 + \pi)^t$).

TABLE 4.2. Special tax incentives

	Canada	France	Germany	Italy	Japan	UK	USA
Tax holidays	No except three provinces	Two years exempt, three years 50% tax holiday	No	Ten-year tax holiday	No	No	No
Investment tax credit or allowance	ITC—slow growth region, R&D	Incremental training/R&D	Yes	No	ITA—incremental R&D, import incentive, energy	ITC/grants	Incremental R&D
Tax-free zones	No	No	Yes	No	No	Yes	Partial exemption for US possessions
Reduced rates of tax	Manufactures Small business	Yes	No	No	No	No	Exempt earnings for qualifying export activities
Accelerated depreciation	Yes	Yes	Yes	No	No	100% in zones	Pollution equipment

allowances are not indexed for inflation (so the real value after the holiday is eroded by inflation) or when governments provide fast write-offs. For example, under a cash-flow tax, the company loses the value of expensing during the holiday and will pay taxes on income generated by holiday investments when the holiday is complete. In some circumstances, holiday investments can be taxed more highly than normal investments in inflation or tax depreciation rates are sufficiently high that the firm's real value of tax depreciation after the holiday is insignificant.

3.3. Other taxes

Governments are very innovative in assessing all sorts of taxes on corporate investments besides the corporate income tax. In Canada, corporate taxes are assessed on the gross assets of companies. In Mexico, the gross assets tax is a minimum tax whereby it is creditable against corporate income taxes. For Mexican companies established in the Maquilidoran region where they are exempt from corporate income tax, the gross assets tax is a final tax. Other minimum taxes can be found in the USA (on profits), and on the net worth of companies (Colombia), turnover (Morocco), and dividends (UK, France, and Germany for integration purposes). Taxes on property (structures and buildings) may be found in many countries.[30]

Some studies have also tried to incorporate non-capital taxes such as sales and payroll taxes in the user cost of capital to calculate the overall impact of the tax system on firms' decisions. However, it is unclear that this is appropriate methodology to follow. Payroll taxes affect labour decisions, not capital decisions. Sales taxes are neutral with respect to capital as long as they are levied on consumption goods, not capital goods. Thus, to correct the user cost of capital to calculate the impact of non-capital taxes on investment is incorrect. Instead, taxes such as capital, payroll, and motor fuel taxes might impact on the cost of producing a product. Therefore it would be more appropriate to calculate the effective tax rates on the marginal cost of production which is increased by taxes on various inputs (subject to the incidence of the taxes). In McKenzie, Mintz, and Scharf (1993), a measure is derived for the impact of taxes on the marginal cost of production which aggregates taxes

---

[30] To incorporate these various special provisions in the user cost of capital, see Estache (1995) and Chen and Mintz (1995) on minimum taxes and Chen and Mintz (1993) on capital and property taxes.

according to a cost structure for the firm. One can then think of taxes as affecting the production decision of the firm rather than a particular input such as capital.

3.4. The effective tax rate on capital

To capture the effect of all the different provisions of the corporate tax system on capital investments, it has now become popular to measure the *effective corporate tax rate* on capital (Auerbach, 1983; Boadway, Bruce, and Mintz, 1984).[31] The effective tax rate is the amount of tax paid as a percentage of the rate of return on capital held at the margin. It is measured by the following formula:

$$T^c = \frac{r^g - r^n}{r^g} \tag{8}$$

with r^g and r^n being the rate of return gross and net of taxes, respectively. For example, in the case of depreciable capital, the gross rate of return on capital is equal to the expression for the income net of economic depreciation $(F/q - (\delta - x))$. The net rate of return on capital is the case when all tax terms are zero (r^n is therefore equal to the weighted average cost of finance, $\beta i + (1-\beta)\rho - \pi$).

In Table 4.3, a comparison of effective corporate income-tax rates for the G7 countries is provided for 1994. Machinery (with relatively low depreciation rates compared with economic depreciation) and inventories (valued on a FIFO basis) tend to be highly taxed while land and

TABLE **4.3.** *Marginal effective corporate tax rates: G7 countries, manufacturing, 1994 (%)*

	Machinery	Buildings	Inventories	Land	Aggregate
Canada	19.4	20.4	34.4	19.4	23.8
France	28.6	25.1	31.4	25.8	28.3
Germany	37.8	27.7	26.2	26.2	31.2
Italy	49.2	38.4	26.9	26.9	38.9
Japan	41.6	32.2	29.4	29.4	35.0
UK	36.9	24.9	41.8	20.3	34.1
USA	21.2	28.4	30.2	16.8	25.4

Source: author's own calculations based on capital stock, economic depreciation and interest rate parameters developed in McKenzie and Mintz (1992).

[31] King and Fullerton (1984) estimate effective tax rates on capital but include both corporate and personal income tax provisions. This is discussed below.

inventories (LIFO basis) are more lightly taxed due to interest expense deductions in the presence of inflation.

3.5. Personal taxation and the cost of capital

As emphasised by King (1977), personal taxation may be an important element in assessing the cost of capital and effective tax rate. To incorporate personal taxes in the effective tax rate, we need to account for personal tax rates on nominal interest income (denoted by m), the accrual equivalent tax rate on nominal capital gains (c)[32] and the dividend tax rate (v). After personal taxes are paid, investors earn interest income at the rate $i(1 - m)$, capital-gain income equal to $\rho(1 - c)$, and dividend income equal to $\rho(1 - v)$. Let β be the proportion of assets held as bonds, $1-\beta$ be the proportion of assets held as equity, a be the proportion of equity income derived as capital gains, and $1 - a$ be the proportion of equity income derived as dividends. Therefore the after-tax rate of return on capital, after correcting for personal taxes and inflation, is equal to the following:

$$r^n = \beta i (1 - m) + (1 - \beta) \rho (1 - \theta) - \pi \tag{9}$$

with θ denoting the average tax rate on equity income ($\theta = ac + (1 - a)v$).

One can measure the effective capital tax rate, T, that incorporates both corporate and personal taxes by using expression (9) for r^n in the right-hand side of equation (8) above. This approach is used in King and Fullerton (1984) and OECD (1991), who measure the effective tax on capital, taking into account both corporate and personal taxes.

The inclusion of personal taxes as part of the effective tax rate measure clearly confronts analysts with the thorniest issue that has to be dealt with when analysing tax systems. This issue is related to the choice of personal tax rates that are relevant in assessing the effective tax rate on capital. Investors could face different tax rates for several reasons:

- *Progressivity of the tax rate schedule at the personal level.* This implies some investors face lower tax rates on capital income than others.

---

[32] Recall that capital gains taxes are assessed only when assets are sold. An accrual equivalent capital gains tax rate is calculated by discounting payable capital gains taxes to reflect the amount of tax paid had an accrual basis been used instead. See Davies and Glendy (1990) for a discussion of different methods of measuring the accrual equivalent capital gains tax rate.

- *Tax exemptions for certain forms of savings.* Some sources of savings, such as pension plan savings, are exempt from taxation.
- *Financial intermediaries.* Banks, insurance companies, mutual funds, and other financial institutions have their own special tax considerations.
- *Foreign investors.* Companies are owned not only by domestic investors but also by foreigners who are subject to a country's withholding and income taxes levied by government where the investor resides.

To deal with all these potential types of investors who can own companies, one requires a financial model that explains the determination of financial policies and rates of return on assets. This issue will be discussed in more detail in the next section, on corporate taxation and financing, although it would be useful to discuss now one particularly relevant point related to financial markets in open economies.

In earlier work on effective tax rates (King and Fullerton (1984), for example), it was assumed that economies were closed to international capital movements. Under this assumption, it is best to measure an aggregate effective tax rate on capital incorporating both the corporate and personal income provisions of a country to evaluate how investment is affected by the tax system. If either corporate tax rates of personal tax rates are increased, both domestic investment and savings, which are equal to each other in equilibrium, would be affected simultaneously.

However, in an open economy, whereby savings are obtained from international sources as well, it is no longer clear what impact personal taxes in a particular country might have on investment and corporate taxes on savings. In a small open economy (Boadway, Bruce, and Mintz (1984) and see also Bovenberg, Andersson, Aramhi and Chand (1990)), rates of return received by investors are determined by international markets. This implies that domestic investment and savings decisions may not influence international interest rates and yields on financial instruments. Thus personal taxes on domestic savings way reduce the return earned by savers, but this would simply reduce capital outflows of savings or increase capital inflows from abroad without affecting the interest rate that governs a firm's investment decision. Similarly, corporate tax provisions reduce investment, increasing (reducing) capital outflows (inflows) without affecting domestic savings decisions that depend on international yields on assets. Given these conclusions, one should *disaggregate* domestic corporate and personal effective tax rates for a small open economy to determine how investment and savings are affected.

These two extreme cases, the closed and open economies, raise important perspectives for policy. For example, in a closed economy, personal taxation reduces both domestic savings and corporate investment. In a small open economy, savings would be reduced, capital outflows would decline, but investment would not be affected, since firms finance capital at the internationally determined interest rate. Thus policies such as reducing tax rates at the personal level could be largely ineffective in increasing corporate investment in a small open economy.

How open are economies to capital movements? Feldstein and Horioka (1981) and Summers (1986) argue that national capital markets are closed since domestic investment and savings are highly correlated, in part due to government policies that interfere with capital flows. French and Poterba (1991) suggest that most equity of corporations is owned by domestic investors (although this does not suggest that foreign savings could be the primary determinant of *marginal* savings). On the other hand, interest rates across countries seem to be closely related through financial arbitrage (Frenkel and Razin, 1987). Recent evidence suggests as well that cross-border financial transactions have increased substantially, from 64 per cent of GDP in 1990 compared with 9.6 per cent in 1980 for the G7 countries (Edey and Hviding, 1995).

This discussion of open versus closed economies becomes relevant in evaluating the impact of integrating corporate and personal taxes on capital income (see Boadway and Bruce (1992) and Devereux and Freeman (1995)). One view is that integration of personal taxes that results in relief for resident shareholders only is not effective in integrating corporate and personal taxes since foreign investors do not obtain the same benefit. The reduction in dividend or capital gains taxes only increases domestic savings without affecting the cost of capital of the company. Thus integration is not necessary. Alternatively, economies may be sufficiently large or distinct (Gordon and Varian, 1989; Burgess, 1988) that domestic savings influence interest rates faced by a country. Under these conditions, a reduction in dividend and capital gains taxes will increase the international supply of savings to an economy and reduce interest rates faced by the economy. In this case, integration is of benefit to investment. Moreover, integration may still be necessary to simplify a tax system and to minimise tax planning opportunities.

3.6. Do taxes affect investment decisions?

A large number of models have been estimated using econometric methods to determine how taxes impact on investment decisions. There are generally three approaches used in the literature.[33]

- *The accelerator model.* The first approach, due to Clark (1917), is to link investment simply to changes in aggregate demand. The accelerator model is based on an assumption that relative prices of labour and capital do not affect the demand for capital. Only output affects investment, so the impact of taxes on investment would only be through the impact on aggregate demand. The model was extended to allow for lags by assuming that output of current and past periods affects current investment.
- *The neoclassical model.* The neoclassical model assumes that profit-maximising firms will use capital and other inputs in production until the marginal product is equal to the price of the factor used in production. In terms of the microeconomic theory, the demand for capital will therefore depend on both output and the rental price of capital and other factors of production. The neoclassical model (Jorgenson, 1963) is based on an underlying production function with a given measure of substitutability of factors in production. As it is assumed that investment responds slowly to changes in output and the user cost of capital, an adjustment is made so that current investment depends on both current and past changes in capital stock. Under the neoclassical model, taxes affect capital output as in the accelerator model, as well as the user cost of capital.

Later versions of the neoclassical model allowed for different formulations. One approach is to avoid specifying a production function, such as one with a given degree of substitutability of factors, but instead to assume a particular profit or cost function and derive the demand for investment using duality (see Bernstein and Nadiri (1987) for an explicit formulation using the dual approach). Feldstein (1982) outlined two other models. The *return over cost* model allows for net investment per unit of output to be correlated with the excess of the marginal return to capital (net of taxes and depreciation) over the cost of finance. The *effective tax rate* model assumes that net increases in capital stock as a percentage of output

[33] A comprehensive review of the literature may be found in Chirinko (1992), who discusses more fully the various approaches used to model investment behaviour. Only the primary ones are considered here.

are positively related to the net rate of return of capital, once correcting for both depreciation and taxes.

A recent neoclassical approach is to use the investment demand function derived from the firm's maximisation decision (the 'Euler equation'), which depends on future investment, the difference between current and future costs or prices of capital, and the return on capital (with the error term depending on both technological shocks and expectation errors). Taxes play an interesting role by affecting both current and future variables. One can thus more easily accommodate anticipated shifts in tax policy.

- The *Q model*. The Q model, due to Brainard and Tobin (1968) but originally conceived by Keynes (1936), is based on the notion that firms will invest in capital if the market value of projects is at least as great as the cost of purchasing capital. Q is measured as the ratio of the market value of a firm's equity and debt liabilities (the present value of its future returns) to its replacement cost of capital. If Q is greater than 1, then the firm invests in capital, while if Q is less than 1, the firm will divest. In principle, the market value of the firm embodies information used by investors to evaluate discounted earnings of the firm. Moreover, keeping in mind that investment is determined up to the point whereby the market value of the marginal unit of capital is equal to its purchase price, *marginal* Q would be the best indicator for investment decisions. However, the marginal Q is difficult to measure, since it requires one to measure the market value of an incremental project decision. Instead, one must measure the *average* Q, which is the total market value of the firm divided by the replacement cost of its capital (see Hayashi (1982), who shows how average and marginal Q are related).

  In Q models, it is hypothesised that investment is adjusted but at a cost that increases by the amount of investment (a quadratic function is usually assumed so that investment is simply a linear function of Q). The Q variable is corrected by reducing the replacement cost of capital by the present value of tax depreciation allowances as well as correcting the market value of equity and debt by personal and corporate income taxes that influence the financing of capital (see Summers (1981)).

Examples of empirical work that employ various approaches to modelling investment behaviour are provided in Table 4.4. Estimates of the impact on taxes on investment are also provided in terms of price and, where appropriate, output effects. Older studies of investment behaviour

TABLE **4.4.** *Selected investment studies*

Study	Period covered	Methodology	Results
Hall and Jorgenson, 1967	1929–63	Neoclassical; time series of US manufacturing and non-manufacturing investments in structures and equipment.	Elasticity of capital to output varies from 0.04 to 0.13.
Summers, 1981	1931–78	Q model with time-series investment.	Doubling investment tax credit raises investment 5.5% in first year and 17.3% in the long run.
Feldstein, 1982	1953–78	Time-series study based on return over cost, effective tax rate model.	Elasticity of investment to return on capital is 0.58 and to output is 0.62.
Chirinko and Eisner, 1983	1973–79	Use of six macroeconomic quarterly models; structures and machinery	Elasticity of investment to user cost is −0.52.
Poterba and Summers, 1983	1950–80	Annual time series of UK firms using a Q model with personal and corporate tax rates.	Dividend taxes impact on investment.
Chirinko, 1987	1951–81	Similar to Feldstein study except that return on capital is lagged.	Elasticity of investment to return on capital is 0.17 and to output is 1.76.
Blundell, Bond, Devereux, and Schiantarelli, 1992	1975–86	Pooled firm-level data using Q model.	Increase of 10% in market value of equity increases investment by 2.5% in the short run.
Auerbach and Hassett, 1992	1953–88	Use of both the Euler and Q model approaches and allowance for changes in tax rates.	Tax policy plays a significant but not necessarily stabilising role in affecting investment.
Devereux, Keen, and Schiantarelli, 1994	1976–86	Pooled firm-level data using neoclassical and Q models allowing for tax losses.	Allowing for tax losses does not improve measured impacts of tax system on investment.
Bernstein and Shah, 1994	1966–84	Industry-level dataset for companies operating in Pakistan based on a model of the user cost of capital.	Short- and long-run impacts allowing for various policy changes. Elasticities are small but investment tax credits have the largest impact per dollar of revenue loss.

have primarily relied on aggregate time-series data. Newer studies have been using firm-level data (therefore both cross-section and time-series) with much better results given better information.

The overall conclusion one derives from recent studies is that taxes affect investment decisions, although the size of the effect is less clear. The firm-level studies find somewhat larger effects but there is still considerable controversy. For example, in Devereux, Keen, and Schiantarelli (1994), the existence of tax losses in the UK did not affect the estimated impact of taxes on investment even though one would expect differences between taxpaying and non-taxpaying companies in terms of their reaction. Investment studies require future effort to incorporate several issues.

First, investment is modelled under the assumption that financing of capital is independent of investment. Yet one would expect a simultaneity between financial and investment decisions for several reasons. Some firms may be constrained in terms of liquidity, so investment projects may be adopted only if sufficient internal sources of funds are available. Also, some types of capital, such as structures and land, may be more easily financed by debt that can use the capital as collateral.

Second, the incorporation of expectations about the future has always plagued investment studies. Although the Q and Euler equation approaches have achieved some success at incorporating the expectations about future variables in the models, they still rely on specific *ad hoc* assumptions such as quadratic adjustment costs for investment.

Third, government decision-making is assumed to be exogenous in most investment models. However, in principle, governments react to changes in the economy such as providing temporary investment tax credits during recessionary periods. If firms anticipate changes in government decisions, then one should model not only investment behaviour but also government behaviour to obtain a better understanding of investment and taxes.

Finally, the analysis of taxation requires good data. The most difficult problem often faced by researchers is that specific tax data on firms, such as the composition of depreciation allowances (by type of asset), the use of tax loss carry-forward and carry-back provisions, and information on more intricate aspects of tax law (such as capitalised expenses in construction or local government taxes), probably result in biased estimates of coefficients (perhaps towards smaller values) for tax variable terms.

4. Taxes and Financing

Corporate taxes are expected to affect financial decisions of firms as investment can be funded by bonds, new equity issues, financial leases, accounts payable, or undistributed profits (retained earnings). Given the deductibility of interest as an expense under the corporate income tax, the tax system may be expected to encourage companies to finance investment with debt. However, corporate financial decisions also depend on the other parts of the tax system that might influence financing, such as personal taxes on capital income and financial transaction taxes. As pointed out in Section 3, the effect of corporate taxation on investment in part depends on how financial decisions are determined.

This area of research is highly controversial, since both theoretical and empirical research have had contradictory conclusions. One of the most important contributions to the theory of finance was due to Modigliani and Miller (1958). Using a model without taxes, they argued that firms are indifferent with respect to the use of debt and equity to finance their capital expenditure. The argument is based on the notion that investors and firms face the same opportunity costs or interest rate when financing assets. If a firm issues £1 of debt in replacement of equity finance, the firm incurs additional interest costs equal to the interest for £1 of debt. Investors, however, reduce their savings in equity assets by £1, which allows them to buy £1 of bonds (and thereby earn interest income equal to the rate of interest). Thus investors are no better or worse off when the firm changes its debt policy. The Modigliani–Miller theorem suggests that a firm's value is independent of financial decisions. In a latter addendum to their paper (Modigliani and Miller, 1963), the authors consider the fact that interest payments on debt are deductible under the corporate income tax. This fact led Modigliani and Miller to a conclusion that taxes might affect financial policy of firms, although they did not consider the role of personal taxes in influencing financial policy.

To see the importance of financial decisions to investment decisions as well as the role of both corporate and personal income taxes, let us consider a simple situation in which the firm can issue either bonds or equity.[34] Suppose that the firm earns a (risk-adjusted) rate of return of Y on capital that is distributed as either equity or bond income. An investor pays corporate taxes at the rate u and personal taxes at the rate θ,[35] with

[34] The financing decision is even more complicated, since there are a number of sources of finance to firms, including retained earnings, new equity issues, collateral debt, unsubordinated debt, leasing, and accounts payable, most of which have different tax implications for firms. As pointed out, interest deductibility favours debt. Leasing may be favourable when the lessor is in a better position than the lessee to use write-offs for capital (Edwards and Mayer, 1991).

[35] As Poterba and Summers (1985) show, the effective tax rate on equity income is an average of the capital gains and dividend tax rates when firms are signalling their attributes to investors in a market. Alternatively, the effective tax rate on equity is the capital gains tax rate if retained earnings are used to finance investment, or the dividend tax rate if new equity is used to finance investment. When firms only finance capital with retained

an after-tax income of $Y(1 - u)(1 - \theta)$. If, instead, the income is paid out as interest, which is not taxed at the corporate level given its deductibility as an expense, then the after-tax earnings of the investor are $Y(1 - m)$. Assuming that the investor is indifferent between bonds and equity, it is therefore necessary for after-tax returns on assets to be the same, which implied that the tax rate on interest income should be equal to the combined corporate and personal tax on equity income: $m = u + \theta(1 - u)$. Otherwise, investors will prefer bonds if the tax rate on bonds is less than that on equity, or prefer equity if the converse is true.

If tax rates are not equal, firms seek to use those sources of finance that minimise taxes for owners. For example, if the tax rate on bond income is less than the combined corporate and personal tax on equity income, then the firm will borrow as much money as possible and invest in both real and financial assets. Such financial arbitrage implies that firms would be 100 per cent debt financed. If the tax rate on equity is less than that on bonds, the firm will issue only equity and, if possible, sell equity short and lend the funds to investors who may deduct interest payments incurred for investments that are expected to earn a profit.

In the above discussion, it is assumed that financial arbitrage requires the gross-of-tax rate of return (i.e. Y) to be the same across the assets, and the net-of-tax rate of return (i.e. $Y(1 - m) = Y(1 - u)(1 - \theta)$) to be the same across the assets. The former case is referred to as 'firm-level arbitrage' and the latter as 'household arbitrage'.[36] There is even a third arbitrage, which is that firms are indifferent between the net-of-corporate-tax cost of debt and equity finance. Using equation (5), the tax cost for debt is $i(1 - u)$ and for equity finance it is ρ. If the firm is indifferent between these two costs, then $i(1 - u) = \rho$.

Which investor tax rates are relevant to measuring the cost of capital and the effective tax rate is difficult to determine. As discussed above, given the progressivity of the income tax system, investor tax rates depend on income. Thus low-income investors may prefer to hold bonds, since they may face a low rate of personal tax on interest relative to the combined corporate and personal tax rate on equity ($m < u + \theta(1 - u)$). High-income investors may prefer equity (if $m > u + \theta(1 - u)$).

All this is further complicated by the presence of multiple corporate tax rates within a country (some types of industries might be taxed at

earnings, dividends are simply a payment in excess of the financial needs of the company. Dividend taxes therefore have no impact on the firm since the dividends are effectively lump-sum payments to investors and the taxes are capitalised in the value of the firm.

[36] King and Fullerton (1984) refer to firm-level arbitrage as the 'fixed p' case and household arbitrage as the 'fixed s' case.

lower statutory tax rates than others), the operation of financial intermediaries (financial institutions, insurance companies, and tax-exempt
pension plans) and, as already mentioned in Section 3, the openness of
markets to foreign investors. Thus the tax rates on investors (m and θ)
and the corporate tax rate (u) may all differ for each type of firm,
depending on the location of the firm and its ownership.

To sort out how taxes might influence financial decisions, models have
been developed to explain the behaviour of financial and investment
markets. Models can be grouped into three types (Myers, 1984):

- *Tax arbitrage models.* One set of models that deal with taxes and
  finance assume that investors and firms determine financial decisions so as to eliminate any differences in tax rates across investors
  or types of investment, so that the Modigliani–Miller theorem is
  restored. For example, in Miller (1977), firms are able to issue as
  much debt or equity as they wish. Individual investors are constrained from borrowing or selling assets short. Under Miller's equilibrium, some marginal investor is indifferent between holding
  equity and debt (for this investor, $m = u + \theta(1 - u)$) while other
  individuals, who are constrained, seek to own as much of an asset as
  possible. Thus low-income individuals or tax-exempt entities such
  as pension plans would invest only in bonds while upper-income
  individuals would only own equity. Firms, however, would seek
  marginal sources of finance from unconstrained investors, who
  would earn the same after-tax rate of return on investments.
  Moreover, individuals will trade assets affecting their taxable
  income, so that differences in tax rates across investors can be
  reduced. Gordon (1986) shows how the Miller model can be applied
  at the international level, which requires one to consider the determination of international exchange rates in the presence of taxes.
- *Static trade-off models.* Static trade-off models suggest firms will
  choose an optimal mix of debt and equity finance but will trade off
  tax benefits with other costs that affect financing. These costs might
  include bankruptcy costs and other transaction costs. In these models, the optimal mix of debt and equity is determined where the tax
  benefit of issuing debt (when $m < u + \theta(1 - u)$) is offset by the
  incremental cost of issuing debt. The implication of these models is
  that the debt to asset ratio, β in equation (5), is optimally determined so that the marginal interest cost (net of corporate taxes),
  which reflects anticipated bankruptcy and other transaction costs, is
  equal to the cost of equity finance. Under the additional assumption

that firms operate with constant returns to scale, one can show that the debt-to-asset ratio is independent of the firm's capital stock and that the firm's weighted average cost of finance (equation (5)) would be used to determine the cost of capital. Thus one can justify a two-stage procedure whereby, the first stage, financing is chosen to minimise the cost of finance and, in the second stage, firms optimally choose their capital stock.

There are several different arguments given for the static trade-off models, two of the most important being related to tax losses and bankruptcy costs.

Tax losses. In DeAngelo and Masulis (1980), firms, facing uncertainty in future returns, trade off the tax benefit of issuing debt when the firm is taxpaying (due to the deductibility of interest expense) with the tax cost of losing corporate tax write-offs should the firm become non-taxpaying. Intuitively, firms issue debt until the personal tax rate on interest income, m, is equal to the expected corporate and personal tax rate on equity income (the expected corporate tax rate is the probability of the firm paying corporate taxes times the corporate tax).[37]

Bankruptcy costs. Several models with bankruptcy costs (Stiglitz, 1972; Stapleton, 1975) have shown that firms will choose an optimal debt policy, trading off the tax benefits of issuing debt with the bankruptcy costs of issuing debt. Bankruptcy costs are real costs such as legal and trustee fees and lost sales resulting from the reorganisation or selling-off of assets of a firm (Altman, 1984). However, as Webb (1983) has shown, investors also face bankruptcy costs. One can restore the Modigliani–Miller theorem by allowing for personal bankruptcy costs that offset the bankruptcy costs of firms.

In a number of empirical studies (for example, Kim (1978)), it was found that the variance of returns affects the financial policy of firms. This would be consistent with the explanations used by static

---

[37] The usual interpretation of the DeAngelo and Masulis model is that the cost of issuing debt results from a firm losing the tax value of fast depreciation deductions or investment tax credits when it becomes non-taxpaying. This is actually the wrong interpretation. As long as there is some reason that corporate income can become negative for tax reasons (for example, when nominal interest expenses are deductible), the firm, when issuing more debt, increases the probability of becoming non-taxpaying so that the only tax on equity income is the personal tax rate on capital gains or dividends which is less than the tax rate on interest income. An optimal debt decision is achieved which trades off the excess tax cost on equity income in taxpaying situations with the excess personal tax costs of issuing bonds when the firm is not paying corporate taxes.

trade-off models. It has also been found that firms that are taxpaying or are able to flow out tax losses to investors under partnership arrangements may be more highly debt financed (Mackie-Mason, 1990a; Gentry, 1994). Also, it was found by Bartholdy, Fisher, and Mintz (1987) that a one-point increase in the statutory corporate income tax rate resulted in almost a three-quarter-point increase in the debt/asset ratio of Canadian-controlled companies.

- *Pecking-order models.* The pecking-order model, as discussed by Myers (1984), predicts that firms finance capital by exhausting the cheapest source of finance before going on to their next more costly source. The least-cost source of finance is retained earnings (cash) followed by risky debt and new equity issues. Thus the financial policy of the firm depends on the accumulated past earnings of the firm as well as its current investment needs: those firms with few reserves or large capital demands would require more finance in the form of debt and new equity than would those with 'deep pockets' of cash reserves or less capital demand.

What are the economic reasons for the pecking-order model? In the past number of years, theories related to informational problems have been developed to explain why firms may be reluctant to seek sources of finance from 'outside' investors who have less knowledge about a firm than 'inside' investors (important contributions include Myers and Majluf (1984) and Miller and Rock (1985)). The lack of knowledge may result from outside investors not being able to judge the quality of projects to be undertaken by the firm or adverse selection (Akerlof, 1970) or be due to moral hazard whereby entrepreneurial actions can affect the expected value of the firm's profits. In the case of lack of knowledge about inside investor opportunities, firms when selling securities to the market find that the security prices reflect the market's perception of the firm's investment opportunity. Owing to the lack of information available to shareholders, share prices reflect the anticipated average quality of investments rather than the true quality firms by using a signal for quality (for example, dividend policy or debt/equity ratios) or investors can screen firms so better managers reveal their true behaviour (for example, use of bond covenants), the high-quality firms will be reluctant to sell shares in the market since the prices of shares held by existing informed shareholders are bid down to a lower level. Thus the sale of equity and risky bonds by firms reduces the value of the firm in the market. This leads to 'bad' firms chasing out 'good' firms so that, in the extreme, the market believes only bad firms would ever issue equity or risky bonds.

For general problems of informational imperfections, it is possible for good prospects to separate themselves from bad prospects by using a signal or for investors to use a screen as an indicator of quality that would be too costly for bad agents to duplicate. In the case of firms signalling quality about their projects, the amount of debt relative to equity may serve as a signal (Ross, 1977; Leland and Pyle, 1977). Since higher-quality firms are able to issue debt incurring lower bankruptcy and agency costs than low-quality firms, one would observe higher-quality firms with greater debt to equity ratios. However, to the extent that high-quality firms must issue debt to finance investment, they would bid down their value, thereby giving up potentially worthwhile investments or, in other words, underinvest in capital compared with a situation with no informational asymmetries. The problem with this theory is that firms may not issue dividends, since it forces firms to borrow more at a higher cost from markets. Yet dividend policy itself can be a signal about the value of the firm.[38] If dividends serve as a costly signal (due to dividends being more highly taxed than capital gains arising from retentions at the personal level), then higher-quality firms should issue more dividends than lower-quality firms, implying that they finance capital with more capital raised from the market. Brennan and Kraus (1987) and Constantinides and Grundy (1989) use signalling arguments to question the 'pecking-order hypothesis' by suggesting that a richer set of financial choices, rather than simply debt and equity, would result in firms overcoming informational problems in markets.

In a model with informational asymmetries between inside and outside investors, corporate tax policy has two effects. The first is the standard one: taxes, through the cost of capital, discourage investment and, given the deductibility of interest expense, may encourage debt financing. The second effect is through the current cash position of the firm. If taxes reduce the cash flow that is available to firms to finance investment, then investment will be ultimately affected as firms must rely on other sources of finance that are more costly to raise from the market. The implication of the

---

[38] See Battacharya (1979), Miller and Rock (1985), and Bernheim and Wantz (1995) for models that deal with dividend signalling. The literature has not made clear which signals are preferred by firms for signalling (dividends, debt policy, new security issues, and so on).

pecking-order models is that personal taxes play little role in affecting investment decisions. Moreover, a rent tax on firms that reduce their cash may affect investment.

Several studies have successfully incorporated cash-flow constraints in explaining investment decisions (Fazarri, Hubbard and Petersen (1988), Hubbard (1990) and, for other references, Chirinko (1992)). It is suggested by these studies that upfront incentives, such as the investment tax credit, are more successful in encouraging investments than downstream incentives, such as lower corporate tax rates or accelerated depreciation.

5. Corporate Taxation and Risk

Investment is an inherently risky decision. When firms commit themselves to new capital projects, they must predict the after-tax returns on investment. These returns are uncertain, so risk, which is the aversion that investors have towards uncertainty, plays an important role in affecting capital decisions. Taxes affect the perception that investors have towards risk, so it is clearly important to determine the degree to which taxes affect the evaluation of risky investments.

When uncertainty is present, investors will balance future gains with potential losses. For example, suppose that an investor can choose a safe asset (for example, a government treasury bill) with a rate of return of 6 per cent per annum or a risky investment with an expected rate of return of 10 per cent per annum. If the investor is just as happy to invest in either asset, then the excess rate of return on the risky asset, 4 per cent, which is the difference between the expected rate of return of 10 per cent and the safe rate of return of 6 per cent, is the monetary return or *risk premium* needed to compensate the investor for risk.

Risky investment arises for a number of reasons. These include the following:

- *Income risk.* This arises from uncertainty with respect to operating income or revenues net of current costs.
- *Capital risk.* This arises from uncertain economic depreciation costs due to unknown wear and tear of capital assets or obsolescence (as future innovations that replace capital are uncertain).
- *Financial risk.* This arises from uncertainty with respect to future interest expenses incurred for borrowed funds. Financial bonds

held by investors may be risky, since firms may be unable to repay the principal and interest on loans. Investors therefore demand a higher rate of interest on bonds taking into account the risk of non-repayment of loans and interest and any associated bankruptcy costs.

- *Inflation risk*. This arises from uncertainty with respect to future inflation rates that will affect future earnings as well as the cost of replacing assets.
- *Irreversibility risk*. As capital may be irreversible (once sunk, it cannot be used for another purpose), uncertainty is increased for investors who have to be concerned about the timing of a project.
- *Political risk*. This arises from uncertainty with respect to uncertain public policies, such as tax rates.

Below, we consider how taxes influence investment in the presence of each type of risk. However, the discussion is best understood by considering some theoretical aspects of how taxes and risk interact.

5.1. Taxation and risk: theory

To understand how taxes may interact with different types of risk, it would be useful to provide an example similar to the one provided at the beginning of this section. Suppose an investment of £100 can earn a return of either 30 per cent or –10 per cent in the following period. Assuming that there is an equal chance of either return being earned, the expected return is 10 per cent. The standard deviation of returns[39] is equal to 20 per cent. If investors are willing to accept £1 in expected income for every £5 in the standard deviation of returns, then the monetary cost of the risk is 4 per cent in terms of the rate of return on the asset. The *risk-adjusted* return in assets is therefore equal to 6 per cent (10 per cent less 4 per cent for risk). Once adjusting for risk, an investor would be willing to hold either risky or riskless assets earning a return of 6 per cent.

Now consider income taxes levied at the rate of 25 per cent on investment returns. An important aspect of tax policy when considering risk is how the government treats losses when incurred by investors. If the

---

[39] The standard deviation is the square root of the probability-weighted sum of squared deviations around the mean ($\sigma = [p_1(x_1 - \bar{x})^2 + p_2(x_2 - \bar{x})^2]^{1/2}$ where p_i and x_i are the probability and return in the ith state respectively).

income tax provides for *full refundability* or a *full loss offset* when losses are incurred, the government issues a cheque equal to its share of losses determined by the rate of tax (in this example, a 25 per cent refund of any losses incurred by the investor). Anything less would be an imperfect loss offset or partial refundability.

At the tax rate of 25 per cent and full refundability, the after-tax rate of return for the investment is 22.5 per cent (when profitable) and −7.5 per cent (when unprofitable). The expected after-tax rate of return on the investment, given that each return is equally possible, is 7.5 per cent and the standard deviation of returns is 15 per cent. One may note that both the expected return and standard deviation are reduced by 25 per cent, which is equal to the tax rate on income. The cost of risk is now 3 per cent (assuming that the investor still likes to have £1 of income to compensate him for £5 in the standard deviation),[40] so the after-tax risk-adjusted rate of return on the investment is 4.5 per cent. Note that if the return on a safe asset that earns a before-tax rate of return of 6 per cent is also taxed at a rate of 25 per cent, then its after-tax rate of return is 4.5 per cent as well. Thus the rates of return on both the risky and riskless assets remain equal to each other, so that the income tax with a full loss offset has no direct impact on relative rates of return. In this sense, a tax system with full refundability is neutral with respect to risk. Implicitly, full refundability of losses allows investors to deduct fully the cost of risk from the tax base so that neutrality is maintained (Mintz, 1982; Gordon, 1985; Gordon and Wilson, 1991).

When governments do not fully refund losses, the tax system can dramatically increase the cost of risk associated with investment. When there is no loss offset at all, the investor earns an after-tax rate of return of either 22.5 per cent or −10 per cent. The expected rate of return on the investment is 6.25 per cent. Thus the income tax at a rate of 25 per cent and with no refundability reduces the expected rate of return by a rate of 37.5 per cent and the standard deviation by only 18.75 per cent. Assuming again that the investor needs £1 in expected income to offset £5 in standard deviation, the risk-adjusted after-tax rate of return on the investment is only 2.5 per cent. This rate of return is far less than the after-tax rate of return of 4.5 per cent of the riskless investment. When

---

[40] We assume that income or wealth does not affect the investor's evaluation of the cost of uncertainty relative to expected returns. As stressed in the literature, taxes that reduce income or wealth could make individuals more averse to risk by requiring a greater amount of income to compensate for risk (Domar and Musgrave, 1944; Mossin, 1968; Stiglitz, 1969).

there is no full refundability, the tax system clearly discourages risky investment.

Under current corporate income tax systems, losses are only partly refundable. Governments may allow losses to be carried back or carried forward for a limited period (in the case of the UK, losses are carried forward indefinitely). When a current year's losses are carried back, the loss is applied against profits earned in qualifying past years, resulting in a refund of corporate taxes. Alternatively, when losses are carried forward, the losses are applied against profits of qualifying future years, resulting in a reduction in future corporate income taxes. However, the losses are not carried forward at a rate of interest, so that the present value of losses is subsequently reduced by the number of years needed to use them against future profits. If losses cannot be used within the qualifying number of years, they then expire without refundability.

At best, therefore, governments permit only a partial refundability of losses. Given the dynamic nature of investment, the presence of carry-backs and carry-forwards complicates considerably the analysis used to model the impact of taxes on risky investments (see Auerbach (1986) and Mayer (1986)). For example, accumulated losses in current years can help shelter taxes on future investments, thereby reducing the amount of tax to be paid on future income generated by marginal investment decisions. Similarly, current taxable profits may be used to absorb future losses, thereby reducing the amount of tax to be paid on current losses (Altshuler and Auerbach, 1990). Thus at each point of time, the effective tax paid on an investment will vary according to the history of the company.

5.2. Taxation, risk, and the cost of investment

As discussed above, there are several sources of risk that affect investment decisions. The effect of taxes in the presence of each type of risk on investment decisions largely depends on the degree to which losses are refundable. As shown above, when losses are not refundable, the impact of taxes is to discriminate against risky investments.

- *Income risk.* When losses are fully refundable, taxes do not impact on the cost of capital in the presence of income risk.[41] However, when losses are not refundable, risky investments are discouraged, as shown in the example above. Tax rates vary depending on the

---

[41] It is assumed that capital is reversible, a point that we turn to later.

history of the firm—effective tax rates are lowest when firms have past losses that shelter income taxation and are highest when firms are starting up or future profits are highly uncertain (Mintz, 1988).

- *Capital risk.* When firms face capital risk, the tax system could penalise risky investments, since governments do not share the gains and losses arising from uncertain economic depreciation (Bulow and Summers, 1984). Under most tax systems, depreciation allowances are based on the historical rather than the replacement cost of investment. Thus the tax depreciation allowances will be too little (generous) when economic depreciation is more (less) costly than expected. Taxes will generally increase the cost of risky capital investments unless tax depreciation allowances and other write-offs (such as investment tax credits) are so generous that the tax system subsidises the replacement cost of investment (McKenzie and Mintz, 1992).

- *Financial risk.* As financial risk increases the cost of borrowed funds for firms, such costs are deductible from corporate income for tax purposes. Thus the tax system provides an implicit deduction for such risks. However, certain costs upon bankruptcy may not be deductible since no income is available to absorb tax losses. Thus the existing asset holders may find that some expenses associated with bankruptcy will not be deductible which, if anticipated, will result in higher interest payments demanded for loans.

- *Inflation risk.* When a tax is fully indexed for inflation as found in a number of Latin American countries, taxes will not affect the risk associated with uncertain inflation rates. However, without indexation, taxes will affect inflation risk faced by firms. Conceptually, the effect of taxes in the presence of inflation risk is similar to the results arising from the lack of inflation accounting for tax purposes. Uncertain inflation affects the future income of businesses, the replacement cost of assets, and inflation-adjusted interest expenses. For example, when inflation is higher than expected, the firm will earn greater profits (which are taxed unless the firm is in a loss position), incur higher replacement cost for assets (which are not accounted for by historical tax depreciation allowances), and incur a capital gain resulting from a lower real value of debt liabilities. The first two impacts of inflation on income and capital costs would increase the tax penalty on capital, while the latter impact on real debt liabilities would lower the effect of inflation on capital costs. The net effect depends on the degree to which firms finance capital with debt.

- *Irreversibility risk.* When capital investments are irreversible, firms face an additional cost associated with the inflexibility of capital (Nickell, 1978; Dixit and Pindyck, 1993). Similarly to the case of capital risk, taxes can increase the cost of irreversible investment, since the cost of inflexibility is not deductible from the corporate income tax base (see Mackie-Mason (1990b) and McKenzie (1994)).

  This point can be illustrated as follows. Using our previous example, suppose that an investment could either[42] (i) be undertaken immediately, thereby earning either a 30 per cent or −10 per cent rate of return with equal chance in the future, or a risk-adjusted return of 6 per cent (the expected return is 10 per cent), or (ii) be delayed one year so that the investment is made knowing a certain 8 per cent rate of return is realised, otherwise no investment is made as the return will be negative.

  Given that capital, once invested, is irreversible, there is a clear gain to the firm to delay implementing the project. The *option* value of delaying the project is the difference between the return on capital by postponing the investment by one period compared with the risk-adjusted return on capital by immediately investing in capital. In other words, a firm would be willing to pay a price to be given the option of rejecting a project in the future should it not be profitable. In this example, the option value of the project is 2 per cent of the investment cost, which reflects the difference between the certain rate of return of 8 per cent after delaying the investment and the risk-adjusted rate of return of 6 per cent if the investment is immediately made. One can think of the option value as a cost in addition to the depreciation and financing costs for irreversible investments.

  With irreversible capital, the effect of taxes will depend on the degree of refundability. With full refundability, and as we determined earlier, the risky investment subject to a 25 per cent tax rate on returns would earn a risk-adjusted return of 4.5 per cent. By delaying one year to resolve uncertainty, the after-tax return would be 6 per cent. Thus, in the presence of taxes, the option value of delaying investment is 1.5 per cent of the cost of investment compared with the 2 per cent option value without taxes.

  When there is no refundability, the risk-adjusted return on investment made immediately would be 2.5 per cent, as determined earlier. Given that delaying the investment would allow the firm to

---

[42] Returns are expressed by taking into account timing differences.

earn a 6 per cent return, then the option value of flexible investments is equal to 3.5 per cent of the investment cost in the presence of taxes rather than 2 per cent without taxes. Thus the option cost of irreversible investment is higher in the presence of non-refundable taxes.

In recent work (McKenzie, 1994), the effective tax rate on irreversible capital has been estimated. In the presence of risk, the effective tax rate is calculated by subtracting the riskless net-of-tax return on capital from the gross rate of return on capital (and dividing the difference by either the risk-adjusted gross or net rate of return on capital). To adjust the gross rate of return on capital for risk, the cost of risk in addition to economic depreciation must be subtracted from the cost of capital. McKenzie estimates effective tax rates for Canada and finds that, in aggregate, the 1992 effective tax rate on riskless reversible investments is 32 per cent, on reversible risky investments is 42 per cent and on risky irreversible investments is 48 per cent when the variability in future income is as high as 10 per cent. Thus the incorporation of risk can significantly affect the effective tax rate. Without more precise estimates of risk, it is difficult to determine the total impact of the tax system on investment (Shoven and Topper, 1992).

- *Political risk.* Policy decisions made by governments can affect the riskiness of investments in three ways.

First, when firms anticipate tax changes, the cost of capital is affected by both current and future tax policy variables. For example, if corporate tax rates are reduced, firms are better off purchasing capital in the current period (when the deductions for expenses are at a high rate of tax) and delaying the earning of income until after the tax rate is lowered. As discussed above, the tax holiday is an example in which tax policies are anticipated to change. The incorporation of changes in tax rates or depreciation rates requires one to consider the time variation in the present value of depreciation allowances.[43]

Second, uncertainty about government policy implies that tax rates and allowances will add to the riskiness of investment. Political risk in terms of future tax policies generally increases the cost of capital.

Third, in the case of irreversible investment, uncertainty of tax policy adds to the option cost of undertaking projects that require

---

[43] See Auerbach and Hassett (1992), who provide explicit formulas for the cost of capital when tax rates change.

capital to be sunk. In addition, the presence of irreversibility adds another dimension to tax policy considerations. When capital is sunk, governments may have the irresistible urge to tax such capital at a high rate in the future.

This endogeneity of government decisions results in a problem of *time consistency* in tax policy whereby governments may wish to take actions in the future that would be different from what would be originally planned (see Kehoe (1989) and Persson and Tabellini (1992)). Once capital is sunk, taxation in future years has no effect on the use of capital. However, investors would anticipate governments taxing such capital heavily and so would fail to undertake investment currently to avoid excessive taxation in the future. Thus, to encourage investment, governments would need to commit themselves *credibly* to not increasing rates of tax on sunk capital in the future. The desire of a government to develop a reputation for not excessively taxing capital in future years may be sufficient in ensuring a commitment. Indeed, one finds that many governments often 'grandfather' old capital from changes in depreciation schedules or increases in excise tax rates. However, some governments may not last for ever, so, without worrying about reputational effects, there is an incentive to shirk from a commitment not to tax old capital unless there is some cost associated with breaking the commitment. Some of the costs that might encourage governments to commit to tax rates that are not excessive on sunk capital include increased tax competition for foreign investment, tax evasion, and concern for particular groups in society (for example, labour). If there is uncertainty about such commitments, tax policy variables will affect the risk cost faced by firms.

6. Who Pays the Corporate Tax?

An old but important question in public finance is the following: 'who pays for the corporate tax?' As discussed in the introduction to this survey, corporations are only institutions but they are favourite subjects for taxation. Yet corporations do not pay taxes—people do! So who pays the corporate tax? Are corporate taxes shifted forwards through higher consumer prices or backwards onto workers and shareholders in terms of lower factor incomes? Is the corporate tax progressive (falling more heavily on the rich) or regressive (falling more heavily on the poor)? Below, several arguments are considered only briefly.

The original contribution of Kryzaniuk and Musgrave (1963) argues that corporations shift forward taxes to consumers as higher prices (thereby lowering the real income of consumers). Their empirical work suggested that corporate after-tax rates of return on capital remain unaffected, suggesting that corporate taxes have no impact on the returns earned by shareholders. Depending on how prices are affected, the shifting forward of the corporate tax can be progressive or regressive. If necessity industries such as housing and food are more highly taxed than luxury good industries, then the corporate tax will fall more heavily on lower-income than higher-income individuals. Otherwise, the converse may be true.

In the seminal work of Harberger (1962), the corporate tax was found to fall largely on shareholders. Harberger considered an economy with labour and capital used in the production of goods offered by a capital-intensive corporate and a labour-intensive non-corporate sector. Capital and labour were freely mobile between the two sectors, although fixed in aggregate. The corporate tax was seen as an additional levy on the corporate sector (where in the USA there is no integration of corporate and personal taxes). In Harberger's model, the corporate income tax has two impacts. First, the corporate tax increases the cost of using capital in the corporate sector, thereby discouraging the use of capital and increasing the demand for labour (this is referred to as the *substitution effect*). Second, the corporate tax increases the cost of goods produced by the taxed sector relative to the untaxed sector, thereby causing the relative price of corporate goods to increase and demand to shift from the corporate to non-corporate sectors (this is referred to as the *output effect*). Given that the corporate sector is more capital-intensive, the shift in demand results in more capital relative to labour being released from the corporate sector than the labour-intensive non-corporate sector would demand. Given that these impacts reinforce each other, the corporate income tax is largely borne by shareholders and is therefore progressive.

The Harberger model is appropriate for closed economies with a fixed capital supply. In dynamic models with variable savings, corporate taxes would reduce capital demands and the amount of savings available. If savings are perfectly elastic with respect to the interest rate, the after-tax return on savings cannot adjust downwards, so corporate taxes would have to be shifted forward. Domestic savings, however, are not perfectly elastic with respect to the interest rate, so a model with dynamic considerations would suggest that the corporate tax would fall in part on shareholders.

In open economies, particularly small ones, the above conclusions are subject to revision. If the interest rate faced by firms is determined by international markets and is not influenced by the domestic demand or supply of capital, the corporate tax cannot affect after-tax returns earned by shareholders. Instead, given the relative immobility of labour, especially unskilled labour, at the international level, the corporate tax will be shifted back on fixed factors (labour and Land). For a small open economy, this implies that the corporate tax could be regressive, especially if lower-paid unskilled workers must bear the brunt of the corporate tax.

There is little economic evidence that can be used to answer the question 'who pays the corporate tax?'. Economic studies on the incidence of taxes will use various assumptions to analyse the impact of the corporate tax on the distribution of income (Whalley, 1984) ranging from full forward shifting to backward shifting. This lack of empirical work on the distributive effects of the corporate tax is rather troubling, since the degree to which corporations are taxed is one of the most important political issues to be found in many industrialised countries.

7. Conclusions

This survey provides an extensive discussion of several topics related to corporate taxation. The topics include: (i) policy objectives, (ii) investment effects, (iii) financing of firms, (iv) risk, and (v) distributive effects.

Yet this survey is not nearly exhaustive enough, since several important topics have not been considered. There has been little discussion of the impact of corporate taxation on inbound and outbound investment, and recent work on the taxation of international capital flows has not received attention here. Questions regarding competition for capital flows and policy harmonisation in an international framework, and the efficiency aspects of corporate tax (especially in an open economy), have also not been considered. Neither have the compliance costs of corporate tax.

Economists, however, have come a long way in the past several decades in understanding the function and effects of the corporate tax. As indicated by the many issues raised by this survey, the corporate tax will remain an exciting topic for analysts for some time to come.

References

Akerlof, G. (1970), 'The market for "lemons": quality and the market mechanism', *Quarterly Journal of Economics*, vol. 84, pp. 488–500.

Altman, E. (1984), 'A further empirical investigation of the bankruptcy cost question', *Journal of Finance*, vol. 39, pp. 1067–89.

Altshuler, R., and Auerbach, A. (1990), 'The importance of tax law asymmetries: an empirical investigation', *Quarterly Journal of Economics*, vol. 105, pp. 61–86.

Atkinson, A., and Stiglitz, J. (1980), *Lectures on Public Economics*, London: McGraw Hill.

Auerbach, A. (1979), 'Wealth maximization and the cost of capital', *Quarterly Journal of Economics*, vol. 93, pp. 433–46.

—— (1983), 'Corporate taxation in the United States', *Brookings Papers on Economic Activity*, vol. 2, pp. 451–505.

—— (1986), 'The dynamic effects of tax law asymmetries', *Review of Economic Studies*, vol. 53, pp. 205–26.

—— (1991), 'Retrospective capital gains taxation', American Economic Review, vol. 81, pp. 167–78.

—— and Hassett, K. (1992), 'Tax policy and business fixed investment in the United States', *Journal of Public Economics*, vol. 47, pp. 141–70.

Bartholdy, J., Fisher, G., and Mintz, J. (1987), 'Taxation and financial policy of firms: theory and empirical application to Canada', Economic Council of Canada, Discussion Paper no. 324.

Battacharya, S. (1979), 'Imperfect information, dividend policy and the "bird in the hand" fallacy', *Bell Journal of Economics*, vol. 10, pp. 259–70.

Bernheim, B., and Wantz, A. (1995), 'A tax-based test of the dividend signalling hypothesis', *American Economic Review*, vol. 85, pp. 532–51.

Bernstein, J., and Nadiri, M. (1987), 'Corporate taxes and incentives and the structure of production: a selected survey', in J. Mintz and D. Purvis (eds.), *The Impact of Taxation on Business Activity*, Kingston, Ontario: John Deutsch Institute for the Study of Economic Policy.

—— and Shah, A. (1994), 'Taxes and production: the case of Pakistan', *International Tax and Public Finance*, vol. 1, pp. 227–43.

Blundell, R., Bond, S., Devereux, M., and Schiantarelli, F. (1992), 'Investment and Tobin's Q: evidence from company panel data', *Journal of Econometrics*, vol. 51, pp. 233–58.

Boadway, R., and Bruce, N. (1984), 'A general proposition on the design of a neutral business tax', *Journal of Public Economics*, vol. 24, pp. 231–9.

—— —— (1992), 'Problems with integrating corporate and personal income taxes in an open economy', *Journal of Public Economics*, vol. 48, pp. 39–66.

—— —— and Mintz, J. (1982), 'Corporate taxation and the cost of holding inventories', *Canadian Journal of Economics*, vol. 25, pp. 278–93.

—— —— —— (1984), 'Taxation, inflation, and the effective marginal tax rate in Canada', *Canadian Journal of Economics*, vol. 27, pp. 286–99.

—— —— —— (1987), *Capital Income Taxes in Canada: Analysis and Policy*, Toronto: Canadian Tax Foundation.

—— —— McKenzie, K., and Mintz, J. (1987), 'The effective tax rates on mining industries', *Canadian Journal of Economics*, vol. 30, pp. 1–17.

Bovenberg, A., Andersson, K., Aramhi, K., and Chand, K. (1990), 'Tax incentives and international capital flows', in A. Razin and J. Slemrod (eds.), *Taxation in the Global Economy*, Chicago: University of Chicago Press.

Bradford, D. (1986), *Untangling the Income Tax*, Cambridge: Harvard University Press.

Brainard, W., and Tobin, J. (1968), 'Pitfalls in financial model building', *American Economic Review*, vol. 58, pp. 99–122.

Brennan, M., and Kraus, A. (1987), 'Efficient financing under asymmetric information', *Journal of Finance*, vol. 42, pp. 1225–43.

Bulow, J., and Summers, L. (1984), 'The taxation of risky assets', *Journal of Political Economy*, vol. 92, pp. 20–39.

Burgess, D. (1988), 'On the relevance of export demand conditions for capital income taxation in open economies', *Canadian Journal of Economics*, vol. 21, pp. 285–311.

Canada: Department of Finance (1994), Economic Reference Tables, Ottawa.

Capital Taxes Group (1991), *Equity for Companies: A Corporation Tax for the 1990s*, London: Institute for Fiscal Studies.

Chen, D., and Mintz, J. (1993), 'Taxation of capital in Ontario and Canada: an interindustry and interprovincial comparison', in A. Maslove (ed.), *Business Taxation in Ontario*, Toronto: University of Toronto Press.

—— —— (1995), 'The impact of the corporate minimum tax on new investment', Ontario Ministry of Finance, forthcoming.

Chirinko, R. (1987), 'The ineffectiveness of effective tax rates on business investment: a critique of Feldstein's Fisher–Schultz Lecture', *Journal of Public Economics*, vol. 32, pp. 369–87.

—— (1992), 'Business fixed investment spending: a critical survey of modeling strategies, empirical results, and policy implications', University of Munich, Centre for Economic Studies, Working Paper no. 27.

—— and Eisner, R. (1983), 'Tax policy and investment in major US macroeconometric models', *Journal of Public Economics*, vol. 20, pp. 139–66.

Clark, J. (1917), 'Business acceleration and the law of demand: a technical factor in economic cycles', *Journal of Political Economy*, vol. 25, pp. 217–35.

Cnossen, S. (1993), 'What kind of corporation tax?', International Bureau of Fiscal Documentation, *Bulletin*, pp. 3–16.

Constantinides, G., and Grundy, B. (1989), 'Optimal investment with stock repurchase and financing as signals', *Review of Financial Studies*, vol. 2, pp. 445–66.

Davies, J., and Glenday, G. (1990), 'Accrual equivalent marginal tax rates for personal financial assets', *Canadian Journal of Economics*, vol. 13, pp. 189–202.

DeAngelo, H., and Masulis, R. (1980), 'Optimal capital structure under corporate and personal taxation', *Journal of Financial Economics*, vol. 8, pp. 3–29.

Devereux, M. P. (1989), 'Tax asymmetries, the cost of capital and investment', *Economic Journal*, vol. 99, pp. 103–12.

—— and Freeman, H. (1991), 'A general neutral profits tax', *Fiscal Studies*, vol. 12, no. 3, pp. 1–15.

—— —— (1995), 'The impact of tax on foreign direct investment: empirical evidence and the implications for tax integration schemes', *International Tax and Public Finance*, vol. 2, pp. 85–106.

—— Keen, M., and Schiantarelli, F. (1994), 'Corporation tax asymmetries and investment: evidence from UK panel data', *Journal of Public Economics*, vol. 53, pp. 395–418.

Diamond, P., and Mirrlees, J. (1971), 'Optimal taxation and public production I: production efficiency' and 'II: tax rules', *American Economic Review*, vol. 61, pp. 8–27, 261–78.

Diewert, W. (1987), 'Comment: corporate tax incentives and the structure of production', in J. Mintz and D. Purvis (eds.), *The Impact of Taxation on Business Activity*, Kingston, Ontario: John Deutsch Institute for the Study of Economic Policy.

Dixit, A., and Pindyck, R. (1993), *Investment under Uncertainty*, Princeton, New Jersey: Princeton University Press.

Domar, F., and Musgrave, R. (1944), 'Proportional income taxation and risk-taking', *Quarterly Journal of Economics*, vol. 58, pp. 382–422.

Edey, M., and Hviding, K. (1995), 'An assessment of financial reform in OECD countries', Organisation for Economic Co-operation and Development, Economics Department, Working Paper no. 154.

Edwards, J., and Mayer, C. (1991), 'Leasing, taxes and the cost of capital', *Journal of Public Economics*, vol. 44, pp. 173–97.

Estache, A. (1995), 'Evaluating the asset based minimum tax on corporations: an option pricing approach', mimeo, World Bank.

Fazarri, S., Hubbard, R., and Petersen, B. (1988), 'Financing constraints and corporate investments', *Brookings Papers on Economic Activity*, vol. 1, pp. 141–95.

Feldstein, M. (1982), 'Inflation, tax rules and investment: some econometric evidence', *Econometrica*, vol. 50, pp. 825–62.

—— and Horioka, C. (1981), 'Domestic savings and international capital flows', *Economic Journal*, vol. 90, pp. 314–29.

French, K., and Poterba, J. (1991), 'Investor diversification and international equity markets', National Bureau of Economic Research, Working Paper no. 3609.

Frenkel, J., and Razin, A. (1987), *Fiscal Policy and the World Economy: An Intertemporal Approach*, Cambridge: MIT Press.

Gentry, W. (1994), 'Taxes, financial decisions, and organization form: evidence from publicly traded partnerships', *Journal of Public Economics*, vol. 53, pp. 223–44.

George, H. (1879), *Progress and Poverty*. Reprinted 1975, New York: Robert Schalkenbach Foundation.

Gordon, R. (1985), 'Taxation of corporate capital income: tax revenues versus tax distortions', *Quarterly Journal of Economics*, vol. 100, pp. 1–28.

—— (1986), 'Taxation of investment and savings in a world economy', *American Economic Review*, vol. 76, pp. 1086–102.

—— and Varian, H. (1989), 'Taxation of asset income in the presence of a world securities market', *Journal of International Economics*, vol. 26, pp. 205–26.

—— and Wilson, J. (1991), 'Measuring the efficiency cost of taxing risky capital income', *American Economic Review*, vol. 79, pp. 427–39.

Hall, R., and Jorgenson, D. (1967), 'Tax policy and investment behavior', *American Economic Review*, vol. 57, pp. 391–414.

Harberger, A. (1962), 'The incidence of the corporation income tax', *Journal of Political Economy*, vol. 70, pp. 215–40.

Hayashi, F. (1982), 'Tobin's marginal Q and average Q: a neoclassical interpretation', *Econometrica*, vol. 50, pp. 213–24.

Helliwell, J. (1969), 'The taxation of capital gains', *Canadian Journal of Economics*, vol. 2, pp. 315–30.

Hubbard, R. (1990), *Asymmetric Information, Corporate Finance and Investment*, Chicago: University of Chicago Press.

Jorgenson, D. (1963), 'Capital theory and investment behavior', *American Economic Review*, vol. 53, pp. 247–59.

Kehoe, P. (1989), 'Policy cooperation among benevolent governments may be undesirable', *Review of Economic Studies*, vol. 56, pp. 289–96.

Keynes, J. (1936), *The General Theory of Employment, Interest and Money*, New York: Harcourt Brace.

Kim, H. (1978), 'A mean variance theory of optimal capital structure and corporate debt capacity', *Journal of Finance*, vol. 33, pp. 45–64.

King, M. (1977), *Public Policy and the Corporation*, London: Chapman & Hall.

—— and Fullerton, D. (eds.) (1984), *The Taxation of Income from Capital*, Chicago: University of Chicago Press.

Kryzaniuk, M., and Musgrave, R. (1963), *The Shifting of the Corporation Income Tax*, Baltimore: Johns Hopkins Press.

Leland, H., and Pyle, D. (1977), 'Informational asymmetries, financial structure and financial intermediation', *Journal of Finance*, vol. 32, pp. 371–88.

Lockwood, B., de Meza, D., and Myles, G. (1994), 'When are origin and destination regimes equivalent?', *International Tax and Public Finance*, vol. 1, pp. 5–24.

McKenzie, K. (1994), 'The implications of risk and irreversibility for the measurement of marginal tax rates on capital', *Canadian Journal of Economics*, vol. 27, pp. 604–19.

McKenzie, K. and Mintz, J. (1992), 'Tax effects and the cost of capital: a Canada–US comparison', in J. Shoven and J. Whalley (eds.), *Canada–US Tax Comparisons*, Chicago: University of Chicago Press.

—— —— and Scharf, K. (1993), 'Differential taxation of Canadian and US passenger transportation', in *Royal Commission on National Passenger Transportation*, vol. 4, Ottawa: Supply of Services, Canada.

Mackie-Mason, J. (1990a), 'Do taxes affect corporate financing decisions?' *Journal of Finance*, vol. 45, pp. 1471–93.

—— (1990b), 'Some nonlinear tax effects on asset values and investment decisions under uncertainty', *Journal of Public Economics*, vol. 27, pp. 301–27.

McLure, C., Jr. (1979), *Must Corporate Income Be Taxed Twice?*, Washington: Brookings Institution.

Mayer, C. (1986), 'Corporation tax, finance and the cost of capital', *Review of Economic Studies*, vol. 53, pp. 93–112.

Meade, J. (1978), *The Structure and Reform of Direct Taxation*, the Meade Report, Boston: Allen & Unwin.

Miller, M. (1977), 'Debt and taxes', *Journal of Finance*, vol. 32, pp. 261–75.

—— and Rock, K. (1985), 'Dividend policy under asymmetric information', *Journal of Finance*, vol. 40, pp. 1031–51.

Mintz, J. (1982), 'Neutral profit taxation, risk taking and optimal profit taxation', *Recherches Économiques de Louvain*, vol. 48, pp. 107–32.

—— (1990), 'Tax holidays and investment', *World Bank Economic Review*, vol. 4, pp. 81–102.

—— and Seade, J. (1991), 'Cash flow or income? The choice of the base for company taxation', *World Bank Research Observer*, pp. 177–90.

Modigliani, F., and Miller, M. (1958), 'The cost of capital, corporation finance, and the theory of investment', *American Economic Review*, vol. 48, pp. 261–97.

—— —— (1963), 'Corporate income taxes and the cost of capital: a correlation', *American Economic Review*, vol. 53, pp. 433–43.

Mossin, J. (1968), 'Taxation and risk-taking: an expected utility approach', *Economica*, vol. 35, pp. 74–82.

Myers, S. (1984), 'The capital structure puzzle', *Journal of Finance*, vol. 39, pp. 572–92.

— and Majluf, N. (1984), 'Corporate financing and investment decisions: when firms have information that investors do not have', *Journal of Financial Economics*, vol. 13, pp. 187–221.

Nickell, S. (1978), *The Investment Decisions of Firms*, New York: Cambridge University Press.

OECD (1991), *Taxing Profits in a Global Economy: Domestic and International Issues*, Paris: Organisation for Economic Co-operation and Development.

Persson, T., and Tabellini, G. (1992), 'The politics of 1992: fiscal policy and European integration', *Review of Economic Studies*, vol. 59, pp. 689–702.

Poterba, J., and Summers, L. (1983), 'Dividend taxes, corporate investment and Q', *Journal of Public Economics*, vol. 22, pp. 729–52.

—— —— (1985), 'The economic effect of dividend taxation', in E. Altman and M. Subrahmanyam (eds.), *Recent Advances in Corporate Finance*, Homewood: Dow Jones Irwin.

Ross, S. (1977), 'The determination of financial structure: the incentive signalling approach', *Bell Journal of Economics*, vol. 8, pp. 23–40.

Royal Commission on Taxation, Canada (1966), *Report*, the Carter Report, Ottawa: Queen's Printer.

Shome, P., and Schutte, C. (1993), 'Cash-flow tax', *IMF Staff Papers*, vol. 40, pp. 638–62.

Shoven, J., and Topper, M. (1992), 'The cost of capital in Canada, the United States and Japan', in J. Shoven and J. Whalley (eds.), *Canada–US Tax Comparisons*, Chicago: University of Chicago Press.

Simons, H. (1938), *Personal Income Taxation*, Chicago: University of Chicago Press.

Stapleton, R. (1975), 'Some aspects of the pure theory of corporate finance, bankruptcies and takeovers: comment', *Bell Journal of Economics*, vol. 5, pp. 707–10.

Stiglitz, J. (1969), 'The effects of income, wealth and capital gains on risk-taking', *Quarterly Journal of Economics*, vol. 83, pp. 262–83.

—— (1972), 'Some aspects of the pure theory of corporate finance, bankruptcies and takeovers', *Bell Journal of Economics*, vol. 2, pp. 458–82.

Summers, L. (1981), 'Taxation and corporate investment: a Q-theory approach', *Brookings Papers on Economic Activity*, vol. 1, pp. 67–127.

—— (1986), 'Tax policy and international competitiveness', National Bureau of Economic Research, Working Paper no. 2007.

US Treasury (1977), *Blueprints for Basic Tax Reform*, Washington: Government Printing House.

—— (1992), *Integration of the Individual and Corporate Tax Systems: Taxing Business Income Once*, Washington: US Government Printing Office.

Webb, D. (1983), 'Contingent claims, personal loans and the irrelevance of corporate financial structure', *Economic Journal*, vol. 93, pp. 832–46.

Whalley, J. (1984), 'Regression or progression: the taxing question of incidence', *Canadian Journal of Economics*, vol. 17, pp. 654–82.

THE WELFARE ECONOMICS OF
TAX COORDINATION IN THE
EUROPEAN COMMUNITY

....

MICHAEL KEEN

International considerations have become increasingly prominent in the analysis and formulation of tax policy. The European dimension, in particular, now pervades almost all areas of taxation in the UK. The purpose of this survey is to raise some of the principal tax issues currently at stake in the European Community (EC), and to describe some of the main tools for thinking about them. The coverage is selective. Institutional detail and administrative issues are discussed only in so far as they raise concerns of deeper economic significance. The focus, moreover, is on welfare aspects of international tax coordination: on the design, that is, of tax arrangements most conducive to economic well-being. Even within this, the focus is narrowed: questions of distributional policy within Member States, in particular, receive less attention than questions of efficiency in relationships between them. This restricted view is intended to bring out more clearly the distinctive issues that arise when the international context of tax policy is recognised; issues that are as yet relatively unfamiliar, but which seem likely to become more pressing in the years ahead.

Section 2 provides general background, with a brief discussion of the general significance for tax design of the single market programme. The bulk of the chapter then addresses the two areas of tax policy in which

I am grateful to Michael Devereux for advice and encouragement in the writing of this chapter, which draws in part on Keen (1990a). Errors and views are mine.

The fundamental tax policy issues facing the European Union have not greatly changed since this chapter appeared in 1993, nor has their institutional context. The text has, therefore, been left essentially unaltered, though I have taken the opportunity to correct some slips and to update information on the references given initially.

First published in *Fiscal Studies* (1993), vol. 14, no. 12, pp. 15–36.

international concerns have, as yet, been most felt: indirect taxation (Section 3) and the taxation of capital income (Section 4).[1] Section 5 briefly concludes.

2. Taxation and the Single Market

Completion of the internal market—and the increasing internationalisation of economic activity more generally—has broadly three kinds of implication for the tax policies of Member States. It imposes formal obligations, tightens informal constraints, and presents opportunities. The obligations are from the Single European Act, which committed Member States to establish, by the start of 1993, '. . . an area without internal frontiers in which the free movement of goods, persons, services and capital is ensured'. While thus implicitly accepting the need for such domestic reforms as this requires, Member States have given up none of their formal sovereignty in tax affairs: taxation is one of the few areas in which each retains veto power. But, however undiminished their formal authority, international integration brings restrictions on member States' effective autonomy in tax matters: free movement of commodities and factors means, in large measure, free movement of their tax bases. In imposing additional constraints on governments in designing their tax systems, one would generally expect the outcome to be worse. The vast differences across Member States in the rate at which they tax cigarettes, for instance, presumably reflect differing priorities in health and distributional policies. To the extent that freer movement of goods reduces the sustainability of such differentials, Member States will perceive real social costs. But there are also opportunities. These come from the prospect of coordinating national policies so as to improve the allocation of the Community's resources. Coordination of tax policies is not the same thing, of course, as centralisation of all tax decisions. That would almost certainly be as unwise as a matter of economic principle as it is unthinkable politically, at least for the foreseeable future. The suggestion is rather that there may exist collective gains from limited measures of harmonisation in particular areas or, more flexibly still, from mutual adherence to some simple rules in tax-setting.

[1] Excellent accounts of these issues, with rather different emphases from the present article, are provided by Smith (1993), Sörensen (1990a) and the contributors to Kopits (1992). There are important links between indirect taxation and the taxation of capital income (Sinn, 1990); for brevity, however, these are not explored here.

These implications all stem from *fiscal externalities* between Member States: from spillover effects, that is, of one country's domestic tax policy on the structure of activities in others. These externalities may be embarrassingly visible, as with the petrol stations that line part of the Belgium–Luxembourg border, or with beer exported from Kent to France to be purchased by British consumers on day trips. Or they may be subtle: to the extent that Germany's exports are capital-intensive, for instance, the relatively high effective marginal tax rate on capital income there may move world prices to her advantage and the detriment of others. They may be the innocent by-product of domestic policies: the capitalisation effects of introducing tax incentives to home ownership, for example, may generate current account deficits. Or they may be the direct consequence of deliberate nationalism in tax-setting.

This last, in particular, is a real and continuing concern in the European context. Member States, being unable to use explicit tariffs against one another, are naturally tempted to use their domestic taxes to similar effect. Excises in particular are marked by what the Commission has delicately called a 'symbiotic' relationship between national tax regimes and national production patterns. The high rate of tax on wine in the UK relative to that on beer, for instance, is presumably not unconnected with the low volume of domestic wine production. The UK alone may be unable to affect the world price of wine, but the heavy tax nevertheless serves to transfer rents from foreign wine producers to Customs & Excise. Similar issues arise in the area of capital income taxation: Luxembourg gains revenue by setting noticeably low tax rates, but in doing so does not make it any easier for the French to enforce taxes on their residents.

Fiscal externalities are most important—or at the least the arbitrage they generate most visible—when, as in these examples, they operate through highly integrated markets. Coordination proposals have consequently centred on the markets for commodities and capital, and it is on these that this chapter focuses. The emphasis, as noted, will be on efficiency issues. This is not to deny the potential importance of distributional aspects of tax policy. In terms of redistribution across Member States, the central institutions of the Community—particularly the Structural Funds—already play a crucial role. In terms of redistribution within Member States, greater mobility of labour in the longer term could have profound effects on the capacity of national governments to levy taxes other than those reflecting such benefits as residency in their jurisdictions confer. When and if such a day comes, innovative tax arrangements will need to be considered. Perhaps, for instance, taxation will be on the basis of citizenship (as in the USA), with the relevant citizenship eventually shifting from that of a Member State to that of the Community. These, however, are deeper issues that we do not address here.

There is though one respect in which the efficiency issues cannot be disentangled from equity concerns. For, even if there are collective gains from the coordination of tax policies, cross-country transfers will generally be needed to ensure that the benefits are shared by all. Quite how severe a restriction this is on feasible tax reform is unclear. Certainly there are no plans for compensation to be paid explicitly in relation to domestic tax reforms, and indeed it would probably be difficult to implement (or even calculate) the compensation needed: it might be difficult for British or Danish politicians to explain or even understand, for instance, why Greece should be compensated for gaining a considerable amount of tax revenue by increasing her tax on cigarettes to a level comparable to that being paid by their constituents. Given the unanimity requirement, the restriction might then seem a serious one. But tax coordination is only one part of the Internal Market programme, opening the way for the 'Hicksian optimism' that the aggregate of a series of collectively desirable reforms will prove individually desirable; or—perhaps more reassuring—for simple horse-trading.

3. Indirect Taxation

This is the area in which coordination has progressed furthest in the EC.

3.1. The basis of taxation

There are broadly two ways in which commodities entering international trade might be brought into domestic taxation. Under the *destination principle*—the norm under GATT rules—they are taxed at the rate of (and revenue accrues to) the country in which final consumption takes place. Implementation of this requires border tax adjustments to ensure that exports leave tax free and imports enter subject to full domestic taxation. Under the *origin principle*, taxation is at the rate of (and paid to) the country of production. In the EC, the destination principle currently remains the central organising idea: this is the rationale, for instance, for the zero-rating of exports under the value-added tax (VAT) regime.

Developments since the launch of the Single Market programme in 1985, however, have raised three important issues of principle.

First, 1 January 1993 brought a significant change in the precise interpretation placed on the destination principle: with the removal of restrictions on movements of tax-paid goods for personal use, the meaning of 'final consumption' in the definition above becomes rather 'purchase for final consumption': what matters, that is, is not where enjoyment of the good takes place, but rather the place of purchase for that enjoyment. Before the start of this year, the underlying principle was that wine drunk in the UK should pay UK tax; now it is that the tax be that of the Member State in which the consumer bought it.

Second, the desire to remove physical border controls between Member States has led to a search for ways of implementing, without physical checks at frontiers, the border tax adjustments required under the destination principle. The Commission's original proposal in respect of VAT was for the abolition of zero-rating of exports, but the introduction instead of some form of clearing-house arrangement—with importers ultimately being refunded from receipts in the country of export—to achieve the same pattern of revenue receipts as under previous arrangements. At least for the present, however, zero-rating has been retained and, instead, a system (akin to postponed accounting) introduced which dispenses with border formalities. These administrative issues will not be discussed here, though they do raise interesting and substantive issues, concerning, for instance, the incentives for Member States to verify claims for refund of tax on imports (see Lee et al., 1988). It is the next, third, issue on which we shall concentrate.

This is the question of whether or not the destination principle should be retained for transactions between firms. For the present, arrangements are explicitly transitional, to be replaced at the start of 1997 by a 'definitive system . . . based in principle on taxation in the Member State of origin of the goods or services supplied'.[2] Precisely what this means seems, as yet, undecided. On a minimalist interpretation, it might simply mean some form of clearing house: a system, that is, for implementing the destination principle without remitting tax on exports. But it might mean what, at first sight, it actually seems to say: movement to an origin basis.[3] There is indeed a strong grain in the tax history of the EC—

---

[2] The Sixth VAT Directive states a similar long-term aim.

[3] More precisely, since the destination basis would be retained between the Community and the rest of the world, movement would be on a 'restricted origin' basis. For brevity, the discussion that follows abstracts from the complications that arise under such a mixed system: for a flavour of these, see Georgakopoulos and Hitiris (1992).

dating back to the Neumark Report (1963)—which favours such a move. The original reason for doing so—the ability to dispense with border tax adjustments, and hence border controls—will to a large extent be removed if the post-1993 arrangements prove successful. Nevertheless, some continue to see the origin basis as a desirable long-run objective in itself. The economics of the comparison between destination and origin bases thus deserves some attention.[4]

In the simplest case, this is a non-issue: origin and destination bases are economically equivalent.[5] To see why, suppose that some commodity (perfume, say) is taxed at 50 per cent in the UK, and at 20 per cent in Italy (both rates tax exclusive). Imagine first that the destination principle is in place, and that the price to UK consumers of a bottle of perfume is £1.50. Then both Italian and UK producers will receive a net of tax price of £1; and if the exchange rate is, say, £1 = 2,000 lire, then the after-tax price of that same bottle of perfume in tax-free Italy will be 2,000 lire (otherwise competitive producers would sell only in one of the two markets). If the origin basis is adopted instead, and tax rates remain the same, will not perfume production in the UK be wiped out? Not necessarily, for the exchange rate may change. Indeed if sterling devalues by a factor that exactly reflects the higher tax on perfume in the UK than in Italy, to £1 = (1.2)/(1.5) × 2,000 lire = 1,600 lire, then there is no reason for prices in either country to change, and hence no need for any change in the real economy: Italian producers will now receive a net of tax price in the UK of £1.50/1.2 = £1.25 (reflecting payment of tax at the Italian rate), but this is now worth 1.25 × 1,600 = 2,000 lire, and so is still exactly equivalent to the net of tax price they receive on domestic sales: there is thus no scope for Italian producers to undercut British.[6]

This equivalence result is striking. But it is also very fragile. For note that the exchange rate adjustment required in the example depended on the precise tax rates assumed: since there is only one exchange rate, if tax rates differ across commodities—as they do—it cannot adjust so as simultaneously to ensure neutrality in respect of all commodities. Uniform taxation is thus essential to the equivalence, and indeed the intuition behind the result is immediate given this assumption: a uni-

---

[4] We do not address the practical problems of implementing an origin basis VAT.

[5] See Berglas (1981) and Whalley (1979). The result itself originates with the Tinbergen Report (1953).

[6] This argument relies on exchange rate adjustment, but that is inessential: internal price and wage movements can have exactly the same effect at a fixed nominal exchange rate. In the example above, what would be needed is for prices in the UK to fall by 20 per cent (= 1 − (1.2)/(1.5)).

form destination-based tax is a tax on a country's consumption, a uniform origin-based tax a tax on its production; and the national budget constraint means these two are the same thing.[7]

As a guide to practical policy-making, the equivalence result is thus of limited value. Allowing for the possibility of tax rates differing across commodities, two questions then arise. The first is essentially positive: what would be the likely impact of shifting from destination to origin bases at unchanged tax rates? This has been addressed by, for instance, Dosser (1964) and Sinn (1989). The latter emphasises, in particular, the non-uniformity inherent in the zero rate applied to investment goods: moving to an origin basis, reallocation of production towards investment goods can then be expected in high tax countries, and reallocation towards consumption goods expected in low tax countries. As will emerge shortly, however, exercises which presume tax structures to remain invariant in the face of a change of basis may be of limited interest: strategic incentives in taxation change profoundly with a shift of base.

The second question is the normative one: which principle best suits the collective interests of the Community? Two dimensions of economic efficiency are important here: each principle satisfies one (under certain conditions) but, in general, not the other.[8] Under the destination principle, imports compete on a level footing with domestic products. Italian and Belgian producers selling identical clothes in Spain, for instance, will receive the same net price as each other and as domestic Spanish firms: none enjoys a commodity tax advantage over the others. Thus the destination principle ensures that relative producer prices are the same throughout the Community. Assuming competitive behaviour, equality of producer prices implies equality of marginal costs, which in turn implies *production efficiency*: collective output could not be reallocated across firms in such a way as to reduce the total costs of its production. Under the origin principle, in contrast, it is the prices that consumers face, rather than those received by producers, that are equated internationally: for price differentials would create an incentive for perfectly legal arbitrage, buying in low price countries to consume in high. The

---

[7] Standard statements of the equivalence result add two requirements additional to uniformity. The first is that there be perfect competition: Lockwood et al. (1994) show, however, that this can be dispensed with. The second is balanced trade: national consumption and production in any period will otherwise differ. Note though that in a representative agent model, equality between the two must hold in present value terms; equivalence, it seems reasonable to conjecture, will then continue to hold even if trade is not balanced in every period.

[8] The arguments that follow ignore transport costs, but are straightforward to amend.

consequence of this is *exchange efficiency*: equality of prices means equality across consumers of their marginal willingness to pay for goods, making it impossible to reallocate collective consumption in such a way as to make some consumers better off and none worse off. The choice thus becomes that between production efficiency (under the destination principle) and exchange efficiency (under the origin principle). The central guiding result in considering this choice is that of Diamond and Mirrlees (1971): assuming 100 per cent taxation of pure profits, perfect competition, and that there are no constraints on the tax instruments that can be deployed, an optimal tax structure will preserve production efficiency. This creates a presumption[9] for a destination-based system (with tax rates generally differing across jurisdictions in reflection, *inter alia*, of differing patterns of consumer demand).

This is a powerful result in thinking about the likely nature of the optimal fully coordinated indirect tax structure for the Community. But such a degree of cooperation—common pursuit of the collective well-being—may not be in prospect for some time. Instead, Member States seem likely to preserve substantial scope for the pursuit of their own self-interest. One must thus also consider the scope and likely nature of non-cooperative tax-setting under the two bases. Being unable to impose tariffs against one another, Member States have an incentive to find domestic tax instruments that have a similar effect. And a tariff can be exactly replicated by combining a destination-based consumption tax with an origin-based production subsidy at the same rate: such a combination will, like a tariff, raise the common price faced by domestic consumers and producers above that received by foreign suppliers. Under the destination basis, one would thus expect to see relatively heavy taxation of importables; under the origin basis, the expectation is of relatively heavy taxation of exportables.[10] The strategic incentives are thus quite different under the two bases. Which is more damaging to the collective well-being is uncertain, but—as shown by Lockwood (1992)—non-cooperative behaviour can overturn the appeal to the destination principle: the outcome under the origin basis may be preferable to that under the destination basis.

---

[9] The Diamond–Mirrlees framework does not fully capture the international aspects of the tax design problem that is relevant here, so that these remarks—and similar ones in Section 4—are in the nature of reasonable conjectures.

[10] These presumptions could be overturned in some models of imperfect competition.

3.2. Harmonisation under the destination principle

For the reasons noted at the start of Section 3.1, the Commission's proposals on rates of indirect taxation are to be seen in the context of retention of the destination principle. At the outset of the Single Market programme, the Commission's objective was 'approximation' of rates ('harmonisation' having become an un-word): not exact uniformity, but convergence within fairly narrow limits (except, that is, for excises, where—given the variation in VAT rates applied to excised goods—the Commission saw no option but uniformity). These limits, moreover—formally proposed in 1987–were explicitly chosen not as being in any sense optimal but rather as a pragmatic compromise between the positions from which Member States began. In terms of VAT, for instance, the proposal was for a reduced rate band of 4–9 per cent and a standard rate of 14–20 per cent. In 1989, the short-term strategy shifted away from targets of this sort and towards the agreement of minimum tax rates. We return to this strategy in Section 3.3. This subsection focuses on the welfare effects of approximation, which remains the long-term goal.

In terms of orthodox tax principles, approximation is at first sight a strange kind of reform: starting with a series of distortions in each country, working out the average distortion and then moving all countries closer to that average is not immediately appealing as a recipe for welfare gain. Surprisingly, it turns out that it does have attractive welfare properties.

Recall from the discussion in Section 3.1 that the only inefficiency under the destination principle is in consumption: if the tax on clothes is heavier in Spain than in Italy, for example, then, at the margin, Spanish consumers value clothes more highly than do Italian. Harmonising commodity taxes—and it is analytically easiest to focus on the extreme case in which the endpoint is full uniformity—has the merit of reducing the collective cost of these distortions.

This is illustrated in Figure 5.1. Imagine that this shows two countries with identical straight-line demand curves for some product, the world price of which is fixed at P. In country 1 the destination-based tax is initially t; in country 2 it is initially lower, at T. In the usual way, there is associated with each tax a triangle of excess burden (the amount by which the welfare lost by the consumer exceeds the revenue raised by the government): ABC in country 1, ADE in country 2. Suppose now that they harmonise their taxes at the average of T and t. Since the length L_1L is the same as L_2L—the linear demand curve implies that, since the absolute change in price is the same in the two countries, so too is the

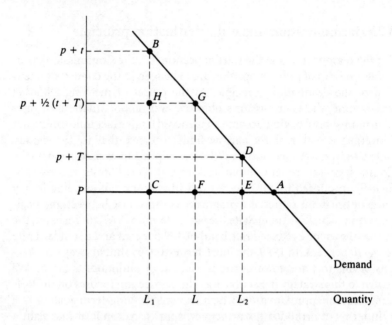

Figure 5.1. The efficiency gain from indirect tax harmonisation

absolute change in demand—the reduction in excess burden in the high tax country 1, *BCFG*, exceeds the increase in country 2, *DEFG*. Collectively, the two countries are better off.[11]

The underlying argument is far more general than the picture. Demands can differ across the two countries, and they can have any logically possible shape; there can be any number of taxed goods; and world prices may respond to changes in the pattern and amount of trade. In these more general circumstances, harmonisation improves collective welfare if the point towards which countries converge, instead of being (as in Figure 5.1) a simple average of their initial tax rates, is a particular weighted average, the weights reflecting the relative slopes of (compensated) demand curves in the two countries (see Keen, 1987). The role of these weights is to ensure that harmonisation has no effect on collective demand for any product, and so has no effect on world prices (leaving *P*

[11] Figure 5.1 points to an alternative intuitive explanation for the result. It is essentially illustrating the familiar feature that, at constant producer prices (on which read on), dead-weight loss is convex in the tax rate. This convexity means that convergence reduces average dead-weight loss over the two countries.

in Figure 1 unchanged): the increase in the demand for wine in the UK, for instance, is then exactly offset by a lower demand in France.

The result also remains valid—in striking contrast to many others in the analysis of trade policy—when firms behave oligopolistically, at least in the simplest such models (see Keen and Lahiri, 1993). With the point of convergence constructed, exactly as before, so as to leave aggregate demand unaffected at the initial producer price, the sole consequence of harmonisation is again to improve the efficiency with which goods are allocated across consumers: moving a fixed total of clothing, for example, from low valuation consumers in Italy to high valuation consumers in Spain. Production decisions are entirely unaffected, so there is no interaction with production or monopoly distortions of the kind that one might have expected to complicate matters.

Nor is the argument affected by introducing third countries, not party to harmonisation. Again the essential observation is that aggregate demand across the participating countries is unaffected. For there is then no direct effect on net exports to others and hence no direct effect on the terms at which the Community trades with the rest of the world. This implies, in particular, that there will be neither loss nor gain to third countries. Or rather, to be precise, there will be only an indirect income effect, reflecting the higher real income that the Community enjoys as a consequence of the improvement in its internal efficiency.

The argument is thus a very general one. Generality, however, is not the same thing as importance. Three limitations of the argument should be emphasised. The first is that harmonisation will generally affect tax revenues. In practice, the situation for most Member States under the proposals described above would not have been as dramatic as in Figure 5.1: many countries would have found the required changes in VAT and the excises broadly offsetting. The revenue concern leads, however, to a more fundamental point. If one were designing a fully optimal indirect tax structure for the Community as a whole—maximising some measure of collective welfare subject to raising such revenue as required for expenditure purposes—it is extremely unlikely that one would recommend the same rate structure for all Member States: it will typically be desirable, for instance, to exploit cross-country differences in elasticities of demand. As a matter of logic, it must then be the case that there will come a point at which further harmonisation—now leading the Community away from the optimum—will lower revenue in at least one Member State.

The second limitation of the argument is that it attaches no weight to the use of indirect taxes for distributional or (particularly in the context of the excises) health policies. The extent to which it is appropriate to pursue these policies through indirect taxation is a matter of broader controversy, but certainly rates in the Community currently seem heavily influenced by such concerns. Hence, so too have been responses to the Commission's proposals: Symons and Walker (1989), for example, find that they would have led to a small increase in inequality in the UK.

The third limitation is that cross-country transfers will generally be required to ensure that both countries share in the collective gain. As noted in Section 2, this may be difficult to arrange. The need for compensation disappears, however, if the starting-point of harmonisation is one in which—along the lines described at the end of Section 3.1—Member States use their domestic commodity taxes, as best they can, as protective devices. In this case harmonisation may generate not only a collective gain but also a direct gain to each country: Keen (1989) establishes conditions under which harmonisation from a non-cooperative equilibrium is Pareto-improving without any need for international transfers. Intuitively, if the UK penalises wine relative to beer in order to serve its own national interest and France subsidises it for the same reason, then obliging the two countries to adopt more similar tax treatments will serve to undo the damage that each inflicts on the other. Harmonisation may thus have coherence as a collective response to fiscal externalities from strategic tax-setting. Revenue effects, moreover, may be less of a concern in this context, the principal motivation behind the initial distortion being not the need to raise money but the desire to secure national advantage.

It is thus possible to make an argument for harmonisation on conventional efficiency grounds. Quite how large the gains are remains an (uninvestigated) empirical matter. They may well be relatively small when weighed against the associated restrictions on internal policies. In any event, the principal argument used by the Commission in support of its proposals is entirely different. It is that without convergence of tax rates the incentives for tax-induced cross-border trade in a border-free Europe (both legal purchases for personal use and illicit smuggling for resale) will be so strong as to jeopardise the probability of the destination principle being implemented.

Harmonisation is thus presented as a price to be paid for retaining the destination principle. As a sweetener, the Commission envisages substantial resource savings from the elimination of border controls: Cecchini (1988) puts the gain at 1.7 per cent of the value of intra-Community trade (against which would need to be set the administrative and compliance costs of the alternative arrangements for border tax adjustments now and eventually adopted). The more fundamental question of whether the price is really one that has to be paid—of whether substantial cross-country divergences in tax rates and the destination principle are mutually exclusive without border controls—remains open: Cnossen and Shoup (1987) argue forcefully that it is not. Indeed the changes of 1 January 1993 can be seen as a bold experiment to discover the answer. Suppose, however, that it proves impossible to sustain cross-country variations in tax-inclusive consumer prices in the absence of physical controls. What would be the implications?

3.3. Tax competition with open borders

At first sight it might seem that the Community would then move *de facto* to an origin basis. If Greece sets a low tax on olive oil, for instance, and makes substantial final sales on that basis to foreigners, then it is indeed effectively taxing on an origin basis. More generally, the arbitrage condition relating prices across Member States would be exactly as under the origin basis: transport costs aside, consumer prices would be equalised. But there are two important differences from the pure origin principle, leaving something that is a hybrid of the two. They reflect a simple asymmetry: individuals are more likely to claim tax refunds to which they are entitled than to volunteer tax payments they owe. The first departure from the origin principle then arises in the allocation of tax revenues. For suppose that Greece attempted to exercise some monopoly power by imposing a heavy tax on all sales of olive oil. Importers could in principle simply appeal to the formalities of the destination principle and reclaim all Greek tax. Roughly speaking, low tax goods would be taxed on an origin basis; high tax goods would be purchased only in so far as enforcement of the destination principle proved feasible, most likely in domestic markets.

The second departure from the origin principle is in the structure of the incentives for strategic tax-setting. Under the origin principle, as noted in Section 3.1., self-interest points to relatively heavy taxation of exportables. Given the inability to enforce high tax rates on domestic production, however, the incentives can be expected to point in the opposite direction: towards setting lower tax rates than other countries, particularly contiguous ones see Mintz and Tulkens (1986), de Crombrugghe and Tulkens (1990), and Kanbur and Keen (1993). To the welfare losses from unproductive arbitrage activities at initial tax rates is thus added a collective welfare loss through tax competition leading to tax rates that are too low. As a further twist on this, one would expect a tendency for tax rates to be especially low in 'small' countries. For the nationalistic incentive to cut taxes is especially strong for such countries: the revenue lost from a small domestic base is liable to be swamped by that gained from cross-border shopping by large neighbouring countries.

The prospect of tax-cutting has thus become a principal concern in discussions of indirect tax policy. Some would welcome unfettered tax competition as a beneficial restriction on governments' inherent tendency to overtax and overspend. Mistrust of the state has been one of the philosophical underpinnings of the attitude of the UK government, which has advocated a 'market solution' to the problem of indirect tax coordination: simply open the borders and, with some safeguards for social policy objectives (i.e. enabling the UK to retain high excises), let tax competition rip. This has the merit of removing any need consciously to identify those aspects of domestic tax policy that have strong international repercussions; these will be made clear by the market rather than second-guessed in Brussels. Except for devout adherents of the Leviathan view of the state, however, the possibility of adverse fiscal externalities is not one to be ignored. More active policy interventions then need to be considered.

Approximation is one obvious response, eliminating (or at least limiting) both the incentive for cross-border shopping and the ability of Member States to compete in tax-setting. But it is a crude device, and the political heat generated by the implied restrictions on domestic social policies—particularly in the UK—led in early 1989 to a substantial restructuring of the Commission's indirect tax proposals. With the advent of a new Commissioner for Fiscal Affairs, Christiane Scrivener, the original approximation proposals were replaced by a more pragmatic approach one—seeking to establish not a target range within which all Member States rates must lie, but rather minimum tax rates that all must impose: a minimum standard rate of VAT of 15 per cent, with one or two reduced rates of at least 5 per cent (and retention of existing zero-rating) came into force at the start of this year, as did minimum excise rates.

The minimum tax strategy has considerable appeal as one that responds to the more damaging and visible consequences of tax competition while preserving a considerable degree of formal discretion in national tax-setting. The objectors, one might think, should be the low tax countries that initially derive considerable benefit from cross-border shopping. But, perhaps surprisingly, they too may gain from the imposition of a minimum tax; and this is so even though the constraint bites only on them, and even in the absence of compensatory transfers. Kanbur and Keen (1993) show, in a simple two-country model of tax competition with open borders, that the introduction of a minimum tax constraint is indeed Pareto-improving. Intuitively, it is clear enough that the high tax country will gain: the outward tide of cross-border shoppers is stemmed. The more striking conclusion that the low tax country also gains arises from the strategic interaction between countries. For the forced increase in the low tax country's rate enables the other—from which the cross-border shoppers come—to raise its tax rate, more secure than before against escape of its domestic tax base. And this higher tax rate abroad diminishes the adverse impact on the haven country of the forced increase in its own rate. Taking into account also the revenue gained from its own residents, the net effect may thus be that revenue increases in the low tax country too. Suppose, to take an extreme case, that the effect of the minimum tax is to raise tax rates by the same amount in two contiguous Member States and that demand in each is inelastic. If the extent of cross-border shopping depends only on the difference in tax rates, then its volume will be unaffected. Tax revenue will therefore increase in both countries.

4. Capital Income Taxation

The issues here are arguably more pressing than those in the indirect tax areas. Technically, they are certainly more complex.

4.1. Residence and source principles

There are two main principles by which income that crosses jurisdictions might be taxed. One is the *residence principle*: under this, income is taxed at the rate of, and revenue accrues to, the country in which the recipient—personal or corporate—resides. The other is the *source principle*, under which tax is paid at the rate of and to the jurisdiction in which the income arises. Broadly, the residence principle taxes a nation's savings, the source principle taxes the income that arises from investments in it. In practice, most governments assert the right to tax both the foreign earnings of their own residents and the income that foreigners derive from activities within their jurisdiction. The potential double taxation that this creates is generally alleviated, however, by the adoption of one of three methods. First, the residence country may simply exempt foreign source income (as, for dividend income, do seven of the Member States, including Germany and the Netherlands). Second, taxes paid abroad may be allowed as a deduction in calculating liability at home: this is rare in practice but, as will be seen, conceptually important. Third, the residence country may credit against domestic liability any taxes paid to the foreign government; this is the norm in the other Member States, and in both the USA and Japan. If this crediting were perfect—requiring that the home government actually give refunds on income from jurisdictions with a higher tax rate than its own—such a situation would be equivalent, from the investors' perspective (though not from that of the revenue authorities) to application of the residence principle. But such refunds are not in fact paid: investments in high tax jurisdictions abroad thus typically bear tax at the foreign rate rather than the lower domestic one. This pushes the present situation towards an effective source basis.

Two other aspects of current practice push in the same direction. The first is deferral: for individuals and subsidiaries operating abroad, no domestic tax becomes due (subject, usually, to some anti-avoidance provisions) until the income is actually brought home, so blunting the impact of home taxes. Indeed for retention-financed investments by subsidiaries abroad, deferral means that the home tax rate and the comparing the repatriation of profits now to their reinvestment abroad and repatriation later, the effects of the home tax system cancel out.[12] The second important aspect is evasion of home taxes on portfolio income from abroad: it is notoriously difficult to ensure that such income is reported to the authorities of the residence country. Only source taxes— principally withholding taxes on interest and dividends—are then paid.

There thus arises a question of principle, analogous to the choice between destination and origin bases discussed above: which is more conducive to the collective good, the residence or the source principle? Discussion focuses on two central efficiency concepts. Precise definitions vary, but the following seem to capture their essence:[13] *capital export neutrality* (CEN) requires that a resident of any particular jurisdiction face the same effective marginal rate of capital income taxation—reflecting the impact on marginal investment decisions of both rates and bases

---

[12] This striking result breaks down if the product markets into which related companies sell are integrated, if tax rates vary over time, or if definitions of the tax base differ between residence and source country: see Keen (1990b) and Leechor and Mintz (1993).

[13] For brevity, this discussion abstracts from issues arising from the distinction between personal and corporate taxes: these are taken up by Devereux (1992).

of taxation—whatever the jurisdiction in which they invest; *capital import neutrality* (CIN) requires that investments in a particular jurisdiction face the same effective marginal tax rate whatever the residence of the investor. If CEN holds, production will be efficient in the sense that output could not be increased by reallocating firms' investments across locations. If CIN holds, the allocation of savings across consumers will be efficient in the sense that all savers, whatever their jurisdiction of residence, will receive the same after-tax return; that is, they will all face the same prices for future in terms of present consumption. These two efficiency criteria—which are simply those of production and efficiency discussed earlier in another guise—are closely related to the two principles mentioned above: it is immediately clear from the definitions that the residence principle is sufficient for CEN, the source principle sufficient for CIN.

Complete identity of tax structures across countries, together with non-discrimination between home and foreign investments, would guarantee both CEN and CIN. Regarding such uniformity as chimerical, the question usually posed at this point is, then, which is the more desirable, CEN or CIN? The starting-point is again the Diamond–Mirrlees production efficiency result invoked in Section 3.1. This leads to a presumption that CEN will typically be a feature of a collectively optimal tax structure, and hence to a presumption in favour of the residence principle. Suppose, to give an example, that Marks & Spencer faces a higher marginal tax rate in Portugal than in the UK. Then when M&S's profit-maximising decisions lead it to equate post-tax returns across jurisdictions, the pre-tax return must be higher in Portugal than in the UK: at the margin, M&S's total output could, therefore, be increased by investing less in the UK and more in Portugal. Given sufficient control over indirect taxes, some tax reform could now be found which distributes that additional output across consumers in such a way that all are better off.

There are a number of caveats to the Diamond–Mirrlees result. It assumes, recall, that pure profits are taxed at 100 per cent, that there is perfect competition, and—as in the tail of the example just given—that there are no constraints on the other tax instruments the government may use. If any of these conditions is not satisfied, the optimal tax structure will generally have neither CEN nor CIN. It is perhaps natural, nevertheless, to seek primacy of one principle over the other. And the argument here has typically been that violating CEN is likely to be much more costly than violating CIN (see, for instance, Giovannini, 1989). Since investment decisions are generally presumed to be highly responsive to rates of return,[14] it is argued, the cost of departing from CEN is likely to be large. The only inefficiency implied by violating CIN, the argument continues, is in the composition of total savings: if UK investors face a higher tax rate than the Germans, then the post-tax return they receive from their investments will be lower, so that both countries could gain if UK investors saved a little less and German a little more. Savings decisions are then claimed to be inelastic, suggesting that this inefficiency is unlikely to be serious. But the argument is not entirely convincing. The magnitude of the interest elasticity of savings (or, what is more relevant here, the intertemporal elasticity of substitution) remains an unresolved empirical question. Moreover, the argument ignores another inefficiency implied by deviations from CIN: if competition is imperfect, tax advantages may enable high (marginal) cost producers to coexist with, or even drive out, low cost. The integration of goods markets is likely to weaken the force of this potentially productive inefficiency: in order to sell in a particular country it may become less important to have a substantial physical presence there. But some lingering doubts on the usual presumption for the residence principle remain. In any event, we currently know almost nothing about the quantitative welfare implications of alternative tax treatments of cross-national direct investment.[15]

There is, moreover, a further practical problem—additional to those mentioned above—in implementing something equivalent to the residence principle for corporate source income. This is the need to undo the consequences of deferral. Doing this in the literal sense of moving to concurrent taxation, the tax practitioners tell us, would be 'a technical nightmare' (Mùten, 1983). One other conceptual difficulty with the conventional argument that CIN should be sacrificed to CEN should be noted: it may be possible to achieve both even without full harmonisation. Suppose, for instance, that the profits earned by a multinational in one jurisdiction are independent of those earned in another. Imagine now that each country adopts a source-basis 'net equity' cash flow tax; taxes corporations within its jurisdiction, that is, on their net distributions (dividends less sales of new equity) to shareholders, whether personal or parent company. Imagine too (for simplicity) that there are no

---

[14] The Ruding Report (Ruding Committee, 1992) provides a very useful survey of the impact of taxation on international investment flows, concluding that the effects are indeed quantitatively signficant.
[15] Even measuring effective marginal tax rates on border-crossing investments, it should be stressed, is difficult, both conceptually and analytically: see, for example, Devereux and Pearson (1989), Keen (1990b), and Sörensen (1990b).

personal taxes. Then the outcome will be fully neutral, and this will be so even if the rates of corporation tax differ across countries and even if no credits are given for foreign taxes paid by subsidiaries (Keen, 1990b). The reason is straightforward: the tax base is then simply the quantity that, in the absence of tax, firms would seek to maximise, and hence their decisions are unaffected. Moreover, such a scheme possesses the CEN property of the residence principle whilst maintaining the administrative advantages of deferral: by giving a credit on new equity injections going into subsidiaries abroad, one undoes the distorting effect of taxing the dividends that come out.

But there is a problem. To the extent that tax rates differ across jurisdictions, firms would have an incentive to use transfer-pricing devices to reallocate their taxable profits. Such an incentive clearly already exists under current arrangements, both within the Community and outside. Paper transactions, however, can be expected to generate relatively little collective welfare loss (though they may well have powerful effects on the level and distribution of tax payments, and are certainly a major concern to tax authorities).[16] With increasing integration of goods markets, however, the same forces that give rise to transfer pricing can be expected to have an increasing influence on real investment decisions, presumably[17] a much more costly form of distortion. For as it becomes less of a prerequisite for access to the market of a Member State that a firm have substantial physical presence there, and as it become harder to maintain effective segmentation of markets, so firms may increasingly find that location decisions are largely a matter for their tax advisers. This leads to a more general point. In the 1980s, discussion of domestic capital income taxation and its reform focused on the distortionary consequences of variations across types of investment in the effective *marginal* rate of taxation. This in turn leads to the suggestion that coordination of tax bases across Member States is at least as important as convergence of statutory rates. When rents are transferable across investments, however, real distortions arise from variations in *average* rates of taxation (a point emphasised, for example, by Tanzi and Bovenberg, 1990). And rates of corporation tax continue to vary widely across the Community, despite

---

[16] As evidenced by, for instance, the controversial Section 482 proposals in the USA.

[17] Presumably, but not—at least from the perspective of collective welfare—necessarily. In efficiency terms it may make little difference whether a particular investment is located in the UK or in Portugal. In terms of their own factor incomes and tax receipts, however, it may make a great deal of difference to the British and Portuguese. Note, too, that transfer pricing may actually serve a useful purpose in so far as it provides a way of arbitraging tax differentials that is less costly to society than distorted location decisions.

the spontaneous rate reductions of the 1980s: retained profits are taxed at 50 per cent in Germany, for instance, and at 33 per cent in the UK.

4.2. Non-cooperative capital income taxation

Capital income taxes, no less than indirect taxes, can be deployed to national rather than collective self-interest. Indeed it is this that largely underlies the case for coordination of policies: the reduction in statutory corporation tax rates just mentioned, in particular, smacks of mutually harmful tax competition. Assessing the merits of alternative forms of coordination thus requires an understanding of the incentives for strategic behaviour. Here, as will be seen, there remain many puzzles.

Consider first a country so small that its decisions have no effect on either goods prices on world markets or the world interest rate. The Diamond–Mirrlees result again applies, pointing as before to production efficiency. For a capital exporting country, this means that the pre-tax return on domestic investments should equal the return available to the nation on the world capital market: and this calls for a deduction system, since it is this that will induce domestic investors to adopt in their own self-interest what is the appropriate perspective in terms of the national interest, regarding taxes paid abroad as akin to business costs at home. Here is the first puzzle: why have not dominant capital exporting countries, like the post-war USA, adopted a deduction system?[18] For a capital importing country, on the other hand, the nationalistically optimal policy depends on whether or not the foreign country credits taxes paid abroad. If it does not, then since any source-based tax would drive a wedge between the return earned in that country and the world interest rate, no source tax will be deployed. If it does, then the source country will wish to impose a source tax at exactly the foreign tax rate, thereby transferring money from the foreign exchequer to itself at no real cost to the investor.

If all countries regard themselves as small and take the tax decisions of others as beyond their influence, then—applying this reasoning simultaneously to all—the non-cooperative equilibrium will have only residence-based taxes: source taxes wither away (Razin and Sadka, 1991). This is a reassuring conclusion for those persuaded of the desirability of CEN: it says that this will be achieved automatically, with no need for

---

[18] It is, however, interesting to note that, in imperial days, the UK did allow a deduction for investments outside the Empire only, but a credit for those within.

explicit coordination. But it is also puzzling, for, as noted earlier, we do not in practice observe universal application of the residence principle. Instead, we observe, for the most important capital exporters, crediting. This leads into another puzzle: why is the credit system so pervasive? Why should the USA, for instance, choose to transfer more to foreign governments in the form of tax breaks than it does in the form of aid? In fact the puzzle is even deeper, for it is by no means obvious how the credit system even survives in the face of self-interested behaviour by governments. For it is an implication of the argument in the preceding paragraph that if, each country were to set its tax rate to its own best advantage, taking others' tax rates as given, the credit system would collapse. It may be useful to spell out exactly why (the formal argument being due to Bond and Samuelson, 1989). Recall that a small capital importing country would always want to charge the same rate of tax as the capital exporting country, so long as the latter credits foreign taxes. At the same time, however, the capital exporter will want to charge a *higher* tax rate than does the importer. For suppose the rates are initially the same. By slightly increasing its tax rate, the capital exporting country would raise tax revenue from its residents' investments abroad above a starting-point of zero. It would also reduce the level of this foreign investment, but, since post-tax returns are being equated by private investors, the national return on the marginal investment abroad (which excludes taxes paid to the foreign government) is less than that on the marginal domestic investment (which includes tax paid to the home government), such a reallocation of investment being to the capital exporting country's advantage. The desires of capital exporter and importer are thus inconsistent; no equilibrium exists. One neat resolution of this is suggested by Gordon (1992) and Bruce (1992). For imagine now that it is costless to evade residence-based taxes but impossible to evade source-based ones. Then, if the capital-exporting country acts as a Stackleberg leader—that is, takes into account the reaction of the other country to its own choice of tax rate— then by crediting foreign taxes it can induce a higher tax rate abroad and so facilitate enforcement of its own source-based taxes.

4.3. Options for coordination

After several false starts, the EC has now established a firm presence in the area of capital income taxation. Two directives are in place: one eliminates withholding taxes and requires crediting of underlying corporation tax on dividends paid to a parent company (other than as provided for in existing agreements to mitigate double taxation); the other establishes common tax rules for mergers. Also in place is an arbitration convention for mitigating the double taxation that might otherwise arise from uncoordinated transfer-pricing adjustments by revenue authorities in different jurisdictions. Directives are also proposed for the abolition of withholding taxes on interest and royalties, and to deal with the consolidation of losses across the EC. Potentially even more fundamental to the long-term development of policy is the report of the Ruding Committee in June 1992. There is no space here to consider these developments in detail; the Ruding Report, in particular, was the subject of a symposium in *Fiscal Studies* (vol. 13, May 1992); once again, the focus is on the broadest strategic choices faced by the EC.

To begin, it is worth emphasising that even perfectly informed and well-intentioned coordination of capital income taxation may be undesirable. For Kehoe (1989) shows that removing the possibility of capital flight would enhance the ability to tax accumulated capital and so might lead to the expectation of capital levies (even if they are genuinely not intended), with consequent damage to current savings decisions. This 'time-consistency' problem—which arises in so far as governments are unable credibly to commit themselves to future tax rates—has been raised in the EC context by, for instance, Sinclair (1990). One would suspect, however, that the opportunity of investing outside the EC is likely to limit its severity (to say nothing of other devices, such as the acquisition of reputation effects, whereby governments might acquire credibility). It is interesting, moreover, to note that evasion may actually serve a socially useful purpose in this context. Boadway and Keen (1993) show that a government unable to commit itself to the tax rate would optimally wish to allow some tax evasion, even if perfect enforcement were costless; for the possibility of evasion alleviates fears of high future tax rates.

Short of full coordination, a number of looser forms of cooperation are possible. The loosest would be piecemeal convergence within the existing broad structure; including, in particular, the elimination of all withholding taxes and the extension of imputation credits across Member States. In welfare terms, such a convergence might be justified in exactly the same terms as was indirect tax harmonisation in Section 2.1 above. The issue then arises as to the relative importance of convergence in bases and in statutory rates. To the extent that narrow bases—generous depreciation deductions and the like—tend in practice to go with high statutory rates, harmonisation of only one or the other may actually increase the dispersion of effective marginal rates, a point whose practical importance is demonstrated by Devereux and Pearson (1995).

But recall that potentially costly distortions arise from the divergences in statutory rates too, which give rise to a host of transfer-pricing problems (using this term in its broadest sense). Indeed, one can think of these problems as analogous to those of cross-border shopping discussed in Section 3.3 above: firms choosing where to take their profits are like consumers choosing where to buy. The earlier analysis concerning minimum tax rates then again applies: all may gain from the imposition of a lower bound on the statutory rate of corporation tax. The Ruding Committee's recommendation of a minimum rate of 30 per cent thus has a coherent theoretical rationale.[19]

A more structured approach to coordination would be to seek thorough application of either the residence or the source principle. For the reasons discussed earlier, the popular favourite here has been the residence principle. Two very practical difficulties, both mentioned earlier, stand in its way, however: those of abolishing deferral, and those of evasion. One response to these is to seek enforcement of the residence principle by imposing heavy source taxes but offering refunds that provide the taxpayer with an incentive for honest declaration (see Giovannini and Hines, 1991). Again, however, administrative problems arise: in particular, a clearing house would be needed to reallocate revenues.

One further alternative—advocated by McLure (1989)—is the adoption of some system of formula apportionment. Under such a system, which is the norm for federal and provincial taxes in North America, a firm's total profits are allocated across jurisdictions by reference to weighting factors that indicate the geographical pattern of its activities. The advantage is that, with appropriate weights, such a scheme prevents income being shifted by paper transactions. So long as tax rates differ across jurisdictions, distortions would arise only in respect of decisions that affect the weights themselves. With a convergence of rates, however, such a system would become in effect a European corporation tax. And such a role for the corporation tax would not be without appeal. Location-specific rents—which are all that can be taxed without any threat from lower taxes abroad—may be limited at the level of Member State, and further eroded by continuing integration. Rents from access to the European market, however, seem likely to be substantial. By taxing them, a well-designed European corporation tax might raise considerable revenue at little welfare loss. Given the difficulty of allocating these rents across Member States, such revenue might even be a natural source for the financing of communal expenditures. The corporation tax thus

---

[19] The case for a maximum rate of the kind they suggest is less obvious. One rationale could be the fear of terms of trade effects of the kind mentioned briefly in Section 2.

becomes, in part, analogous to the common external tariff. For one of the traditional functions of the corporate tax, after all, is to tax foreigners.

5. Concluding Remarks

Some surveys answer questions, others pose them. This one has been largely of the latter type. Not enough is known, for instance, about the relative merits of destination and origin principles outside the simplest cases. Nor is the prevalence of crediting fully understood. Other issues have only been touched on here, while still others beginning to appear on the policy agenda—particularly those associated with greater mobility of people—have been set aside altogether. It seems more than likely that international aspects of taxation will come ever more to the fore in the years ahead, not only in the EC but also, for instance, in the context of North American free trade. The tools and arguments outlined here may help to address them.

References

Berglas, E. (1981), 'Harmonization of commodity taxes', *Journal of Public Economics*, vol. 16, pp. 377–87.

Boadway, R., and Keen, M. J. (1993), 'Evasion and time consistency in the taxation of capital income', mimeo, University of Essex.

Bond, E., and Samuelson, L. (1989), 'Strategic behaviour and the rules for international taxation of capital', *Economic Journal*, vol. 99, pp. 1099–111.

Bruce, N. (1992), 'Why are there foreign tax credits?', mimeo, University of Washington.

Cecchini, P., with Catinat, M., and Jacquemin, A. (1988), *The European Challenge, 1992: The Benefits of a Single Market*, Brookfield, Vermont: Gower.

Cnossen, S., and Shoup, C. S. (1987), 'Coordination of value-added taxes', in S. Cnossen (ed.), *Tax Coordination in the European Community*, Deventer: Kluwer Law and Taxation.

Crombrugghe, A. de, and Tulkens, H. (1990), 'On Pareto improving commodity tax changes under fiscal competition', *Journal of Public Economics*, vol. 41, pp. 335–50.

Devereux, M. P. (1992), 'A note on efficiency criteria in the international taxation of income from capital', mimeo, Keele University.

—— and Pearson, M. (1989), *Corporate Tax Harmonisation*, Institute for Fiscal Studies Report Series No. 35, London: IFS.

———— (1995), 'European tax harmonisation and production efficiency', *European Economic Review*, vol. 39, pp. 1657–81.

Diamond, P. A., and Mirrlees, J. A. (1971), 'Optimal taxation and public production I: Production efficiency', *American Economic Review*, vol. 61, pp. 1–27.

Dosser, D. (1964), 'Welfare effects of tax unions', *Review of Economic Studies*, vol. 31, pp. 179–84.

Georakopoulos, T., and Hitiris, T. (1992), 'On the superiority of the destination over the origin principle of taxation', *Economic Journal*, vol. 102, pp. 117–26.

Giovannini, A. (1989), 'National tax systems versus the European capital market', *Economic Policy*, vol. 9, pp. 346–74, 381–6.

———— and Hines, J. (1991), 'Capital flight and tax competition: are there viable solutions to both problems?', in A. Giovannini and C. Mayer (eds.), *European Financial Integration*, Cambridge: Cambridge University Press.

Gordon, R. (1992), 'Can capital income taxes survive?', *Journal of Finance*, vol. 47, pp. 1159–80.

Hartman, D. G. (1985), 'Tax policy and direct foreign investment' *Journal of Public Economics*, vol. 26, pp. 107–21.

Kanbur, R., and Keen, M. J. (1993), 'Jeux sans frontières: tax competition and tax coordination when countries differ in size', *American Economic Review*, vol. 83, pp. 877–92.

Keen, M. J. (1987), 'Welfare effects of commodity tax harmonisation', *Journal of Public Economics*, vol. 33, pp. 107–14.

———— (1989), 'Pareto-improving indirect tax harmonisation', *European Economic Review*, vol. 33, pp. 1–12.

———— (1990a), 'Aspects of tax coordination in the European Community', in D. Purvis (ed.), *Europe 1992 and the Implications for Canada*, John Deutsch Institute Policy Forum Series No. 21, Queens University, Kingston.

———— (1990b), 'Corporation tax, direct foreign investment and the single market', in L. A. Winters and A. J. Venables (eds.), *European Integration: Trade and Industry*, Cambridge: Cambridge University Press.

———— and Lahiri, S. (1993), 'Domestic tax reform and international oligopoly', *Journal of Public Economics*, vol. 51, pp. 55–74.

Kehoe, P. J. (1989), 'Policy cooperation amongst benevolent governments may be undesirable', *Review of Economic Studies*, vol. 56, pp. 289–96.

Kopits, G. (ed.) (1992), *Tax Harmonization in the European Community*, International Monetary Fund Occasional Paper No. 94, Washington DC: IMF.

Lee, C., Pearson, M., and Smith, S. (1988), *Fiscal Harmonisation: An Analysis of the Commission's Proposals*, Institute for Fiscal Studies Report Series No. 28, London: IFS.

Leechor, C., and Mintz, J. (1993) 'On the taxation of multinational corporate investment when the deferral method is used by the capital exporting country', *Journal of Public Economics*, vol. 51, pp. 75–96.

Lockwood, B. (1993), 'Commodity tax competition under destination and origin principles', *Journal of Public Economics*, vol. 52, pp. 141–62.

214   *Michael Keen*

Lockwood, B., de Meza, D., and Myles, G. D. (1994), 'When are destination and origin regimes equivalent?', *International Tax and Public Finance*, vol. 1, pp. 5–24.

McClure, C. E. (1989), 'Economic integration and European taxation of corporate income at source: some lessons from the US experience', *European Taxation*, August, pp. 243–50.

Mintz, J., and Tulkens, H. (1986), 'Commodity tax competition between member states of a federation: equilibrium and efficiency', *Journal of Public Economics*, vol. 29, pp. 133–72.

Mùten, L. (1983), 'Some topical issues concerning international double taxation', in S. Cnossen (ed.), *Comparative Tax Studies: Essays in Honor of Richard Goode*, Amsterdam: North-Holland.

Neumark Report (1963), 'Report of the Fiscal and Financial Committee', in *The EEC Reports on Tax Harmonization*, Amsterdam: International Bureau of Fiscal Documentation.

Razin, A., and Sadka, E. (1991), 'International tax competition and the gains from tax harmonization', *Economics Letters*, vol. 37, pp. 69–76.

Ruding Committee (1992), *Report of the Committee of Independent Experts on Company Taxation*, Brussels: CEC.

Sinclair, P. J. N. (1990), '1992: The whys and wherefores', in D. Purvis (ed.), *Europe 1992 and the Implications for Canada*, John Deutsch Institute Policy Forum Series No. 21, Queens University, Kingston.

Sinn, H.-W. (1989), 'Tax harmonization and tax competition in Europe', *European Economic Review*, vol. 34, pp. 489–504.

—— (1990), 'Can direct and indirect taxes be added in comparisons of international competitiveness?', in H. Siebert (ed.), *Reforming Capital Income Taxation*, Tuebingen: Mohr.

Smith, S. (1993), ' "Subsidiarity" and the co-ordination of indirect taxes in the European Community', *Oxford Review of Economic Policy*, vol. 9, no. 1, pp. 67–94.

Sörensen, P. B. (1990a), 'Issues in the theory of international tax coordination', Bank of Finland, Discussion Paper No. 4.

—— (1990b), 'Taxation and the cost of capital in direct foreign investment', mimeo, University of Copenhagen.

Symons, E., and Walker, I. (1989), 'The revenue and welfare effects of fiscal harmonisation for the UK', *Oxford Review of Economic Policy*, vol. 5, pp. 61–5.

Tanzi, V. in H. Siebert (ed.), *Reforming Capital Income Taxation*, Tuebingen: Mohr.

Tinbergen Report (1953), 'Report on problems raised by the differential turnover tax system applied within the common market', European Coal and Steel Community.

Whalley, J. (1979), 'Uniform domestic tax rates, trade distortions and economic integration', *Journal of Public Economics*, vol. 11, pp. 213–21.

H30   # TAXATION AND THE ENVIRONMENT

STEPHEN SMITH

1. Introduction

Environmental policies in the UK and other industrialised countries
have to address an increasing range of concerns. These include not just
the long-standing problems of controlling localised pollution from
industrial effluents, but also more recently recognised problems of international pollution (e.g. acid rain) and global ecological balance, especially the risks of damage to the ozone layer and of an accelerated
'greenhouse effect'. These new problems call, in many cases, for extensive
and, in some cases, costly changes to the existing patterns of production
and consumption, and for major new investments in pollution control.
The search for policy instruments that can achieve the necessary adjustments at least economic cost has brought renewed attention to the
potential benefits of using market mechanisms in environmental policy—incentives to encourage the private sector to make decisions which
are less damaging to the environment.[1]

This survey chapter reviews the possible contribution that taxation
could make to the efficient achievement of environmental policy objectives. The chapter is in eight sections. The next section describes the

The author has received financial support from the ESRC Research Centre at the Institute
for Fiscal Studies. He is grateful to Lans Bovenberg, Sam Fankhauser, David Pearce, John
Pezzey, and David Ulph for comments on a first draft of this chapter; remaining errors are
his responsibility alone.

First published in *Fiscal Studies* (1992), vol. 13, no. 4, pp. 21–57.

[1] For recent surveys of the case for market mechanisms in environmental policy, see
Helm and Pearce (1990), Nicolaisen, Dean, and Hoeller (1991), and Muzondo, Miranda,
and Bovenberg (1990).

main ways in which tax instruments have been employed in environmental policy, and identifies in particular three types of environmental tax measure—'Pigouvian' taxes on polluting emissions, 'approximations' to Pigouvian taxes, and cost-sharing or 'mutualisation' taxes. The main issues raised by each of these three types of fiscal instrument are then discussed in turn in Sections 3–5. Section 6 surveys empirical studies of the effects of various possible environmental taxes, including the burgeoning empirical literature on a carbon tax. Section 7 then considers environmental taxes in the context of public finance, and surveys the arguments over the distributional and revenue aspects of environmental taxes. In Section 8 some conclusions are drawn, identifying the main areas where the debate in the literature appears to have found scope for a useful fiscal dimension to environmental policy.

2. Types of Environmental Tax

Within the broad heading of environmental tax instruments, a number of distinct types of measure may be identified.

2.1. Pigouvian taxes

This group of market-based instruments are those which involve tax payments which are directly related to metered or measured quantities of polluting effluent. A tax per unit of measured pollution output of this sort conforms most closely to the type of tax envisaged in the early discussion by Pigou (1920) of the correction of externalities. In European countries, a number of instances can be found of taxes on measured polluting emissions; whilst some are set at a very low level, others are levied at rates liable to have a substantial impact on polluter behaviour and to raise significant revenues (Opschoor and Vos, 1989). In the USA, although a number of examples of such taxes can be found, recent policy has tended to make greater use of marketable permits in applications where some form of market-based environmental mechanism could be employed.

Measured emission taxes have generally tended to be considered as an alternative to 'command-and-control' systems of pollution regulation, and in Section 3 we set out the main considerations identified in the choice between regulatory policies and environmental taxes. Section 3 also briefly considers the merits of emissions taxes in comparison with two other possible market-based instruments, subsidies and tradable permits.

2.2. Approximations to Pigouvian taxes

Changes in the rates of indirect taxes (excise duties, sales taxes, or value added taxes) may be used as an indirect alternative to the explicit taxation of measured emissions. Goods and services which are associated with environmental damage in production or consumption may be taxed more heavily (e.g. carbon taxes and taxes on batteries and fertilisers), whilst goods which are believed to benefit the environment may be taxed less heavily than their substitutes (e.g. the reduced taxes on unleaded petrol).

Under this heading we may also include various tax expenditures designed to provide incentives to reduce pollution. For example, the direct tax system, particularly accelerated depreciation provisions in corporate taxation, may be used to provide incentives for the installation of certain types of pollution control equipment.

The scope for restructuring of indirect taxes for reasons of environmental policy can be wide. Sometimes, new taxes have been introduced, or other tax changes have been made, to achieve a specific environmental objective, and have been explicitly identified as 'environmental taxes'. Increasingly, however, policy towards the structure of existing indirect taxes on goods such as energy, vehicles, and motor fuels is taking account of environmental concerns, and the evolution over time of the level and structure of existing indirect taxes is being shaped by environmental concerns.

This group of tax instruments where fiscal restructuring is used as an indirect 'proxy' for pollution measurement raises a rather wider range of issues than the taxation of measured emissions—including questions of integration and compatibility with existing tax policies and administrative procedures. The debate over these issues is assessed in Section 4.

2.3. Mutualisation taxes

In many cases environmental taxes have in practice been used principally for purposes of revenue-raising, rather than to provide incentives to reduce polluting emissions (Opschoor and Vos, 1989). Where environmental taxes have been employed in this way, it has generally been to raise revenues for particular public expenditures related to environmental protection—for example, to recover the costs of administering a system of environmental monitoring or regulation, or to pay for public or private expenditures on pollution abatement measures. Thus, for example, in France a number of specific taxes on polluting emissions—most notably on water pollution—raise revenues which are earmarked according to a 'principle of mutualisation' to expenditures on pollution abatement which benefit the taxpayers of the tax concerned. Similar earmarked pollution taxes are to be found in a number of other countries, with the principal aim of raising revenues for particular purposes; the taxes concerned may or may not also have an incentive effect on the level of polluting emissions.

3. Pigouvian Taxes

The need for public intervention to control environmental pollution arises because of the 'externalities' involved in pollution—the costs that the polluting individual or firm imposes on other members of society.[2] Without government intervention, a polluter may have no reason to take these external costs into account. Decisions about the level of production and consumption activities which give rise to pollution, about the choice of technology, the use of pollution abatement measures, and the disposal of waste products, will then all be taken purely on the basis of the 'private' costs and benefits to the individual polluter. In particular, the atmosphere and water systems may be treated as free methods for disposing of unwanted waste products, despite the fact that unrestricted pollution of the atmosphere, or of groundwater, rivers, and seas, may impose costs on other firms or individuals.

Environmental policy needs to draw a balance between the costs of pollution and the costs of controlling pollution. Whilst there may be some forms of pollution which it would be desirable to eliminate entirely, this will generally be the exception rather than the rule. Ideally,

---

[2] See Cornes and Sandler (1986) for a theoretical treatment of externalities and Newbery (1980) for a survey of policy approaches to externalities. The definition of externalities is far from straightforward; see Meade (1973) and Arrow (1970) for contrasting views.

pollution should be restricted up to the point where the benefits to society as a whole from further reductions in pollution are less than the costs of controlling pollution through the installation of control devices or the curtailment of polluting activities. In economic terms, therefore, pollution should be controlled up to the point where the marginal cost of further abatement measures just outweighs the gain from reduced emissions.[3]

For a single polluting firm (for example, a firm discharging organic matter into a river) we can draw marginal abatement cost (MAC) and marginal damage cost (MDC) functions as shown in Figure 6.1. The marginal abatement cost will generally rise (strictly will not fall) with more stringent control, since the MAC curve assumes a ranking of measures, such that the least costly are implemented first. Often the marginal damage cost will also rise with emissions, reflecting a tendency for large amounts of pollution to cause proportionately greater damage to the environment than small amounts of pollution. This might be the case if the environment has some natural assimilative capacity—as in the case of the ability of water systems to assimilate organic matter. In the figure, E* represents the efficient level of pollution control. At E*, the marginal abatement cost and marginal damage cost are equal, at a level C*.

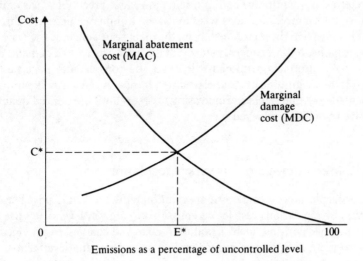

Figure 6.1. Balancing the costs and benefits of pollution abatement

---

[3] See Baumol (1972) and Baumol and Oates (1988).

In theoretical terms, the appropriate level of abatement is achieved where the marginal social cost of reducing pollution by an additional unit is equal to the marginal social benefit of a one-unit reduction in pollution. Achieving this level, whether through tax policies or through other measures, requires information on both the structure of marginal abatement costs and the structure of marginal damage costs. As the survey by Cropper and Oates (1992) shows, considerable progress has been made in recent years in refining the methods for obtaining the information needed to determine the optimal level of pollution abatement. Extensive research has, for example, been undertaken into the valuation of marginal environmental improvements, using both indirect inference from the market prices of housing and other commodities affected by environmental conditions, and direct survey evidence ('contingent valuation') of the values which individuals place on environmental improvements. Johansson (1990) discusses the degree of convergence of estimates obtained using the range of available methods, and considers explanations for some of the observed discrepancies.

In practice, the context for many environmental policy decisions is already more tightly defined than in the above analysis of 'optimal' pollution control (Baumol and Oates, 1971). Many countries have already undertaken quantitative commitments to reduce greenhouse gas emissions, for example, and may wish to use environmental taxes to achieve these targets. In these circumstances, the main issue concerns the scale of the response to tax changes, in terms of the price elasticity of demand for the taxed products. Although there may be considerable uncertainty about the magnitude of these elasticities, measures can always be implemented on a gradual basis, increasing tax rates until the desired quantitative response is achieved.[4]

3.1. Market mechanisms versus regulation

In principle, any given pattern of pollution reduction could be achieved either by regulations restricting emissions to a given level or by use of market mechanisms, such as pollution taxes and charges, to provide an appropriate incentive to reduce emissions to the same level. Thus, in Figure 6.1, a charge of C^* per unit of pollution could be used to reach the

---

[4] It should be noted, however, that it will not always be possible to use a trial-and-error process of this sort to *discover* the information about marginal abatement costs needed to set an environmental tax at the optimal rate, since polluters may respond strategically in these circumstances.

optimal level of emissions, E^*, or regulations could require the polluter to abate emissions to the same level. However, whilst charging mechanisms and regulations can be used to equivalent effect in the context of this simple example, in practice there are both advantages and disadvantages to the use of emissions taxes.

3.1.1. Static cost minimisation

The costs of reducing polluting emissions may in practice vary between polluters for a variety of reasons. Different firms may use different technologies, some of which may be more able to accommodate reductions in polluting emissions than others. Similarly, the costs to individual households of reducing their use of particular polluting products may vary as a result of differences in tastes or individual circumstances. An efficient pollution abatement policy would seek to reflect these individual differences in abatement cost, and would concentrate reductions in pollution where they can be achieved at least cost.[5] Empirical studies of the costs of pollution abatement using different abatement rules, summarised by Tietenberg (1990), show that the gains from efficiently allocating emission reductions between polluters can be substantial. In a study of the cost of achieving strict abatement standards for nitrogen oxide pollution in Baltimore, USA, Krupnick (1986) shows that efficient abatement would involve about one-sixth of the cost of uniform reductions in pollution imposed using command and control. Similar large gains from the efficient pattern of abatement, compared with uniform regulatory requirements, are found by other key empirical studies, including Atkinson and Lewis (1974) and Seskin, Anderson, and Reid (1983).

The principal argument in favour of emissions taxes or other market-based approaches to pollution control is that they are more likely to achieve an efficient allocation of pollution abatement across polluters than is a policy based on regulation. Extensive information about individual costs and circumstances would be required for a regulatory authority to allocate pollution abatement efficiently across individual polluters, and regulatory policies will tend to have to rely on rules which can only approximately reflect individual circumstances. In contrast,

---

[5] In addition, an efficient pattern of response to pollution problems might involve relocation by firms or households; White and Wittman (1982) discuss the possible contribution of pollution taxes to efficient location decisions. It has been recognised that certain types of abatement and defensive measures can complicate greatly the achievement of an optimal level of pollution abatement (Coase, 1960; Shibata and Winrich, 1983).

using the price mechanism in the form of a tax per unit of emissions economises on the information needed—those polluters with the lowest abatement costs in effect 'select themselves' in response to the signal provided by the tax.

3.1.2. Dynamic incentives for innovation

In addition to these 'static' cost-minimisation properties of emissions taxes, taxes and other environmental market mechanisms may also provide a 'dynamic' incentive for the development of further cost-effective methods of pollution control. The source of these dynamic improvements is the fact that, even at the static optimum, the environmental tax continues to be paid on remaining units of emissions—thus providing an incentive to search for technological innovations that will reduce still further the optimal level of emissions (Wenders, 1975; Magat, 1978; Milliman and Prince, 1989).

Emissions taxes[6] will give a greater incentive for such innovations than command-and-control regulations, which merely constitute an incentive for the minimum necessary compliance. However, it is not clear whether emission taxes, alone, can be expected to secure the first-best level of innovation. Carraro and Topa (1991) show a model in which emissions taxation leads to less than the first-best level of environmental innovation.[7]

3.1.3. Vulnerability to regulatory failure

Market instruments such as emissions taxation may be less exposed to the risk of regulatory 'failure' than certain forms of quantitative regulation. One important source of regulatory failure is the asymmetry of information between regulators and their subjects (Vickers and Yarrow, 1988). Where a substantial amount of information about the circumstances or characteristics of individual firms is required to implement a particular policy, the firms may be in a strong position to control the

---

[6] Tradable permits, whether auctioned or distributed free, will also provide a similar incentive for innovation, since the necessary permits have a cost or opportunity cost to any source which continues polluting. However, depending on the rule for permit issue over time, this incentive could be less than with an emissions tax (Maleug, 1989). This result arises because the firm which innovates reduces the aggregate demand for permits, and thus reduces the value of any permits which it holds.

[7] There are, of course, well-known 'public-good' arguments for the subsidy of R&D, especially of fundamental research.

flow of information to the regulator in such a way as significantly to affect the way the policy is applied. Although there may be little difference in the amount of information required for administration and enforcement between a uniform rule on emissions levels (e.g. one setting an upper limit to emissions) and an emissions tax, a regulatory policy which sought to take more account of the circumstances of individual firms would be much more vulnerable to regulatory failure. The efficient allocation of emissions abatement between firms depends on the marginal costs of abatement to each firm, and this information can only be obtained by the regulator from the firms themselves.

3.1.4. Revenues

The revenue raised from emissions taxes may be regarded as an additional benefit from their use, in that it may reduce the amount of revenue which has to be raised from existing taxes, and hence reduce the net aggregate dead-weight loss from raising public revenues (Terkla, 1984). At the same time, however, as discussed in Section 7, there are also issues about the burden of the tax payments on households or firms, and their distribution, to be taken into account.

3.1.5. Monopoly

Buchanan (1969) discusses a possible limitation of environmental taxes in circumstances where polluting firms have a degree of monopoly power. Where companies have market power, they may reduce output below that which would occur in perfect competition, in order to maintain higher prices. An environmental tax raises the marginal cost of production and consequently a monopolist will reduce output even further, away from the social optimum. An environmental tax set at a level that would lead to an efficient amount of pollution abatement by firms in a competitive industry will typically not be efficient if applied to a monopoly. In an empirical investigation of the significance of this argument, however, Oates and Strassmann (1984) found that the welfare costs of output restriction by monopolies were rather small and the inefficiencies in Pigouvian taxation from this source consequently unimportant.

3.1.6. Non-uniform damage

Where the *concentration* of pollution, either in particular localities or over certain time periods, is of importance, more complex forms of tax instrument will be needed than where the concentration of pollutant emissions is irrelevant.[8] A straightforward tax per unit of effluent discharge (or, more generally, pollutant emitted) would not discourage geographic or temporal concentrations of pollution, whilst at the same time it could mean that firms in areas where pollution was less damaging might be charged more than the value of the damage created. Where policy is, none the less, constrained to use only uniform taxes, there is then a straightforward trade-off between the efficiency gain from taking into account the diversity of abatement costs, and the efficiency costs of inadequately differentiating between polluters with different marginal abatement benefits (Seskin, Anderson, and Reid, 1983). A number of papers have considered the use of zoned taxes or other non-linear tax systems to reflect the fact that pollution in particular localities or at certain times causes greater damage (Tietenberg, 1978; Kolstad, 1987).

One case where determination of the appropriate time profile of tax rates is particularly complex is that of a carbon tax, used to control greenhouse gas emissions. One reason for this is that the problem is one of a stock externality: the damage relates primarily to the total stock of greenhouse gases in the atmosphere rather than to the rate of emissions (Nordhaus, 1991). Also, as Sinclair (1992) observes, the choice of a tax profile is further complicated by the fact that the fuels concerned are an exhaustible resources. Policy measures to regulate the rate at which the resource is depleted will need to take account of the natural changes over time in the pricing of the resource, reflecting its scarcity. Sinclair's conclusion that, in steady state, the optimal carbon tax rate should *decline* over time is challenged by Ulph, Ulph, and Pezzey (1991), who argue that a steady state will in general not arise, and that in many cases the optimal carbon tax will rise initially, and then fall as the exhaustion constraint starts to bite.

3.2. Pollution taxes versus subsidies

In principle, subsidies can be used to provide a similar incentive to reduce pollution to that provided by a tax or charge on each unit of pollution. A subsidy, on each unit of pollution *abatement* compared with the existing situation, would lead individual polluters to reduce pollu-

---

[8] Cases where the geographical concentration of pollution is of no concern at all are rare; the emission of carbon dioxide (and its impact on global warming) probably provides the only significant practical example.

tion by the same level, and make the same choice of technology as they would if faced with a tax at the same level on each unit of pollution.

There are, however, four principal points of difference between the use of incentive mechanisms based on subsidies and mechanisms based on taxes and charges.

3.2.1. *Definition of the subsidy baseline*

Since the equivalent subsidy has to be paid on each unit of pollution abated, rather than on each unit of pollution emitted, it is necessary to define a baseline level of emissions against which current emissions will be compared. In principle, this requires a complex 'counterfactual' assessment of what would have happened in the absence of policy. A more straightforward alternative, using the emission levels at the start of the policy as the baseline, may initially be a reasonable approximation, but would become increasingly out of date; in addition, as Kamien, Schwartz, and Dolbear (1966) point out, it could encourage polluters to increase pollution at the outset, to qualify for higher subsequent subsidy.

3.2.2. *Effects on entry and exit*

Whilst taxes and subsidies can provide the same incentive at the margin, as Bramhall and Mills (1966) observe, they have different effects on the level of profits earned by polluters. This may affect the evolution over time of the industry structure, since the pollution abatement subsidy could reduce the rate of exit from the industry. Whilst the reduction in exits (e.g. bankruptcies) may be seen as having political advantages, it has the unhappy consequence that the level of pollution from the industry as a whole could actually rise, if policy were based on pollution abatement subsidies rather than pollution taxes.[9]

3.2.3. *Public expenditure*

One obvious difference is that subsidies add to public expenditure, and thus require other taxes to be raised to finance them, whilst pollution taxes raise tax revenue, and thus permit other taxes to be reduced. The potential value of the revenues from environmental taxes is discussed in detail in Section 7.

[9] See Baumol and Oates (1988: ch. 14) for further discussion. Pezzey (1992) discusses the conditions under which a scheme including subsidies would achieve efficient abatement and efficient entry/exit decisions.

3.2.4.   *Concealed protection*

One important practical consideration which counts against the use of subsidies in environmental policy is the risk that over time these subsidies may come to constitute a form of protection for the industries concerned. The appropriate level of subsidy to reflect environmental objectives may be difficult to define with any precision, and the appropriate pattern of payment across firms may, as argued above, rest on a number of difficult judgements. In these circumstances, the borderline between justified and unjustified subsidy may be blurred, and it may be relatively easy for protectionist pressures to lead the subsidy to be increased. Such indirect or concealed protection in the guise of environmental policy has been the focus of discussions in a number of international fora. Amongst the countries of the OECD, it has been a major reason for the adoption of the Polluter Pays Principle (PPP), which is based on the most readily verifiable rule, a baseline of zero subsidy in environmental policy (OECD, 1974).

On the other hand, Bovenberg (1992) argues that subsidies may in some circumstances be promising instruments for unilateral environmental policy, since they will lead to smaller changes in the pattern of trade and factor flows than environmental taxes, and will thus involve smaller economic adjustment costs. This argument for the use of subsidies is perhaps strongest in the context of the gradual adoption by countries of policies to control an international environmental externality. For example, the temporary impact of the unilateral introduction of a carbon tax on the trade of the country which moves first may be large; a policy based instead on subsidy would reduce the need for trade to adapt to what the 'first movers' hope is only a temporary situation, before other countries have adopted similar measures.[10]

3.3.   Pollution taxes versus tradable permits

US policy towards market instruments in environmental policy has evolved in a rather different direction from that taken in Western Europe. Little use has been made of emissions taxes in the USA, but there has been considerable interest in the use of systems of tradable pollution permits, including a much-documented river pollution application in Wisconsin (O'Neil et al., 1983), permit trading for lead in petrol, and

---

[10] Similar arguments can be made for using regulation or 'grandfathered' tradable permits instead of taxes in these situations.

extensive scope for emissions trading in various parts of the air pollution control system. There has been some discussion of the reasons US policy has evolved in this distinctive direction (Burtraw and Portney, 1991), and extensive consideration of practical lessons that can be derived from US experience (see, e.g., Tietenberg, 1990).

The principal theoretical consideration in the choice between taxes and tradable permits relates to the impact of uncertainty. Where policy can be based on complete information about both the costs and benefits of pollution control, a chosen optimal level of pollution abatement can be attained either using quantity-based instruments (such as tradable permits) or using price-based systems of regulation (charges or taxes). Important differences emerge, however, between quantity- and price-based regulation in how the outcomes are affected by uncertainty about the costs and benefits of abatement (Weitzman, 1974).

A system of tradable permits guarantees the quantitative reduction in pollution, but at uncertain cost, whilst a price-based mechanism such as an environmental tax has an uncertain impact on the quantity of emissions, but fixes the marginal cost to polluters of emission controls. The choice between the two types of environmental market mechanism thus turns on whether policy error regarding the costs of pollution control would be more damaging than uncertainty about the quantitative reduction in pollution.

The practical experience of tradable permits also suggests one other major problem area, which is the efficiency of the permit market. Permit markets have tended to be thin, and the supply of permits for trading, in particular, has been small, perhaps because the rules of the schemes have been too vague about the long-term basis for permit allocation and have imposed various restrictions on permissible trades (Hahn, 1989). Permit trades will also not take place at the efficient level if polluters are large and can affect the price at which permits are traded (Hahn, 1984; Misiolek and Elder, 1989).

On the other hand, permits have the attraction that they can be introduced without significantly increasing the average financial burden on existing polluters by a system of 'grandfathering'—a free distribution of permits to existing polluters. This may, it is suggested, ease acceptance compared with taxes and charges where there may be public scepticism about any commitment to use revenues to compensate, on average, those industrial or social groups affected by the introduction of an environmental tax.[11] Issues of tax burden and compensation with environmental taxes are discussed in more detail in Section 7.

[11] Pezzey (1988, 1992) points out that polluters may believe themselves to have *de facto*

4. Approximations to Pigouvian Taxes

The environmental tax instruments discussed in the previous section were payments *directly related* to polluting emissions—for example, the taxes operated by some countries for effluent discharges into rivers; the tax is directly related to polluting emissions, in the sense that the amount of tax paid depends on the quantity emitted, and hence on the amount of pollution caused. In this section we consider an alternative group of environmental taxes based on an *indirect* relationship between the amounts paid in tax and the environmental problem which the tax seeks to influence. This group of environmental tax measures would include, for example, changes in the rates of taxation on petrol, introduced for environmental reasons. In such a case, the incentive to reduce polluting emissions takes an indirect form, in that the tax is not levied directly on the quantity of emissions, but instead is levied on a base which is assumed to be linked in some dependable relationship to the amount of pollution caused.

Both types of environmental tax have a role to play in environmental policy. The choice between a tax directly related to emission quantities and a tax which is more indirectly linked to the pollution it aims to control will depend on considerations of two sorts, administrative cost and 'linkage'. Broadly speaking, as McKay, Pearson, and Smith (1990) argue, there is likely to be a trade-off between lower administrative cost and better linkage; in many cases, environmental taxes based on measured emissions will have higher administrative costs than taxes which are levied on some other base, but will be better linked to the amount of pollution caused, and will thus provide a more precisely targeted incentive to reduce pollution. The balance between these two considerations is, however, likely to differ from case to case.

4.1. Administrative cost

The administrative costs of any new tax will normally be greater, the less scope there is for the tax to be incorporated in existing systems of administration and control. Where the assessment, collection, or enforcement of the tax can be 'piggy-backed' on to corresponding operations already undertaken for existing taxes, the costs of an environmental tax measure

'property rights' in their current pollution, and that grandfathering may simply reflect this situation.

may be significantly less than where wholly new administrative apparatus and procedures are required.

The vast majority of existing taxes are levied on transactions—the value of goods and services sold, the value of incomes paid or received, and so on. The scale economies that can be achieved from administrative integration of environmental taxes are likely to be greatest where environmental taxes, too, are levied in a form based on transaction values. Thus, for example, the differentiation of the rates of existing taxes (which may be seen as the limiting case of a tax reform closely compatible with existing tax administration) may gain considerably from combined administration. On the other hand, there are likely to be few gains from combining the administration of a tax on measured emission quantities with existing transaction-based taxes.

It is necessary to bear in mind that most administrative piggy-backing is unlikely to be wholly costless from the point of view of the administration of existing taxes. Greater complexity is likely to increase administrative costs in all areas— though the extent of this will depend on the existing degree of complexity in the tax structure.

New environmental taxes based on measured emissions quantities will require, as a minimum, the additional costs to be borne of a system for the assessment or measurement of the emission quantities on which the tax is to be levied. These costs will depend on the following.

4.1.2. Measurement cost per source

This will vary depending on the technical characteristics of the emissions (flow, concentration, stability, and so on), the substances involved, and the range of currently available measurement technologies. Recent scientific and commercial developments in measurement and control are likely to have substantially widened the range of technologies available for monitoring the concentrations and flows of particular substances in effluent discharges, and hence to have increased the range of pollution problems for which charging on the basis of direct measurement is likely to be a feasible and cost-effective option. It is also probable that the *future* pace of development and commercialisation of such technologies will in part be stimulated by a greater use of direct emissions charging.

4.1.3. Number of emissions sources

Direct charging for measured emissions quantities will be less likely to be worthwhile, the more separate emission sources there are. An extreme example of this is the case of non-point-source pollution—in other words, where no identifiable pipe, outlet, or chimney provides a 'point source' at which emissions can be measured. The leaching of agricultural fertilisers and pesticides into the water system are examples of non-point-source pollution; for such pollution problems, direct measurement is likely to be costly and/or highly imprecise.

4.1.4. Scope for integration with normal commercial activities

The costs of a system of emissions measurement will generally be reduced if the measurement of emissions can be integrated with activities that would naturally take place for normal commercial reasons. Not merely does this reduce the additional costs of measurement for tax purposes, but it also tends to reduce the risk of false or misleading information being provided, since there are non-tax reasons for accurate measurement.

Even if, despite the administrative costs, Pigouvian taxes on emissions are still preferred to 'approximate' environmental taxes, the existence of significant administrative costs of taxation would be likely to mean that the range of tax instruments employed will be more restricted than would be the case if tax administration were costless. As Yitzhaki (1979) observes, explicit consideration of administrative costs, so that the number of tax instruments is included as a decision variable in optimal tax analysis, voids the need to treat optimal taxation as a second-best problem, with arbitrary restrictions on the tax instruments available. Polinsky and Shavell (1982) consider another issue raised by administrative costs in the context of Pigouvian taxation—whether it is desirable to take administrative costs into account in choosing the appropriate rate at which Pigouvian taxes should be levied. They conclude that the answer varies depending on the relationship between administrative costs and the number of polluters; for example, where the administrative costs are a fixed amount per polluter and are borne by government, it may be appropriate to set the Pigouvian tax rate above the level of the external cost, so as to reduce the administrative cost, but this rule will not be appropriate where the costs of administration are borne by the polluters themselves.

4.2. Linkage

Where the costs of an environmental tax system based on direct charging for measured emissions are high, restructuring of the existing tax system may provide an alternative way of introducing fiscal incentives to reduce environmental damage.[12] The effectiveness of changes in the existing tax system in achieving an efficient pattern of pollution abatement will depend on the degree to which the taxation is closely linked to the pollution which it aims to control. If the tax rises, does it encourage taxpayers to seek to reduce this tax burden by reducing the processes or activities which give rise to polluting emissions; or are they, instead, just as likely to find ways to reduce their tax payments that do not change their level of pollution?

This issue of linkage is central to any case for or against using fiscal instruments other than those based on direct charging for measured emissions: where the linkage between tax base and pollution is weak, the tax may fail to have the desired impact on pollution, and may, at the same time, introduce unnecessary and costly distortions into production and consumption decisions.

'Indirect' environmental tax policies depend on the existence of a stable relationship between the tax base and pollution, but relationships which are observed to be stable in the absence of policy measures can turn out to be unstable once a tax is introduced. A good illustration of this phenomenon is given by Sandmo's (1976) account of Norway's attempt to introduce a system of charging for domestic refuse collection by charging for the special sacks which householders were required to use for their refuse. The logic for the system was that the number of sacks used would be a rough proxy for the quantity of refuse collected from each household. Unfortunately, the charging scheme, once implemented, tended to change the relationship between sacks used and refuse collected. Some households tended to economise on sacks rather than to economise on refuse, and responded to the tax by overfilling the sacks, or by dumping refuse, causing environmental problems elsewhere.

A number of papers have considered the appropriate structure of taxation where the only administratively feasible policies involve some degree of approximation in the linkage between tax base and pollution damage. The issue of linkage has been represented in these models in two different ways. One group of papers has considered models where administrative limitations require that all individuals causing

---

[12] Plott (1966); Holtermann (1976); see also Young (1977).

externalities are taxed at the same rate, but where the externalities from some are more damaging than those from others. In the context of Pigouvian taxation of emissions, these could be cases where taxing different polluters at different rates, according to the damage from their emissions, required a large element of judgement, which thus tended to expose the system to lobbying or regulatory capture. In the case of conventional product taxes, an example might be the use of a tax on coal to encourage smoke abatement; although smoky chimneys may be more damaging in densely populated areas, it would be impracticable to tax coal at different rates in different areas, since it would be almost impossible to prevent urban dwellers from buying their coal from rural suppliers.[13]

Diamond (1973) considers the rate at which such a uniform tax should be levied. In the case where there is separability between the externality and consumption, the appropriate tax rate is simply the weighted average of the marginal contributions to the externality, where the weights are given by the sensitivities of demand for the good which generates the externality. Where the separability assumption is relaxed, so that externalities affect demand as well as utility, calculation of the optimal tax rate is more complex, and 'perverse' cases cannot be ruled out, in which it would be appropriate to subsidise the good causing the externality.

Where linkage is poor, it may be possible to improve matters by going beyond taxation of the good associated with the externality; complements or substitutes to the externality-causing good may be taxed or subsidised. Like Diamond (1973), Green and Sheshinski (1976) and Balcer (1980) consider cases where individual externality effects differ (and where the optimal Pigouvian tax would therefore be at different rates). However, they focus on cases where goods exist that are complements (or substitutes) to the externality-generating good. Depending on the interaction between demand for the complement (or substitute) and the externality, it may be possible to improve on the taxation of the externality-causing good alone, by taxing or subsidising the complementary or substitute good. For example, if the objective is to deal with urban congestion, high petrol taxes might be supplemented by subsidies to urban public transport and taxes on urban parking spaces. Sometimes the appropriate policy rules will appear counter-intuitive. Balcer shows a simple case where a subsidy to a complementary good would be appropriate, and Wijkander (1985) discusses cases where the policy rule is

---

[13] In practice, of course, market instruments in this case are likely to be easily dominated by a simple regulatory rule, forbidding the use of smoky fuels in urban areas.

complicated by the cross-effects between various complements or substitutes to the externality-causing good.

Other papers have represented the linkage issue differently. Sandmo (1976) represents the problem as one where goods can be used for two purposes, only one of which generates the externality; this could be a case where some consumption uses of a good cause more pollution than others (e.g. use of petrol in urban and rural areas) or, as in Henry (1989), where the good causes more pollution in one production use than in another. It is assumed that the good can be taxed, but that it is not possible to differentiate between its different uses. Again, the analyses confirm the value of taxing or subsidising complements or substitutes, as well as taxing the good associated with the externality, and again it proves possible to find counter-intuitive policy prescriptions. Perhaps the most important advantage of representing the issue in this way is that it focuses attention on the key practical question of *how* the externalities are generated: what is the technological relationship between the taxed commodity and the externality, and is this relationship likely to be stable?

Where there are a wide range of available techniques which differ widely from one another in the relationship between tax base and pollution, linkage is likely to be more of a problem than where the range of technologies is small and the tax-base–pollution relationship broadly stable across production techniques. Technical data about the range of available production techniques and their environmental attributes will thus help to assess the practical relevance of linkage problems for any particular environmental tax.

McKay, Pearson, and Smith (1990) observe that a particularly severe problem of linkage arises where it is sought to influence pollution emissions from a production process through taxes on *inputs*, and where significant scope exists for pollution abatement through effluent 'cleaning' at the end of the production process. One case in point is the scope for cleaning the sulphur dioxide emissions of coal-fired power-stations by fitting 'scrubbers' (flue gas desulphurisation equipment, or FGDs). Where effluents can be cleaned in this way, taxes on production inputs will not be an effective way of encouraging an efficient pattern of pollution abatement. Such a tax (e.g. a tax on sulphurous coal) may discourage the use of polluting materials in production, but will provide no incentive to clean up effluents from the process. Although pollution may be reduced, the way in which pollution reductions are achieved will not necessarily be the most efficient.

Environmental taxes on fuel inputs may thus be more appropriate to deal with carbon dioxide emissions, where effluent cleaning is not currently a commercially viable option, than with sulphur emissions, where important effluent-cleaning technologies are available.[14] However, it should be noted that what is at issue is not merely the existence of (commercially viable) alternative technologies, but also the potential for them to be developed, since an efficient pollution tax will create an incentive for new technologies, involving less pollution, to be developed. The acceptability of a carbon tax on fuel inputs instead of a tax on measured carbon emission quantities depends in part on a judgement about how rapidly such technological developments are likely to take place, and about how far their future development might be inhibited by the choice of a tax on inputs rather than on measured emissions.

5. Mutualisation Taxes

In practice, one of the common characteristics of environmental taxes has been hypothecation or 'earmarking' of the revenues, for example, to expenditures on environmental policy measures, or for the use of environmental agencies or funds. Thus, water charges levied in a number of European countries are earmarked to expenditures on water quality management, and feedstock taxes in the USA are earmarked for the 'Superfund', which finances the clean-up of hazardous waste dumps. Indeed, as Opschoor and Vos (1989) conclude, most of the initiatives to introduce environmental taxes have arisen because of the need to find revenue sources which can be assigned to finance environmental expenditures, rather than for their incentive value.

This suggests that the issue of earmarking may need to be considered from two angles. First, there is the question of whether there is a case for earmarking the revenues from an environmental tax introduced for incentive purposes. Secondly, there is the question of whether public expenditures on environmental measures should be financed specifically from the revenues of particular taxes; if so, are there reasons to finance such expenditures from eco-taxes, rather than from general tax revenues?

---

[14] A number of countries, including Sweden and Finland, have already introduced carbon taxes on fuels (Hoeller and Wallin, 1991).

5.1. Earmarking environmental tax revenues

In the case of the use of revenues from environmental taxes introduced to correct market incentives so as to reflect the environmental costs associated with polluting emissions or the production or use of particular commodities, the 'conventional' view of public economics is that earmarking is a potential source of inefficiency in fiscal decision-making. Whilst the assignment of particular revenue sources to particular expenditure headings may be made in a way that initially allocates tax revenues efficiently across expenditure headings, over the longer term, tax revenues and expenditure requirements can move out of line. Requiring the revenues from environmental taxes to be used for given purposes would mean that the amounts spent on these purposes would change over time according to the trend in the revenues from environmental tax, rather than according to spending needs. Alternatively, earmarking could lead to inefficiencies in the pattern of taxation, as the rates of tax come to be driven by the revenue requirements for the earmarked budget headings, rather than by the balance between the costs and benefits of particular tax levels.[15]

On this view, there is no reason to believe that 'earmarking' the revenues from environmental taxes would lead either to appropriate levels of expenditure on environmental improvements or to appropriate levels for the environmental tax. These inefficiencies would, moreover, be likely to be magnified over the course of time.

This view of earmarking, however, depends on assumptions about the underlying political and administrative process that may be unrealistic. Earmarking is contrasted unfavourably with a situation where taxes and public expenditures are set 'optimally' as the outcome of a process which sets taxes so as to minimise the costs of taxation and allocates expenditures across particular headings so as to maximise the overall benefits of public spending. In practice, political decisions about taxation and public spending may reflect a wider range of pressures—including, perhaps, bureaucratic pressures tending to the over-expansion of public expenditure programmes (Buchanan, 1963). In these circumstances, public support for new taxes may be weakened by the concern that the revenues could be diverted to undesired purposes. Earmarking of a new environmental tax to some popular expenditure heading may then be a strategy

---

[15] Oates (1991) discusses a related issue—namely, whether the rates of an environmental tax should be determined by the Ministry of Finance or the Ministry of the Environment. He argues that the latter would be preferable, since the Ministry of Finance may allow revenue considerations to dominate environmental policy efficiency.

which would generate greater political support for the measure than if the revenues were simply to be allowed to augment the general resources of government. By 'ring-fencing' the revenues to 'desirable' expenditure headings, the measure may command greater public support.

5.2. Financing environmental expenditures

The above arguments reflect the 'conventional' debate over earmarking—a discussion of whether it is appropriate for the revenues from a particular tax to be devoted to particular spending headings or to the general exchequer. However, in practice, the context in which environmental taxes have been introduced has often been rather different from that being presumed here—usually the issue has not been what to do with the revenues from an existing environmental tax, but rather to find revenue sources that would be appropriate to finance environmental expenditures. In this context, environmental taxes are seen not as incentive mechanisms, but principally as revenue-raising devices, to provide revenues for a programme of public environmental expenditures (Hahn, 1989).[16]

The principal issue is the identification of revenue sources which would be 'appropriate' to the expenditures in question. One criterion for appropriateness might be given by the concept of benefit taxation: taxpayers should contribute financially towards the cost of public expenditures in proportion to the benefits they derive from them (Musgrave and Musgrave, 1984: ch. 11).

Where the expenditure programmes are general, yielding benefits distributed widely across the population, environmental taxes are unlikely to constitute or approximate benefit taxes. However, the benefit tax argument would seem more applicable in cases where both the expenditure programmes and the taxes were confined to particular sections or groups of the population. These groups may be defined either geographically—in the case of local taxes to finance local environmental expenditures—or in terms of a particular sector or industry. Thus an environmental tax might be levied on a particular sector, to finance public expenditures on abatement measures which benefited that sector, or on cleaning up pollution attributable to that sector.

One obvious attraction of the earmarking of an environmental tax levied on a particular sector to environmental spending benefiting that

---

[16] This is in practice a particularly important motivation for environmental taxes in developing countries, where other options for raising tax revenues may be very limited.

sector is that it may overcome some political opposition to aspects of the policy—either to the use of public revenues to subsidise the costs of a particular sector or, where the tax has an incentive function, to the sectoral impact of the revenue burden; earmarking of this form provides sector-by-sector 'compensation'.

Linking sectoral spending and revenue-raising also formally complies with the restrictions imposed on subsidy schemes by the OECD Polluter Pays Principle; subsidies that would have been regarded as contrary to this principle if paid for out of general tax revenues are regarded as consistent with the requirements of the PPP if the cost is shared amongst the beneficiaries.

However, despite the formal conformity of such sectoral earmarking with the requirements of the PPP, there are reasons for concern about its extensive application. Certain types of environmental policy measure require public involvement and common financing; those that have the character of 'public goods' (e.g. joint effluent treatment facilities, or research expenditures) are unlikely to be provided to an efficient level if they have to rely on the uncoordinated actions of individual firms. However, it is less clear that any justification can be found for public subsidy to measures that benefit one firm alone. Indeed, financing such subsidies from the proceeds of environmental taxes levied on the sector may distort desirable signals about the appropriate level of activity in the sector; they may inhibit exit from the sector (and possibly attract new entrants), leading to a long-run higher level of sectoral activity than would be desirable, and, conceivably, increasing rather than reducing the aggregate level of pollution (Oates, 1991).[17]

Finally, even in the 'public good' case where sectoral expenditures can be justified, it is not obvious that environmental taxes, rather than other levies related perhaps to employment, assets, or output, are the appropriate way of sharing the cost of providing the common facilities. If it is felt desirable that payment should be in proportion to benefits received, it is then a purely empirical matter whether the pattern of benefits is more closely approximated by the environmental tax or by payments of some other tax.

---

[17] Lans Bovenberg has pointed out that the problem of efficient entry/exit may be less severe than is suggested here if tax revenues decline over time, because the long-run elasticity exceeds the short-run elasticity. In this case, part of the subsidy is only temporary, and may not attract new firms.

6. Empirical Studies of the Effects of Environmental Taxes

A growing literature on environmental taxes has tried to assess the likely scale of responses to environmental tax measures. How large would environmental taxes have to be, and what would be their impact on pollution, and on economic variables, including the level and distribution of incomes, prices, exchange rates and international competitiveness, employment, government revenues, and so on? Given the scale of this literature, it is impracticable to provide an exhaustive survey here; this section can merely indicate the range of approaches adopted, and highlight conclusions from a few selected papers.

In practice, whilst policy measures taken in a number of countries have included environmental taxes on narrowly defined commodities (e.g. taxes on plastic bags, batteries, non-returnable containers, and so on), most of the quantitative research has examined more broadly specified environmental taxes, such as carbon taxes (taxes on energy sources related to the amount of carbon dioxide they will produce in combustion), other taxes on domestic or industrial energy use, and taxes on motor vehicles and motor fuels. Besides the fact that these are the areas where environmental taxes might be expected to have the most significant impact, the poor availability of data on past spending and prices tends to restrict the scope for more detailed modelling of environmental taxes on narrowly defined commodities, or on commodities (such as leaded petrol) defined by particular environmental attributes.

With the exception of the literature on the economic effects of a carbon tax, most of the empirical research has focused on estimating the impact of environmental taxes on the use of the taxed commodity, and occasionally on closely related sectors, and has paid less attention to wider economic effects, including macroeconomic adjustment and general equilibrium effects. The studies which seek to estimate elasticities of demand and substitution can be divided into time-series estimates at an aggregate level, and estimates using micro-data on individual firms, industries, or households.

6.1. Time-series estimates at an aggregate level

Estimates at an aggregate level have included time-series estimates of aggregate energy use by industry, by consumers, or by the economy as a whole, time-series models of motor-vehicle ownership and vehicle fuel expenditure, of agricultural fertiliser use, and so on. The data requirements of such studies are comparatively small, but there are frequently difficulties in distinguishing price effects from other trended variables such as income, output price levels, and so on. For the UK, a number of studies of aggregate energy demand are summarised in Hunt and Manning (1989).[18]

Brännlund and Kriström (1991) study the impact of a tax on chlorine effluent from the bleaching process in the pulp industry, using a model which takes into account possible effects on forestry and the sawn timber industry. They found that a tax which increased the price of chlorine by 50 per cent would reduce the quantity of chlorine used by some 14 per cent, but that it would have negligible repercussions for forestry and the timber industry.

The likely impact of a tax on agricultural fertilisers can be derived from a number of studies of the price elasticity of the demand for fertilisers. Burrell (1989) provides a useful survey of this literature. Estimates from linear programming models and from econometric models have tended to diverge widely, with rather higher elasticities being obtained from the latter.

Time-series models can often be particularly informative about the timescale of likely responses to an environmental tax. One recent study which has generated important new information about the likely dynamics of changes in energy use in response to an energy tax is the paper by Ingham and Ulph (1990), which models the age ('vintage structure') of the capital stock in considerable detail. It points out that the scope for changing energy efficiency is much less with existing plant and machinery than when new machinery is installed, and shows that to achieve quick results, a much higher level of taxation would be required than if energy consumption changes were sought over a longer time period.

6.2. Estimates using micro-data

Estimates at a micro-level using data for industries or individual firms tend to be seriously constrained by the lack of relevant data. Changes in the classification of industry or trade statistics mean that industry-level data rarely contain an adequate number of yearly observations for robust

---

[18] See also Ingham, Maw, and Ulph (1991).

estimation, and detailed data on individual firms' expenditures on inputs are frequently unobtainable for reasons of commercial confidentiality.

There has been a growing amount of research on the spending patterns of individual households, using data from large-scale household surveys which can be used to assess the impact of environmental taxes on consumer goods. Household expenditure and income data from a number of years of budget surveys are now available for a number of OECD countries, and allow elasticities of demand and substitution to be estimated at a micro-level for a range of goods (e.g. Blundell, Pashardes, and Weber (1989) and Decoster and Schokkaert (1989)). Usually the models operate at a comparatively broad degree of aggregation, although domestic energy spending and spending on vehicles and petrol are usually separately distinguished. Blundell et al. (1992) provide a comparative analysis of the impact of a 'carbon tax' using consumer-spending models from five European countries (Belgium, France, Italy, Spain, and the UK), whilst other, single-country, studies of energy taxes or carbon taxes using these models have included Johnson, McKay, and Smith (1990) and Symons, Proops, and Gay (1992). Whilst all of these papers are based on a model which treats domestic energy purchases as a single aggregate, and which cannot therefore model the substitution between household fuels that might occur as the result of a carbon tax, Baker and Blundell (1991) present separate equations for household spending on gas and on electricity, based on micro-data from the UK Family Expenditure Survey.

Wider economic effects have been investigated using economic models of two sorts. As Boero, Clarke, and Winters (1991) describe, each approach has particular strengths and weaknesses, and these need to be borne in mind in assessing the results obtained.

6.3. Simulation using macroeconomic models

Macroeconomic models can be used to investigate the economy-wide repercussions of environmental taxes, by embedding estimated models of commodity demands in a full system of equations representing supplies and demands for all commodities and factors of production, and financial relationships. These models can then be used to simulate the wider implications of environmental taxes and the revenues raised from them—including effects on prices, international competitiveness and the exchange rate, employment, and so on. Linked macroeconomic models for a number of countries can be used to investigate how these effects might be altered if policies to introduce environmental taxes were subject to international coordination, rather than introduced by a single country acting alone. Linked simulations of the macroeconomic effects of a carbon tax are reported in Detemmerman, Donni, and Zagame (1991) and Standaert (1992), and a range of international estimates are surveyed in Hoeller, Dean, and Nicolaisen (1991) and Bradley and Fitzgerald (1992). Barker and Lewney (1990) use a sectoral macro-model of the UK economy to simulate the macroeconomic effects both of a carbon tax and of the regulation of water quality. Lanza and Scabellone (1991) use a sectoral model of Italian energy demand to simulate the impact on an index of atmospheric pollution of the European Community's proposal to harmonise the structure of indirect taxes (which would require changes to the taxation of petrol and other energy), and Agostini, Botteon, and Carraro (1991) simulate the impact of various *ad valorem* and specific energy taxes on energy-related pollution in Italy.

The principal uses made of most macroeconomic models have been to study and forecast short-run changes in economic conditions, and there is an obvious question about the extent to which they are suitable for simulating the longer-term implications of major structural changes in the economy, that would be implied by substantial 'carbon taxes' for example. Considerable recent research effort, however, has gone into improving the long-run dynamics of a number of models, to allow them to be used for longer-run simulation exercises.

6.4. Simulation using computable general equilibrium models

Computable general equilibrium (CGE) models are, by contrast, designed to investigate the long-run process of economic adjustments to policy changes, by examining how relative prices of all goods and factors of production would have to adjust to achieve equilibrium in all markets.[19] CGE models tend to pay little attention to the short-run dynamics of the economic adjustment process, in contrast to most macroeconomic models. Also, estimation can play quite a small role in the construction of CGE models; relevant elasticities may be gathered

---

[19] See Shoven and Whalley (1984) and Borges (1986) for surveys of this approach.

from a range of existing sources or simply assumed, and the model 'calibrated' so that it is consistent with data for a particular 'benchmark' year. As a result, statistical criteria to evaluate the reliability of the models and the precision of simulation results are difficult to obtain; the models, in effect, calculate the implications of policy change, *given* a particular structure of the economy, supply and demand elasticities, and so on. Because of their long-run focus, however, CGE models have been increasingly applied to the analysis of major environmental taxes.

This literature has grown explosively. Proost and van Regemorter (1990), for example, look at the impact of a carbon tax using a CGE model for the Belgian economy, and Conrad and Schröder (1990, 1991) describe various aspects of the effects of environmental taxes using a German CGE model. Other studies include Glomsrød, Vennemo, and Johnsen (1990) for Norway, Blitzer et al. (1990) for Egypt, Bergman (1991) on Sweden, and Burniaux et al. (1992), which discusses the OECD's global CGE model, GREEN, in which a number of regions are modelled.

One particular focus of studies based on CGE models of the effects of a carbon tax has been the international distribution of gains and losses from the tax. Since a move towards substantial policy measures to restrict carbon dioxide emissions is likely to require international agreement on coordinated emission reduction measures, knowledge of the pattern of gains and losses across countries is an important prerequisite for international negotiation. Whalley and Wigle (1991) show that the form taken by the carbon tax is critical in determining the distribution of gains and losses; a tax based on energy consumption would impose large losses on the major energy-producing countries, whilst a tax based on energy production would substantially compensate energy-producing countries for the reduced demand for their natural resources by entitling them to a substantial share of the carbon tax revenues.

7. Environmental Taxes in the Context of Public Finance

7.1. Revenues

The revenues that would be raised from environmental taxes on particular raw materials or products associated with pollution will be a function of the responsiveness of demand and supply to price. The more effective the tax is in restraining production and use of the taxed good, the lower will be the revenue derived from the tax. In some sense, therefore, revenue issues arise in inverse proportion to the environmental effectiveness of an environmental tax; the tax is paid and revenues obtained only where the good continues to be produced and consumed.

The effects on revenues of an environmental tax are likely to change over time. Since, in general, supply and demand responses to the imposition of an environmental tax are likely to be rather greater in the long run (when taxpayers' patterns of production and consumption can be freely adjusted) than in the short run (when taxpayers' production and consumption decisions may be constrained by existing capital equipment), there may be circumstances where the revenues to be obtained from the environmental tax could decline over time. Where long-run supply and demand responses to the environmental tax are large, reflecting the existence of close substitutes which are less heavily taxed, the opportunities and problems posed by the tax revenues and the burden of additional tax payments will be short-lived.

In practice, forecasting the long-run revenue effect of environmental taxes is unlikely to be a precise matter. Not only are there likely to be important uncertainties regarding the size and timing of the effects of the tax on production or consumption of the good in question, but also demands and hence revenues will be a function of the overall economic climate and level of economic activity. Economic growth may increase demands for the polluting good, partly (or fully) offsetting the effects of the environmental tax. Where the price elasticity of demand for the taxed good is low, and the income elasticity is high, the increases in demand due to growth are likely to be large relative to the reductions in demand due to the environmental tax. Thus one concern is considering the use of tax on energy to control environmental problems associated with energy use is that the price elasticity of energy demand is so low that a steeply rising energy tax would be needed merely to keep energy demand constant in the face of rising incomes.

7.1.1. A 'double dividend'?

There has been some interest in the potential of environmental taxes to reduce the overall costs involved in raising fiscal revenues. Does the revenue raised from environmental taxes constitute an additional benefit from their use, in the sense that it allows other taxes, which may have large distortionary costs, to be reduced? Some commentators (e.g. Pearce

(1991) and Oates (1991)) have drawn attention to a potential 'double dividend' from environmental taxes—the possibility that, in addition to their environmental benefits, they have a second source of gains in the sense that the revenue raised from the environmental taxes allows other taxes, with possible distortionary effects on labour supply, investment, or consumption, to be reduced.

As Oates (1991) observes, economic efficiency in raising public revenues requires that the marginal dead-weight burden from each revenue source be equal; in other words, that there should not be scope to raise the same revenues at lower dead-weight cost by changing the pattern of public revenues. The distinctive feature of environmental taxes is that they have negative dead-weight burden over a certain range of tax rates; rather than imposing costs by distorting the pattern of economic activity, they correct existing distortions which arise through the failure to price environmental externalities correctly. Starting from a situation where the environmental benefit of tax changes has not been taken into account, reallocating the pattern of public revenues will then allow the overall dead-weight burden of raising revenues to be reduced.

Empirical studies of the marginal distortionary costs (excess burden) of existing taxes show that these costs can be appreciable—for example, Ballard, Shoven, and Whalley (1985) estimate the marginal excess burden of public revenues in the USA at 20–30 cents for each extra dollar of tax revenue—and, if environmental tax reform permits a reduction in these costs, this may be a significant policy consideration. Terkla (1984) compares the environmental benefits from pollution abatement using emissions taxes with estimates of the dead-weight loss that would be incurred in raising the same revenue through general taxation, and finds that the reduction in excess burden is of a similar order of magnitude to the net environmental benefits.

Revenue considerations will not always imply that the rage of the environmental tax should be increased above the rate that would be appropriate if there were no need for public revenues. As Lee and Misiolek (1986) show, the optimal level of pollution abatement will depend on the elasticity of tax revenues with respect to the tax rate; if a marginal increase in the tax rate reduces tax revenues, then it will be appropriate for a lower tax rate to be set, and for the level of pollution abatement to be lower with a revenue-raising instrument than with an instrument that does not raise revenues.

A corollary of the double dividend argument is that the optimal level of pollution abatement will not be independent of the environmental policy instrument used. Where increasing the rate of the environmental tax increases tax revenue, instruments such as regulation or grand-fathered tradable permits which forgo revenue will have a higher *total* marginal abatement cost (taking into account the marginal dead-weight burden of raising public revenues as well as the 'conventional' marginal abatement costs) that environmental tax instruments, which can use the extra revenue raised to reduce the distortionary costs of other taxes. In this case, an efficient policy will set a higher level of pollution abatement if the tax instrument is used than if an environmental policy instrument is employed which does not raise revenues.

There has been some discussion of the precise nature of the double dividend claim. A paper by Ulph (1992) has sought to clarify the precise meaning of the argument, and to separate clearly the 'revenue' and 'pollution' distortions involved. A key issue is the definition of the yardstick against which the distortionary cost of the tax system is to be assessed. Ulph takes as a yardstick the 'first-best' pattern of production and consumption, where unlimited use of lump-sum taxes is feasible and where the externality is corrected optimally, and measures both environmental and revenue distortions as deviations from this pattern.

Ulph (1992) considers whether the introduction of an environmental tax, from a starting-point without any form of environmental control, would be expected to reduce the excess burden of tax revenues, whilst *at the same time* yielding environmental benefits. He concludes that this depends on the size of the revenues that would be raised from the environmental tax, relative to the revenue needs of the public sector. Obviously, where the public sector has no need for revenue, the revenues from an environmental tax do not substitute for other taxes; indeed, if the revenues cannot costlessly be returned to taxpayers, the revenues raised would represent a cost. Also, he argues that, where the need for tax revenues is large relative to the revenues that would be obtained from correcting the externality in the first-best situation, there may be a tendency for revenue considerations to induce an excessive *reduction* in consumption of the polluting commodity—as discussed above, taking the revenue from marginal abatement into account may justify abatement beyond the first-best level. It is possible, therefore, that there could be a greater externality distortion but a lower revenue-raising distortion with a tax system that included environmental taxes than with a tax system which did not take account of the externality. Only where the revenues from the environmental tax are broadly of a similar order to the revenue needs of the public sector is it likely that both the pollution and revenue distortions will be simultaneously improved by the use of an environmental tax.

Bovenberg and de Mooij (1992) argue that the distortionary cost of taxation needs to be considered in a more complex general equilibrium context, in which factor supplies and demands are taken into account. Taxes on goods, for example, will tend to distort not only the pattern of spending on goods, but also labour supply. How far taxes on particular goods affect labour supply will depend on the income elasticity of demand; taxes on luxury goods will have a greater disincentive effect than uniform goods taxation, and taxes on necessities will have less disincentive effect. Bovenberg and de Mooij argue that the additional distortions to labour supply and other markets from the environmental tax will be greater, the greater the initial degree of distortion in the economy; where an economy is initially highly distorted, the double dividend argument will then be weaker than where the initial marginal excess burden of taxation was small.

Pearson and Smith (1991) observe that there is a close link between the impact of an environmental tax on the excess burden of taxation and the distributional impact of the environmental tax. Where policy-making operates on the basis of a trade-off in taxation between efficiency and equity objectives, it would generally be possible to reduce the excess burden of taxation by relaxing the distributional constraint. If the distributional objectives are weakened, it will be possible to increase the lump-sum, non-distortionary element within the tax structure, and this will reduce the excess burden of raising a given revenue. An environmental tax which is sharply regressive will tend to increase the lump-sum, non-distortionary component of the tax system, and this will, in turn, tend to reduce the overall welfare costs of raising revenue. This provides a further way in which, in practice, environmental taxes could reduce the distortionary costs of the tax system. However, they would in part do so, only to the extent that the distributional incidence of the tax system is permitted to become more regressive; if the original distributional incidence is restored, this source of efficiency gains would be eliminated.[20]

7.2. Distributional aspects of environmental taxes

Although both regulatory and market-based environmental policies may have distributional implications in terms of their impact (both costs and benefits) on households at different levels of incomes, the pattern of tax

---

[20] A similar point is made by Bovenberg and de Mooij (1992).

payments associated with the use of environmental taxes and other revenue-raising market-based instruments raises particular concerns.

The introduction of environmental taxes on energy is, in particular, likely to raise significant distributional concerns, reflecting the importance of energy expenditures in the budgets of poorer households (Dilnot and Helm, 1987; Smith, 1992). This distributional sensitivity of energy taxation is recognised in the indirect tax policies of many OECD countries, which apply lower levels of taxation to certain domestic energy products than to other goods and services.

What matters in assessing the distributional incidence of the burden of an environmental tax is the final incidence (i.e. the households which ultimately bear the burden of the tax) rather than the formal incidence (i.e. who makes the tax payments). Assessing the pattern of final incidence of a general energy tax, such as the proposed European carbon tax, will be complex. In addition to the direct distributional effects working through the prices of direct household purchases of energy, there will also be various indirect distributional effects, for example, as a result of the taxes imposed on industrial purchases of energy. These indirect effects reflect the fact that the ultimate incidence of all taxes is on households—the burden of taxes on business can in principle always be traced to the households or individuals who are the shareholders or owners of each business, or to its suppliers, employees, or customers. In addition to an analysis of the distributional incidence of energy taxes on consumer energy spending, a full analysis of the effects of a general tax on energy will also need to assess which of these various groups shoulders the ultimate burden of an energy tax on industrial energy use, and what place they occupy within the income distribution. Sophisticated general equilibrium modelling will thus be needed if all aspects of the distributional incidence of a general energy tax are to be quantified.

One important aspect of this, in the cases of taxes on natural resources such as energy, is the extent to which the burden of the tax will be borne by the owners of the resources, rather than by resource consumers. In a freely competitive market, the balance between energy consumers and the owners of energy resources (energy producers) will be a function of the price elasticities of energy supply and demand. The more price elastic is energy supply, and the more inelastic is energy demand, the more the burden of a tax on energy will tend to be borne by energy consumers rather than the owners of energy resources. Given the likely low price elasticity of energy demand, there is good reason to believe that a large part of the burden of a carbon tax would be borne by energy consumers rather than energy resource owners. This conclusion would be even stronger in the case of an energy tax introduced by only some countries; the impact of the tax on global energy demand would be smaller than where a worldwide energy tax was introduced.

7.2.1. Taxes on consumer expenditures

As far as the direct effect on energy products bought by private households is concerned, additional taxes on domestic energy would be likely to have a regressive distributional impact (i.e. the additional tax would constitute a larger proportion of the expenditures for poorer households), although this effect may be offset by the broadly progressive distributional impact of taxes on motor fuels. An initial indication of the magnitude of these distributional effects can be obtained from survey data on consumers' expenditure: for example, Poterba (1991) shows that a carbon tax in the USA would have a broadly regressive distributional impact, although he stresses that the regressivity appears less severe if a measure consistent with a 'life cycle' concept of distributional incidence is employed.[21] Pearson and Smith (1991) show that a carbon tax on consumer energy purchases would have a broadly neutral distributional effect in many European Community countries, but the tax would have a much more regressive impact in the UK and Ireland. Scott (1991), too, finds that a carbon tax would have a regressive incidence in Ireland.

Whilst analyses based on the existing pattern of consumer spending can indicate the approximate distributional incidence of environmental taxes on particular goods or services, the approximation is poorer where households respond to the imposition of the tax by changing their pattern of spending away from the taxed items. Where behaviour changes, there are two types of distributional effect that may be of interest— changes in tax payments and welfare costs. The changes in tax payments will usually be less than the changes estimated on the basis of unchanged spending patterns, although they could be greater, if households substituted towards items that were already heavily taxed. The pattern of welfare costs may also be unevenly distributed across households, with poorer or richer households making a greater adjustment in their pattern of spending.

The conclusions of studies of the distributional effects of a carbon tax have varied, but there is a broad measure of agreement that, in some

---

[21] Poterba (1989) makes a similar observation regarding the distributional incidence of existing excise taxes in the USA. See, however, Smith (1992), who finds less difference between distributional analyses based on current income and a lifetime income proxy, expenditure.

countries at least, a significantly regressive distributional impact could be expected. Pearson and Smith (1991), for example, in a study of the $10 per barrel carbon tax proposed by the European Community, find that, for the poorest 20 per cent of the UK population, the additional payments of tax on household purchases of energy and motor fuels would be equivalent to more than 2 per cent of their total spending, compared with less than 1 per cent for the richest 20 per cent.

7.2.2. Taxes on industrial inputs

The indirect distributional effects of fiscal changes affecting industrial inputs have been less extensively studied and measured than the direct distributional effects of taxes imposed on goods purchased directly by final consumers. One reason for this is that the data requirements are much more substantial, encompassing information on both firms and individuals. A second reason is the complexity of the effects involved, and the absence of any simple rules of thumb for assessing which are likely to be of greatest importance.

If higher prices for industrial inputs are passed on to consumers in the form of higher prices for industrial outputs, there will be distributional effects given by the pattern of consumer spending and the price changes for different industrial outputs. However, there may be various other distributional effects. If consumer demand switches away from energy-intensive goods and services, this may affect the profits of firms producing energy-intensive goods, and thus the incomes of their owners and the wages and employment prospects of their employees. Depending on the complementarity or substitutability of different factors in production, effects could be felt on the return to capital and labour even outside the sectors directly affected.

The balance of these various effects on the distributional incidence of environmental taxes on industrial inputs cannot be predicted a priori. Some important considerations affecting the strength of different effects include the degree of monopoly in factor and product markets, whether international competitors face similar taxes, the degree of substitutability of different factors in production, and the speed of adjustment.

One simple quantification approach, however, which sidesteps many of the most intractable measurement issues, is to use data on the input–output structure of the economy to calculate the impact of a tax on inputs on the relative prices of different outputs, assuming that the tax is fully passed on to consumers and that no changes take place to the pattern of inputs used in production. The change in relative prices can then be applied to data on the pattern of consumer spending to assess the distributional impact of the input tax.

These assumptions are strong, and probably only a reasonable approximation in the short term. Over a longer time period, the assumption of no factor substitution in production is clearly restrictive.[22] However, despite the limitations of the method, it has been used in a number of studies (Common, 1985; Symons, Proops, and Gay, 1992) to provide a reasonably straightforward source of information on the first-round distributional effects of environmental taxes on industrial inputs.

7.2.3. Offsetting policies

The substantial revenues raised from a carbon tax provide scope for policy measures to offset undesired distributional effects—for example, by reducing other taxes. The way in which the additional tax revenue is used will be critical in determining the overall distributional impact of a carbon tax. If the revenue is used in a way which maximises the 'double dividend' efficiency gains, it will tend to be used to reduce tax rates. This will confer much greater benefits on better-off households, and the overall distributional impact of the carbon tax will remain regressive. The revenue could, however, be used in a way which returned at least as much, on average, to poorer income groups as they paid in carbon tax, by making a lump-sum return of revenues. Designing an effective lump-sum redistribution mechanism within existing tax and social security systems is complicated (Johnson, McKay, and Smith, 1990), but could be approximated through a package involving increases in state pensions, social security benefits, and income tax allowances.[23] It is clear, however, that these measures are not those that would be chosen if it was intended to maximise the efficiency gains from reductions in other taxes that the carbon tax would permit. There is thus a clear trade-off between efficiency and equity in the use of the revenues, and double dividend efficiency gains can be achieved only by sacrificing the distributional neutrality of the package.

---

[22] Clearly the assumption on fixed coefficients and no factor substitution allows the carbon tax to have little impact on carbon emissions from production—the only reduction in carbon emissions under these assumptions comes from changes in final consumption spending.

[23] It will be noted that some of these measures constitute public expenditure rather than tax measures. We see no difference in principle between increasing public expenditures by increasing the level of social security benefits and increasing 'tax expenditures' by raising tax allowances, and the former cannot be avoided if poorer households are to be adequately compensated.

8. Conclusions: The Scope for Fiscal Measures in Environmental Policy

Environmental taxes hold out the prospect of more cost-effective pollution control than regulatory policies which are limited by the informational capacity of regulatory authorities. Much of the academic underpinning for this claim is well established and the subject of a broad measure of agreement. The previous reluctance of policy-makers to contemplate such measures has been the subject of considerable discussion (Hahn, 1989), and Buchanan and Tullock (1975) have suggested that some of the political resistance may reflect the interests of existing firms in policy instruments such as regulation which can deter competition from new entrants. However, there are now signs that the political process may at last be starting to explore the scope for practical applications of environmental taxes.

The key issue in formulating fiscal policies towards the environment is the choice between pollution taxes based on measured emission quantities and environmental taxes with an indirect linkage between the tax base and pollution. How far can environmental policy objectives be achieved by restructuring existing taxes, such as indirect taxes on goods and services, and how far will it be necessary to institute new tax mechanisms based on explicit pollution monitoring and control? The issue has been set out in this chapter as a trade-off between the administrative costs involved in 'purpose-built' taxes based on emissions, and the risks of inadequate 'linkage' between tax base and pollution if 'approximations' based on product taxes are employed. One half of this trade-off has been well explored in the literature; for example, the risk that an environmental tax might make matters worse where polluting and non-polluting technologies cannot be distinguished, and the possible contribution of taxes on related goods in correcting inadequate linkage, have been studied in a number of papers. The elements in the administrative cost side of the equation have been rather less well explored. Indeed, since administrative costs would seem to lie at the heart of an explanation for limiting the use to be made of externality taxes, it is surprising that the literature on this is so sparse.

On the empirical side, major strides are being made in quantification of the effects of various possible environmental market mechanisms, with a particular focus on assessing the importance of general equilibrium effects. There is a rich agenda for further work in this area. Besides quantifying the effects of environmental taxes on commodity demands, the pattern of competitiveness and production, prices and exchange rates, the income distribution, and so on, empirical general equilibrium models could also be used to assess the effects of raising revenue through efficiency-enhancing taxes on the overall welfare costs of the tax system. More generally, now that policy-makers are beginning to contemplate environmental taxes like the carbon tax which could raise substantial revenues, quantification of the whole range of public-finance aspects of environmental taxes will be of increasing relevance. Models which simulate the effects of environmental taxes within a general equilibrium framework, and disaggregated models able to look at the impact on different groups, will both be useful in assessing the scope that environmental taxes would provide for other taxes to be reduced, and what the overall effects would be on the efficiency and equity of the tax system.

References

Agostini, P., Botteon, M., and Carraro, C. (1991), 'Fiscal policy to reduce air pollution in Italy', Greta Associati, GRETA Working Paper no. 91.03.

Arrow, K. J. (1970), 'The organisation of economic activity: issues pertinent to the choice of market versus non-market allocation', in R. H. Haveman and J. Margolis (eds.), *Public Expenditures and Policy Analysis*, Chicago: Markham.

Atkinson, S. E., and Lewis, D. H. (1974), 'A cost-effectiveness analysis of alternative air quality control strategies', *Journal of Environmental Economics and Management*, vol. 1, pp. 237–50.

Baker, P., and Blundell, R. W. (1991), 'The microeconometric approach to modelling energy demand; some results for UK households', *Oxford Review of Economic Policy*, vol. 7, no. 2, pp. 54–76.

Balcer, Y. (1980), 'Taxation of externalities: direct versus indirect', *Journal of Public Economics*, vol. 13, pp. 121–9.

Ballard, C., Shoven, J., and Whalley, J. (1985), 'General equilibrium computations of the marginal welfare costs of taxes in the United States', *American Economic Review*, vol. 75, pp. 128–38.

Barker, T., and Lewney, R. (1990), 'A green scenario for the UK economy: macroeconomic modelling of environmental policies: the carbon tax, the Polluter Pays Principle and regulation of water quality', in T. Barker (ed.), *Green Futures for Economic Growth: Britain in 2010*, Cambridge: Cambridge Econometrics.

Baumol, W. J. (1972), 'On taxation and the control of externalities', *American Economic Review*, vol. 62, pp. 307–22.

Burniaux, J.-M., Martin, J. P., Nicoletti, G., and Martins, J. O. (1992), 'The costs of international agreements to reduce CO_2 emissions', *European Economy*, Special Edition no. 1 ('The Economics of Limiting CO_2 Emissions'), pp. 271–98.

Burrell, A. (1989), 'The demand for fertilizer in the United Kingdom', *Journal of Agricultural Economics*, vol. 40, pp. 1–20.

Burtraw, D., and Portney, P. R. (1991), 'Environmental policy in the United States', in D. R. Helm (ed.), *Economic Policy towards the Environment*, Oxford: Blackwell Publishers.

Carraro, C., and Topa, G. (1991), 'Taxation and the environmental innovation', Fondazione Eni Enrico Mattei, Nota di Lavoro 4.91.

Coase, R. H. (1960), 'The problem of social cost', *Journal of Law and Economics*, vol. 3, pp. 1–44.

Common, M. S. (1985), 'The distributional implications of higher energy prices in the UK', *Applied Economics*, vol. 17, pp. 421–36.

Conrad, K., and Schröder, M. (1990), 'An evaluation of recent proposals in environmental policy: an applied general equilibrium approach', Mannheim University, Institut für Volkswirtschaftslehre und Statistik, Discussion Paper no. 412–90.

—— —— (1991), 'The control of CO_2 emissions and its economic impact: an AGE model for a German state', *Environmental and Resource Economics*, vol. 1, pp. 289–312.

Cornes, R., and Sandler, T. (1986), *The Theory of Externalities, Public Goods and Club Goods*, Cambridge: Cambridge University Press.

Cropper, M. L., and Oates, W. E. (1992), 'Environmental economics: a survey', *Journal of Economic Literature*, vol. 30, pp. 675–740.

Decoster, A., and Schokkaert, E. (1989), 'Equity and efficiency of a reform of Belgian indirect taxes', *Recherches Économiques de Louvain*, vol. 55, pp. 155–76.

Detemmerman, V., Donni, E., and Zagame, P. (1991), *Increase of Taxes on Energy as a Way to Reduce CO_2 Emissions: Problems and Accompanying Measures*, report prepared for the Commission of the European Communities, DG XII.

Diamond, P. A. (1973), 'Consumption externalities and imperfect corrective pricing', *Bell Journal of Economics and Management Science*, vol. 4, pp. 526–38.

Dilnot, A. W., and Helm, D. R. (1987), 'Energy policy, merit goods and social security', *Fiscal Studies*, vol. 8, no. 3, pp. 29–48.

Glomsrød, S., Vennemo, H., and Johnsen, T. (1990), *Stabilisation of Emissions of CO_2: A Computable General Equilibrium Assessment*, Oslo: Central Bureau of Statistics.

Green, J., and Sheshinski, E. (1976), 'Direct versus indirect remedies for externalities', *Journal of Political Economy*, vol. 83, pp. 797–808.

Hahn, R. W. (1984), 'Market power and transferable property rights', *Quarterly Journal of Economics*, vol. 99, pp. 753–65.

—— and Oates, W. E. (1971), 'The use of standards and prices for prote the environment', *Swedish Journal of Economics*, vol. 73, pp. 42–54.

—— —— (1988), *The Theory of Environmental Policy*, second Cambridge: Cambridge University Press.

Bergman, L. (1991), 'General equilibrium effects of environmental CGE modeling approach', *Environmental and Resource Economics*, v 43–61.

Blitzer, C. R., Eckaus, R. S., Lahiri, S., and Meeraus, A. (1990), 'A gen librium analysis of the effects of carbon emission restrictions on growth in a developing country', paper presented at a World Bank on Economic/Energy/Environmental Modeling for Climate Polic 22–3 October, Washington, DC.

Blundell, R., Pashardes, P., and Weber, G. (1989), *What Do We L Consumer Demand Patterns from Micro-Data?*, IFS and Londo School, Micro to Macro Paper no. 3, London: Institute for Fiscal

—— et al. (1992), *The Simulation of Indirect Tax Reforms in Comparative Study Using Demand Systems Based on Household* IFS Report, forthcoming, London: Institute for Fiscal Studies.

Boero, G., Clarke, R., and Winters, L. A. (1991), *The Ma Consequences of Controlling Greenhouse Gases: A Survey*, Depart Environment, Environmental Economics Research Series, Lond

Borges, A. M. (1986), 'Applied general equilibrium models: an a their usefulness for policy analysis', *OECD Economic Studies*, no

Bovenberg, A. L. (1992), 'Policy instruments for energy conservati ronmental policy in the Netherlands', in F. Laroui and J. W (eds.), *An Energy Tax in Europe*, Amsterdam: SEO Foundation Research of the University of Amsterdam.

—— and de Mooij, R. A. (1992), 'Environmental taxation and l distortions', mimeo, Erasmus University Rotterdam.

Bradley, J., and Fitzgerald, J. (1992), 'Modelling the economic ef taxes: a survey', in F. Laroui and J. W. Velthuijsen (eds.), *An Europe*, Amsterdam: SEO Foundation for Economic Re University of Amsterdam.

Bramhall, D. F., and Mills, E. S. (1966), 'A note on the asymmet and payments', *Water Resources Research*, vol. 2, pp. 615–16.

Brännlund, R., and Kriström, B. (1991), 'Assessing the impact of charges', Stockholm School of Economics, Economic Res Research Paper no. 6457.

Buchanan, J. M. (1963), 'The economics of earmarked taxes', *Jo Economy*, vol. 71, pp. 457–69.

—— (1969), 'External diseconomies, corrective taxes and m *American Economic Review*, vol. LIX, pp. 174–7.

—— and Tullock, G. (1975), 'Polluters' profits and political control versus taxes', *American Economic Review*, vol. 65.

—— (1989), 'Economic prescriptions for environmental problems: how the patient followed the doctor's orders', *Journal of Economic Perspectives*, vol. 3, no. 2, pp. 95–114.

Helm, D., and Pearce, D. (1990), 'Economic policy towards the environment', *Oxford Review of Economic Policy*, vol. 6, no. 1, pp. 1–16.

Henry, C. (1989), *Microeconomics for Public Policy*, Oxford: Clarendon Press.

Hoeller, P., Dean, A., and Nicolaisen, J. (1991), 'Macroeconomic implications of reducing greenhouse gas emissions: a survey of empirical studies', *OECD Economic studies*, no. 16, pp. 45–78.

—— and Wallin, M. (1991), 'Energy prices, taxes and carbon dioxide emissions', OECD Economics and Statistics Department, Working Paper no. 106.

Holtermann, S. (1976), 'Alternative tax systems to correct for externalities, and the efficiency of paying compensation', *Economica*, vol. 43, pp. 1–16.

Hunt, L., and Manning, N. (1989), 'Energy demand elasticities: some estimates for the UK using the cointegration procedure', *Scottish Journal of Political Economy*, vol. 36, pp. 183–93.

Ingham, A., and Ulph, A. (1990), 'Carbon taxes and the UK manufacturing sector', University of Southampton, Discussion Paper in Economics and Econometrics no. 9004.

—— Maw, J., and Ulph, A. (1991), 'Empirical measures of carbon taxes', *Oxford Review of Economic Policy*, vol. 7, no. 2, pp. 99–122.

Johansson, P.-O. (1990), 'Valuing environmental damage', *Oxford Review of Economic Policy*, vol. 6, no. 1, pp. 34–50.

Johnson, P., McKay, S., and Smith, S. (1990), *The Distributional Consequences of Environmental Taxes*, IFS Commentary no. 23, London: Institute for Fiscal Studies.

Kamien, M. I., Schwartz, N. L., and Dolbear, F. T. (1966), 'Asymmetry between bribes and charges', *Water Resources Research*, vol. 2, pp. 147–57.

Kolstad, C. D. (1987), 'Uniformity versus differentiation in regulating externalities', *Journal of Environmental Economics and Management*, vol. 14, pp. 386–99.

Krupnick, A. J. (1986), 'Policies for controlling nitrogen dioxide in Baltimore', *Journal of Environmental Economics and Management*, vol. 13, pp. 189–97.

Lanza, A., and Scbellone, P. (1991), 'Environmental effects of the EC energy tax harmonisation proposals: a quantitative study for the Italian economy', *Ricerche Economiche*, vol. 45, pp. 529–52.

Lee, D. R., and Misiolek, W. S. (1986), 'Substituting pollution taxation for general taxation: some implications for efficiency in pollution taxation', *Journal of Environmental Economics and Management*, vol. 13, pp. 338–47.

McKay, S., Pearson, M., and Smith, S. (1990), 'Fiscal instruments in environmental policy', *Fiscal Studies*, vol. 11, no. 4, pp. 1–20.

Magat, W. A. (1978), 'Pollution control and technological advance: a dynamic model of the firm', *Journal of Environmental Economics and Management*, vol. 5, pp. 1–25.

256   *Stephen Smith*

Maleug, D. A. (1989), 'Emissions trading and the incentive to adopt new pollution abatement technology', *Journal of Environmental Economics and Management*, vol. 16, pp. 52–7.

Meade, J. E. (1973), *The Theory of Economic Externalities: The Control of Environmental Pollution and Similar Social Costs*, Leiden: Sijhoff.

Milliman, S. R., and Prince, R. (1989), 'Firm incentives to promote technological change in pollution control', *Journal of Environmental Economics and Management*, vol. 17, pp. 247–65.

Misiolek, W. S., and Elder, H. W. (1989), 'Exclusionary manipulation of markets for pollution rights', *Journal of Environmental Economics and Management*, vol. 16, pp. 156–66.

Musgrave, R. A., and Musgrave, P. B. (1984), *Public Finance in Theory and Practice*, New York: McGraw-Hill.

Muzondo, T. R., Miranda, K. M., and Bovenberg, A. L. (1990), 'Public policy and the environment: a survey of the literature', International Monetary Fund, Working Paper no. WP/90/56.

Newbery, D. M. G. (1980), 'Externalities: the theory of environmental policy', in G. A. Hughes and R. M. Heal (eds.), *Public Policy and the Tax System*, London: George Allen & Unwin.

Nicolaisen, J., Dean, A., and Hoeller, P. (1991), 'Economics and the environment: a survey of issues and policy options', *OECD Economic Studies*, no. 16, pp. 7–43.

Nordhaus, W. (1991), 'To slow or not to slow: the economics of the greenhouse effect', *Economic Journal*, vol. 101, pp. 920–37.

O'Neil, W., David, M., Moore, C., and Joeres, E. (1983), 'Transferable discharge permits and economic efficiency: the Fox river', *Journal of Environmental Economics and Management*, vol. 10, pp. 346–55.

Oates, W. E. (1991), 'Pollution charges as a source of public revenues', University of Maryland, Department of Economics, Working Paper no. 91–22.

—— and Strassmann, D. L. (1984), 'Effluent fees and market structure', *Journal of Public Economics*, vol. 24, pp. 29–46.

OECD (1974), *The Implementation of the Polluter Pays Principle*, Recommendation adopted by the OECD Council on 14 November 1974, C(74)223, Paris: Organization for Economic Co-operation and Development.

Opschoor, J. B., and Vos, H. B. (1989), *Economic Instruments for Environmental Protection*, Paris: Organization for Economic Co-operation and Development.

Pearce, D. (1991), 'The role of carbon taxes in adjusting to global warming', *Economic Journal*, vol. 101, pp. 938–48.

Pearson, M., and Smith, S. (1991), *The European Carbon Tax: An Assessment of the European Commission's Proposals*, IFS Report, London: Institute for Fiscal Studies.

Pezzey, J. (1988), 'Market mechanisms of pollution control: "polluter pays", economic and practical aspects', in R. K. Turner (ed.), *Sustainable Environmental Management: Principles and Practice*, London: Belhaven Press.

—— (1992), 'The symmetry between controlling pollution by price and controlling it by quantity', *Canadian Journal of Economics*, vol. 25, forthcoming.

Pigou, A. C. (1920), *The Economics of Welfare*, London: Macmillan.

Plott, C. R. (1966), 'Externalities and corrective taxes', *Economica*, vol. 33, pp. 84–7.

Polinsky, A. M., and Shavell, S. (1982), 'Pigouvian taxation with administrative costs', *Journal of Public Economics*, vol. 19, pp. 385–94.

Poterba, J. M. (1989), 'Lifetime incidence and the distributional burden of excise taxes', *American Economic Review: Papers and Proceedings*, vol. 79, pp. 325–30.

—— (1991), 'Tax policy to combat global warming: on designing a carbon tax', in R. Dornbusch and J. M. Poterba (eds.), *Global Warming: Economic Policy Responses to Global Warming*, Cambridge, Mass.: MIT Press.

Proost, S., and van Regemorter, D. (1990), 'Economic effects of a carbon tax—with a general equilibrium illustration for Belgium', Katholieke Universiteit Leuven, Centrum Voor Economische Studien, Public Economics Research Paper no. 11.

Sandmo, A. (1976), 'Direct versus indirect Pigovian taxation', *European Economic Review*, vol. 7, pp. 337–49.

Scott, S. (1991), 'Theoretical considerations and estimates of the effects on households', in J. Fitzgerald and D. McCoy (eds.), *The Economic Effects of Carbon Taxes*, Policy Research Series Paper no. 14, Dublin: Economic and Social Research Institute.

Seskin, E. P., Anderson, R. J., and Reid, R. O. (1983), 'An empirical analysis of economic strategies for controlling air pollution', *Journal of Environmental Economics and Management*, vol. 10, pp. 112–24.

Shibata, H., and Winrich, J. S. (1983), 'Control of pollution when the offended defend themselves', *Economica*, vol. 50, pp. 425–37.

Shoven, J. B., and Whalley, J. (1984), 'Applied general-equilibrium models of taxation and international trade: an introduction and survey', *Journal of Economic Literature*, vol. 22, pp. 1007–51.

Sinclair, P. (1992), 'High does nothing and rising is worse: carbon taxes should keep declining to cut harmful emissions', *The Manchester School*, vol. 60, pp. 41–52.

Smith, S. (1992), 'The distributional consequences of taxes on energy and the carbon content of fuels', *European Economy*, Special Edition no. 1 ('The Economics of Limiting CO_2 Emissions'), pp. 241–68.

Standaert, S. (1992), 'The macro-sectoral effects of an EC-wide energy tax: simulation experiments for 1993–2005', in F. Laroui and J. W. Velthuijsen (eds.), *An Energy Tax in Europe*, Amsterdam: SEO Foundation for Economic Research of the University of Amsterdam.

Symons, E., Proops, J. and Gay, P. (1992), 'Carbon taxes, consumer demand and carbon dioxide emission: a simulation analysis for the UK', Institute for Fiscal Studies, Working Paper no. W92/6.

258   *Stephen Smith*

5

5

Terkla, D. (1984), 'The efficiency value of effluent tax revenues', *Journal of Environmental Economics and Management*, vol. 11, pp. 107–23.

Tietenberg, T. H. (1978), 'Spatially-differentiated air pollutant emission charges: an economic and legal analysis', *Land Economy*, vol. 54, pp. 265–77.

—— (1990), 'Economic instruments for environmental regulation', *Oxford Review of Economic Policy*, vol. 6, no. 1, pp. 17–33.

Ulph, A., Ulph, D., and Pezzey, J. (1991), 'Should a carbon tax rise or fall over time?', University of Bristol, Department of Economics, Discussion Paper no. 91/309.

Ulph, D. (1992), 'A note on the "double benefit" of pollution taxation', University of Bristol, Discussion Paper no. 92/317.

Vickers, J., and Yarrow, G. (1988), *Privatisation: An Economic Analysis*, Cambridge, Mass.: MIT Press.

Weitzman, M. L. (1974), 'Prices vs quantities', *Review of Economic Studies*, vol. 41, pp. 477–91.

Wenders, J. T. (1975), 'Methods of pollution control and the rate of change in pollution abatement technology', *Water Resources Research*, vol. 11, pp. 383–96.

Whalley, J., and Wigle, R. (1991), 'The international incidence of carbon taxes', in R. Dornbusch and J. M. Poterba (eds.), *Global Warming: Economic Policy Responses to Global Warming*, Cambridge, Mass.: MIT Press.

White, M. J., and Wittman, D. (1982), 'Pollution taxes and optimal spatial location', *Economica*, vol. 49, pp. 297–311.

Wijkander, H. (1985), 'Correcting externalities through taxes on/subsidies to related goods', *Journal of Public Economics*, pp. 111–25.

Yitzhaki, S. (1979), 'A note on optimal taxation and administrative costs', *American Economic Review*, vol. 69, pp. 475–80.

Young, L. (1977), 'Alternative tax systems to correct for externalities and the technical options of firms', *Economica*, vol. 44, pp. 415–20.

INDEX